# BRANDSTORM

# BRANDSTORM

SURVIVING AND THRIVING IN THE NEW
CONSUMER-LED MARKETPLACE

## LIZ NICKLES

### WITH SAVITA IYER

palgrave
macmillan

BRANDSTORM
Copyright © Liz Nickles, 2012.

All rights reserved.

First published in 2012 by
PALGRAVE MACMILLAN®
in the United States—a division of St. Martin's Press LLC,
175 Fifth Avenue, New York, NY 10010.

Where this book is distributed in the UK, Europe and the rest of the world,
this is by Palgrave Macmillan, a division of Macmillan Publishers Limited,
registered in England, company number 785998, of Houndmills,
Basingstoke, Hampshire RG21 6XS.

Palgrave Macmillan is the global academic imprint of the above companies
and has companies and representatives throughout the world.

Palgrave® and Macmillan® are registered trademarks in the United States,
the United Kingdom, Europe and other countries.

ISBN: 978–0–230–34168–5

Library of Congress Cataloging-in-Publication Data is available from the
Library of Congress.

A catalogue record of the book is available from the British Library.

Design by Newgen Imaging Systems (P) Ltd., Chennai, India.

First edition: November 2012

10 9 8 7 6 5 4 3 2 1

Printed in the United States of America.

I dedicate this book to Valerie Solti, a unique and inspiring role model and friend, along with her family, who have given me, among many other things, an understanding of the Solti motto, "Never give up."
And to my son Drew Murray—a brand in the making.

Liz Nickles, August 2012

# CONTENTS

# PREFACE

Branding today is a moving target. There can be no definitive answers in an age when technology constantly shifts the playing field. By the time you read this, many of the facts will have changed, as they changed daily as the book was written. An almost limitless number of brand stories can be told, and this book is not an attempt to tell them all or create a formula or scholarly treatise but to offer a perspective. We see it as the beginning of a conversation about a critical issue that has crossed the line from the conference room and the classroom to a ubiquitous presence and fact of everyday life, accessible and transparent as never before.

# ACKNOWLEDGMENTS

The experts who generously contributed to this work are, each within his or her field, the best of the best, and we are grateful to every one of them and honored to have their insights included in this book: Marvin Amorri, Laurie Ashcraft, Tynicka Battle, Charlotte Beers, Harry Bernstein, Robert C. Blattberg, Mary Helen Bowers, Kumar Chander, Maura Corbett, Jason Damata, Alexandre De Miguel, Craig Dubitsky, Ray Gaulke, Mike Godwin, Susan Gunelius, Doug Hall, Vance Hedderel, Steven Hess, Adrian Ho, Chad Jackson, Rolf Jensen, Richard Kirshenbaum, Glenn Laudenslager, Moray MacLennan, Erik Martin, Leandra Medine, Mickey Murray, Jonice Padilha, Milton Pedraza, Christine Pepper, James Piereson, Don Pintabona, Martin Riese, Jim Salzman, Dan Schwabel, Robert Scott, Todd Semrau, John Sicher, Hank Stewart, Watts Wacker, Roger Warner, Scott Williams, and Dr. Kimberly Young.

Every effort has been made to acknowledge and accurately quote, represent, and credit the views and works of these and all experts and authors who are cited in this book. The brand landscape is in constant flux, however, and some facts may evolve by the time of publication.

We wish to thank Laura Yorke, supporter from the start, Carol Mann, Eliza Drier, and the Carol Mann Agency, as well as Emily Carleton, Laura Lancaster, Carla Benton, Lauren Dwyer, Andrew Varhol, and the team at Palgrave Macmillan, who believed in this book and are the ultimate professionals.

I would like to offer special personal thanks to Charlotte Beers, whose work sets the bar for anyone in branding and marketing, and to Richard Kirshenbaum, who literally wrote the book.

And thank you to Savita Iyer for her insightful work, collaboration, and friendship.

A career is a long road, never navigated alone, and so I thank my inspiring community of friends, many of whom are brands in themselves, particularly: Zoe de Givency, Tamara Asseyev de Gabriac, J. C. Compton, Jean Doumanian, Taryn Edwards, Noel Harwerth, Mickey Kelly Murray, John Maienza, Joan Marie Pasquesi, Patricia Piereson, Carolynn Rockafellow, Diane Silberstein, Dorry Swope, and Gregg Wilson. Thank you to Karen and Jim Reid, Rye Page, Will, Anne, and the late Bernice Hokin, Lois Sturiale, and John Nelson— family who have supported me forever in many ways.

—LIZ NICKLES


I'd like to thank Liz Nickles for giving me the opportunity to work on this book. I greatly enjoyed working with you, Liz, and appreciate your guidance, intelligence, wit, sense of humor, and friendship.

I'd like to say a special thank you to the good friends who supported me during this project, especially Mary Helen Bowers, Wendy Connolly, Christine Tsarsi, and Liz Wolf.

Thank you to my family in Switzerland, and thank you to Farshid Ahrestani for taking over the house when I checked out.

And, finally, a special thank you to Sasha and Keya Ahrestani, for patiently waiting for the homemade Fondant.

—SAVITA IYER

# INTRODUCTION:
# THE BOSS IS BACK

In a horrifying headline incident, a two-hundred-pound pet chimpanzee, taken from animal keepers and raised and nurtured as a member of a human family, turned on a friend of its keepers and ripped her face off. That 2009 rampage, which left a woman disabled and animal lovers in shock, could be a metaphor for what is happening with branding today. Once the controlled and petted properties of a cadre of trained brand keepers—including advertising agencies, corporations, intellectual property attorneys, and political, monarchial, and religious leaders—within the past decade, brands have become democratized. David Ogilvy, the grandfather of branding back in the days when Madison Avenue was the olive in the ad men's martini, might be stunned to see his beloved branding has become a toolbox open for business to anyone who can log onto the Web or send a tweet. Today, marketers worldwide have realized that perilous truth: Brands, once so carefully nurtured and strategically fed into the consumer marketplace by skilled professionals, have been hijacked and shot into cyberspace by those same "target consumers" marketers thought were putty in their hands. In a kind of branding Bruce Lee, consumers have flipped the paradigm and threaten to take control of the brandosphere.

Suddenly, brand proliferation threatens to challenge, if not pull down, the sacred cows—and the cash cows—of the corporate world, as Brandzillas, or monster brands, spring forth fully formed seemingly overnight. Once, Brandzillas were prized and rare creatures, built brick by brick; now, it's click by click. Once upon a time, it took decades for the Model T to become "Ford" or a hat maker from the south of France to become "Chanel." Brands were built carefully and strategically, one consumer at a time, until something monumental resulted, like one of those scale models of Winchester Cathedral constructed with tweezers out of toothpicks and airplane glue. The term "five-year plan" was a mantra in corporate boardrooms. Brands were given room to build—and to breathe. Everyone knew things took time, a plan, and a marketing budget to draw consumers to the brand and then convert them to followers. If you did a fantastic job with a great product, those followers might morph into what they called "avids," intense champions of the brand. That was brand nirvana.

That was then.

Today, a sixteen-year-old from a small town practically off the map in Canada, working from his home computer with his mother's help, got two billion viewers online, averaging hundreds of thousands of views per day. That would be Justin Bieber, and whether you're into his music or not, that's not just a brand, that's a Brandzilla.

Madison Avenue, go choke on an olive.

*Whoa! Where did this come from?* When did the "experts," the P&G-trained, Harvard-educated MBAs lose control? When, like the chimp, did the lovingly hand-raised brands turn around and bite their keepers in the neck? As iconic brands struggle to remain relevant to once-loyal-now-fickle consumers, comprehension does not come easily as companies face challenging new questions:

- When did branding become a hand-to-keyboard combat sport?
- How does a marketing department at a multibillion-dollar consumer products or entertainment company compete with a bunch of thirteen-year-olds with Twitter accounts? Or can it?
- Will "civilian" Brandzillas run amok and disenfranchise corporate marketing departments—or push their staffers out of their jobs?
- If branding is the new Wild West, who's the new sheriff?

Massive change brings equally massive opportunities for those who are aware. Technology and a newly informed consumer have leveled the playing field, leaving these opportunities—and pitfalls—more accessible than ever. But new levels of transparency and speedup have also turned what only a few years ago might have been potholes into potential craters of disaster.

Leading off the May 2, 2011, issue of *Adweek*, the go-to trade journal of the advertising industry, was a cover story claiming that branding is "the driving force of the modern world," increasingly important in an often cold, impersonal, global universe. Brands are emotional touchpoints that help people make decisions about how they relate to each other and to themselves. But this is power with a double-edged sword. The increasing importance of and reliance on branding, combined with unprecedented access and laser-targeted delivery, has set a precipitous course, one in which the balance of brand power has radically shifted back to the consumer.

At stake is a global advertising budget of about $500 billion (as of 2011). The U.S. advertising spend in 2010 was $131.1 billion.[1] That's a lot of money, and when you consider that our little buddy Justin Bieber launched a global brand with a budget of about zero, you have to wonder how well it is being spent. Are companies pouring resources into buggy whips? The fact is, in building out their sophisticated marketing systems and models and budgets, marketers seem to have forgotten, or are just starting to remember, one simple fact: They were never actually in control. They just played the role, as if trapped in a global reality TV show (cue Jon Hamm in a gray flannel suit on *Mad Men*). Consumers were always, in fact, in control because they created the brands. If there is no demand, a product fails and disappears, and there is no brand.

Marketers always thought they knew best. They created the script, and from the advent of television, they created and perpetuated their own version of reality, where families looked alike and women wore aprons. To better achieve this, they retreated behind the two-way mirror for focus-group research, where consumers were examined like they were specimens in a bell jar, so their behavior could be better dissected, motivated, and controlled. I was behind the mirror in focus groups where, if a consumer got too vocal in his or her opinions, the moderator was instructed to divert the discussion away from that person, like a teacher controlling a preschool kid going off-road in the story circle. If the dissenter became really pushy, he or she was slipped a note by the facilitators that they had a "phone call" and was removed from the group to restore a more milquetoast dynamic. If any individual had a strong opinion, he or she was considered to be a negative influence on the group, a "controller," and was often discounted. The lowest common denominator was sought. Marketers seemed to have forgotten that they were never in control—and consumers always were.

But the advent of the Internet forever shattered the rule of the two-way mirror. Technology has put marketers on notice that the boss is back. The consumer has siezed the helm. A thirteen-year-old can go from a kid on a street corner to a global phenom in a matter of minutes. A broken-haired blond in a bubble bra can attract more online followers than the President of the United States. A young mob with mobile phones and Twitter accounts can bring down a regime in the Middle East. No marketing genius on the corporate planet could ever lay claim to these kinds of accomplishments.

But some people could: the people who, throughout history, have set the template for today's Twitterers, who broke through when there was no technology to tap. These were the original Brandzillas, who related on a gut level to their audience in such a way that two centuries later, if someone says, "Let them eat cake," we know exactly who said it first. Nike said, "Just do it," but these Brandzillas showed us how it was done. They were the Brands of the People, made by the people. The original social marketers. And they're *baa-aack*.

## THE BRANDZILLA EFFECT

The greatest Brandzillas have proved to have indelible staying power. They were mainly products of the Louis XIV School of Brand Management. For instance, if you were Louis XIV and decided to brand yourself the Sun King, you told the stonemasons of France to chisel a sunburst on every bridge and building in Paris, and that was pretty much that (those sunbursts are still there; check them out the next time you are in Paris). If you were Henry VIII and decided you didn't like the way your subjects or, say, your wife were not aligning with your personal brand strategy, you could always pull out a royal decree, or order a beheading or a drawing and quartering or two or fifty, to get everybody's attention and put things back "on brand." Those crafty monarchs of old even knew how to brand with color; in fact, they—not Ralph Lauren or Martha Stewart—started the trend. We all know about royal purple, or "to the purple born." But did you know about the color dark green? The pigment that produced dark green in ancient times was among the most expensive, so it was used almost exclusively by, and became identified with, the ultrawealthy. Today, that deep hunter green is a staple of the Ralph Lauren brand palette—as well as the color of the Queen of England's Land Rover.

Fast forward a few centuries from Louis XIV. The branding experts have handed down the strategies that turned Coca-Cola into Coke, permanently enriching dentists throughout the world; morphed a shoe named after a winged Greek goddess into the mantra "Just Do It," sending humankind jogging into the streets; and, on the flip side of the coin, created a mesmerizing monster, Adolf Hitler, who, for a while at least, had millions of German nationals saluting him and waving swastikas, and even the likes of Charles Lindbergh and the Duke of Windsor (the former King Edward VIII)—admiring him, saluting him, and soaking up his rhetoric.

Today, brands are not just tools of the powerful. We have evolved to a symbiotic relationship with brands, one that has been supercharged in the past ten years in a way that makes the brand power of all previous centuries cumulatively seem like a pinpoint on an anthill. The first two videos of Lady Gaga were viewed online by more than four times the total number of inhabitants of France at the time of vintage Brandzilla Marie Antoinette. Digital technology massively amplifies human behavior—whatever it may be, the end result is basically lots of people doing it lots of times.

The Brandzilla Effect means that Brandzillas can be found curled up in the cribs of our infants, embellishing our bodies, and even tattooed onto them. The core delivery system for brand messaging is no longer the TV set or the printed page. It's human beings. Consumers have become "brand ambassadors," walking billboards, flaunting brands' logos and recruiting others to the brand. The one-way street sign is now pointing both ways. In a sense, marketers should be relieved. It's sort of like having a player piano—a lot of the work is done! Once upon a time not so long ago, brands had to work like Sisyphus and spend like Diamond Jim Brady on a binge to capture attention, and even then only the strongest and biggest survived. Now, anyone can not just have a brand, but *be* a brand. In fact, thanks to the Brandzilla Effect, being without a personal brand today is akin to walking around naked.

When I began my career as a baby copywriter at the venerable J. Walter Thompson advertising agency in Chicago, brands were like house pets—tame, domesticated, and controllable. We in advertising were the breeders, wranglers, and curators—experts at creating, training, and controlling them, at projecting the image to which we wanted consumers to respond.

We had a certain swagger to our step. We were the Brand Masters. We could turn lead to gold. Since you paid for this book, I'll let you in on a branding secret, known by a select few. You know a certain tropically named fruit punch that is sold in a box that kids drink with a straw by the gallon? It was originally famously Red. Just Red. And Red was dying on the vine. In need of brand CPR, a brilliant professional inventor with a Proctor & Gamble pedigree named Doug Hall, whose company was (and is) called the Eureka Ranch (which claimed, only partly tongue-in-cheek, to channel the ghost of Benjamin Franklin), was called in to pound on Red's chest. Hall and his team came up with a game-changing idea—kids love brightly colored drinks, like blue, but blue kid drinks on the market at the time gave rotgut a run for its money. The company's original cash cow, the Red drink, tasted great, everyone, including kids, agreed. So—why not put the fruit juicy red taste in a blue drink? In other words, Red and Blue tasted exactly the same, but Blue had the immediate advantage of tasting better than other blue drinks that were out there. "The taste was the same taste, but by putting the fruit juicy Red in every color, to kids, the taste perception was better," says Hall. "In tests, there was a twenty-point difference in liking the product, drinkability, and other positive characteristics." The brand was not only saved, it was expanded—into Green, Yellow, and other colors of the rainbow. The reality was that nothing changed except the color—and kids' perceptions.[2] (This is not a unique instance. In a taste test involving Budweiser's "Lizards" ad campaign, Bud drinkers who had seen and been captivated by the commercials reported that the beer tasted much better.[3]) Via branding, consumers were convinced that this was an entirely new product and swore it tasted differently than Red. From the day of the launch, this line has been a best seller. Your kids probably had one of the colors for lunch. OK, this is not turning water into wine, but it's still some sort of brand alchemy. Today, some ten-year-old would read the label as part of his ongoing consumer advocacy science project, blow the whistle online, and two million kids and their parents would know the story. But Harry Potter and his wand would have had nothing on the marketing magicians. "Most marketing problems are product problems," says Doug Hall. "They are products that are not worth marketing." The solution was in finding—or inventing—a better solution to the product problem. The Blue drink was not just a rip-off of Red—Hall feels that would not have succeeded. In fact, it was a better Blue.

Branding once had a touch of Lazarus to it, capable of reviving the dead or near-dead, if not the merely irrelevant or obsolete. For instance, my consulting partner, Laurie Ashcraft, and I did the original research and worked on the positioning that recast the image of Sears from lawnmowers, tools, "brown goods," and a doorstop catalog to "The softer side," shifting the focus of the brand from the catalog and the workshop to a habitat for women. This paved the way for the perfect fit of name brand models, Sears as a fashion brand—and the Kardashians' clothing line.

Back then, there were tactics to create, launch, defend, or destroy brands. We ad agency compatriots knew and deployed them all, like arrows in our marketing quivers. We could create a "Kodak moment" on a dime—all it took was a puppy and a media budget. One particularly effective tactic, nicknamed "The Roadblock," involved buying all the air time at a particular time, on every network (which at the time numbered exactly three and was actually achievable), so that any human being in the immediate country watching TV in that time period would be "roadblocked" by the brand message. It was thus possible for a brand to "own dinnertime," for instance. (Those were also the archeologically quaint days when people actually sat down for dinner all at the same time as a family.) Every night at 6:30 P.M., the commercial would appear like clockwork, until the brand had been fused into viewers' hungry consciousness. Consumers surrendered like Pavlov's media dog and associated dinnertime with, for instance, Hamburger Helper or Pillsbury Crescent Rolls.

Mind control had a potentially shattering downside—as I realized with horror when I worked on branding a new Boeing aircraft. It's not my intention to insert myself self-importantly into a tragic disaster, but here are the facts of what happened. I worked on the concept and wrote the copy for a hopefully irresistibly charming cartoon ad campaign that urged fliers, in supergraphic type, to ASK! to fly on a particular new kind of jumbo jet, extolling its many virtues. In research, the campaign tested to be extremely effective. It was chosen by the client as the launch campaign. Champagne toasts all around! Then, only months after the campaign broke, one of the aircrafts crashed on takeoff from Chicago's O'Hare International Airport, in our own city's backyard, killing everyone aboard. The crash site was not far from the expressway I drove daily, and I saw the terrible black smoke. And I wondered—did even one passenger get on that plane because of one of those charmingly convincing ASK! ads that we were so proud of? I couldn't bear to work on the account anymore, not that it made a difference to anyone, particularly the victims and their families, or even to my ad agency, any more than a copywriter refusing to work on a cigarette campaign ever stopped anyone from smoking. Any step in the creation of an ad or a commercial is part of a team-driven ecosystem and does not live alone. But, at some point, you have to look at your link in the chain and take responsibility for your role, however seemingly small. At least I told that to myself as I stared at the big ASK! headlines of the ads. But where did my own responsibility start and end? Other disturbing thoughts followed: Did that ice cream jingle send somebody somewhere into a diabetic coma? Did the gasoline ad contribute to the oil shortage? Did pushing cake mix push women's rights back a hundred years? You could drive yourself crazy. But it was frightening to think of the power advertising messages really could wield, or that we liked to think they did. Eventually I learned to get over myself—I hope. But still.

Today, even the thought of that kind of path to influence is laughable. The boardroom, backroom, editing room, and even the throne room are no longer the branding cockpit. Technology has allowed Justin Bieber to have as much social impact as J. Walter Thompson ever had at the height of its powers—or almost any corporate chief had, for that matter. More, in fact. Kim Kardashian has as many Twitter followers as President Barack Obama—and she started in the bedroom, forget the boardroom. Within a matter of weeks, social media can brand a political revolution in Iran that rocked the world the "Twitter Revolution." Consumers are at the wheel, and marketers are racing to catch up. Not for nothing are some big brands shifting their marketing spend away from online display ads to social media.[4]

For marketers, the double-whammy is that the digital consumer has taken a cue from Toto and pulled back Oz's curtain. The Wizard is wearing the Emperor's new clothes. In a world where authenticity is increasingly the watchword, as Watts Wacker, futurist and CEO of FirstMatter, notes, "There are only two things a brand can't promise: trust and authenticity. Only your consumers can give that to you."[5]

Today, it takes only nine and a half seconds to impact a brand—for better or worse: the time it takes to send and download a digital file. Those nine and a half seconds are the new brand frontier. This is the paradigm shift, but it's also the opportunity.

What will you do with your nine and a half seconds?

# Chapter 1

# THE BRANDZILLA EFFECT

She was an instant celebrity, a household name by the age of twenty. A crowd of 6,000 attended her first public appearance. Later, as many as 50,000 fans turned out to view her as she passed by. Her appearance at a theater caused three dislocated arms, two broken ribs, and three crushed feet. A swarm of fawning female groupies copied her style of dressing and even her trademark gliding walk. A cardinal was caught crashing one of her parties. A twelve-year-old boy threw himself at her feet, calling her his "goddess." She played piano and sang moderately well. She was known for her towering, three-foot hairstyles, artistically crafted to create a commentary, incorporating everything from ropes of real pearls and diamonds to a sailing ship to an entire vegetable garden including an artichoke, a carrot, some radishes, and a head of cabbage. She was known for wearing masks in public. Her hairdresser, who tended her famous "pouf" while standing on a ladder, became a celebrity in his own right. One of her gowns was so heavily encrusted with jewels, embroidery, and swags of gold-threaded fabric that it had to be transported on a stretcher. Her style was copied by women internationally, yet it was indelibly her own. Her picture was displayed daily in newspapers and the fashion press. Tormented by the lack of privacy brought about by her position and her fame, she cleverly foiled her followers by having shutters for the windows they peered through covered in mirror. What she wore to the revolution may have actually caused a revolution. Her name became history's shorthand, synonymous first with purity, then with luxury, and finally with ignominy. She called herself the mother of her people, but, in the end, they called her a monster. She was far more than a brand. She was a Brandzilla.

She was an instant celebrity, a household name by the age of twenty. Five thousand people waited two hours for her in blistering heat, screaming at one of her appearances; at another, a fan clinically died in the crush and was brought back to life by medics. Over a billion people turned out to view her before she was twenty-five. She is known for her towering, three-foot hairstyles, artistically crafted to create commentary, incorporating everything from jeweled lobsters to bare bones, to stalagmites, to oscillating rings. One of her outfits was made entirely of frog puppets; another involved forty pounds of raw meat; still another contained her in an egg that had to be carried in on a stretcher. She was known for wearing masks in public. Her stylist became a celebrity in his own right, her style copied by a generation of fans, yet indelibly her own. Her picture is displayed daily in every possible media, and she adorns the covers of the fashion press. Her fans consider her to be their mirror. She calls them Little Monsters, and she calls herself Mother Monster. She has caused a cultural revolution, and she has been called one of the most influential people in the world. She is far more than a brand. She is a Brandzilla.[1]

More than three and a half centuries separate these iconic women—Marie Antoinette and Lady Gaga—yet they share the distinction of being among the most towering brands that ever stalked the earth. Marie Antoinette, the French Queen, endures in the face of the era of Facebook; her heritage and tragic legend are perhaps stronger than ever because the impact and endurance of a brand is built on the human connection, not the electronic one. In a world where the word "brand" has become so ubiquitous that the term has almost two billion entries on Google, there is a special stratosphere for those brands that defined not just themselves but the world around them. Because Lady Gaga's "Little Monsters" are right: Brands are indeed mirrors of ourselves, our society, and our trends because we make them so. Was it apocryphal when the curious peeped into Marie Antoinette's windows at Versailles and saw themselves mirrored back? Brands are reflections of what our world wants at a particular moment in time, whether consciously or not. Brands can represent an idealized life, or they can become part of the fiber of our lifestyle, to the point that the name of the brand becomes synonymous with our desires, our fears, our hopes. When you speak of a "Kodak moment," reach for a Kleenex, or have been "Madoffed," you've been branded. When you say someone has a "spartan" attitude, you get an instant picture of strength, austerity, and toughness.

The attributes of the brand—strength, sentimentality, softness, or scandal—transfer from the actual brand to us. Suddenly, we're part of the story, and that's what sticks with us. Today, the average adult gets as many as 3,000 media impressions a day. How many do you remember? Yet, some brands manage to make themselves indelible, winding their way into our vocabulary, our culture, the frame of reference against which we measure ourselves and conduct our lives. That stupid, smiley jingle that helped you remember the name of the toothpaste until you got to the store? Small change. We're talking about the kinds of brands that millions of people remember for decades, even centuries. We're talking about Brandzillas.

The term "brand" as we know it actually comes from the identifying mark that was used on livestock. They stoked up the old branding iron in the campfire until it was red-hot and sizzled it onto some critter's skin until it was scarred, leaving an identifying mark—once branded, forever branded. Makes you wonder—how much have we evolved? How much has changed today, when logos swing on every woman's shoulders and feet, and body art inks social statements into skin? With every logo you wear, every catchphrase you hum, every penny you pay for water that doesn't come from the tap, you've been branded. Brands exist because of our innate territorialism. They no longer just mark our boundaries or our possessions. They mark *us*.

Brandzillas are Brands on Steroids. Like the ancient Greek gods on Mount Olympus, Brandzillas toss their lightning bolts, shoot their love arrows, and impose their passion on us mortals. As Marie Antoinette learned to her peril, it's not always about eating cake. But you can admire the lightning storm without being struck by lightning. Nobody is bound, gagged, and forced to be a Brand Victim. If you want to wear a three-foot hairdo and sashay through the Hall of Mirrors, or slap a Nike swoosh on your head and dribble down center court, that's a personal choice. It takes an interactive, two-way agreement to become a Brand Victim, a contract between you and the brand. There's a reward on both sides—admiration, votes, worship, and profits versus acceptance, self-image, a sense of belonging, or a path to where you wish you belonged.

## BRANDS = BIG BUCKS

A strong brand is worth more—or, conversely, has more to lose—than a weak or nonbrand. That's a no-brainer: SpongeBob SquarePants macaroni and cheese costs seventeen cents an ounce. The nonbranded equivalent costs ten cents. SpongeBob SquarePants macaroni is more profitable than no-name macaroni. Five-year-olds in a recent study overwhelmingly preferred SpongeBob SquarePants macaroni and cheese to nonbrand macaroni and cheese (forget that recent research has shown that kids are actually dumber after watching SpongeBob SquarePants[2]). Lady Gaga sells more albums than an unknown. That doesn't even take math. Although, for purists and academics, math does exist. Clearly, somebody with considerable math skills came up with this equation for the value of a brand name (see the formula below).

I have no clue what this means—and I don't know where this formula originated. However, let's face it, does it really matter? It doesn't take a doctorate in quantum physics to recognize an überbrand—a

$$\frac{\text{Value of Firm}_0}{\text{Sales}_0} = \text{After} - \text{tax Operating Margin}$$

$$\times \left[ \frac{(1+g) \times \left(1 - \dfrac{(1+g)^n}{(1+\text{WACC})^n}\right)}{\text{WACC} - g} + \frac{(1+g)^n \times (1+g_n)}{(\text{WACC} - g_n)(1+\text{WACC})^n} \right]$$

Brandzilla—when you see one. If you can't figure it out, I have two words for you:

KIM KARDASHIAN

Or maybe, if you're Sears, she's working for you at this point, or, more accurately, you're working for her. You think that's ridiculous? A few years back—like two—no respectable company would hire as their spokesperson a woman who had made a sex tape. Today—bring it on! Kim was given a credit card under her own brand by a major financial company. Wait—did you know that she claims she dropped *them* because their rates turned out to be too high, she thought, for her fans? Who was in control there? Not the credit card company. That's the Brandzilla Effect in action.

## PASSING THE CROWN

Enter the new brand royalty. We don't have Louis XIV or Marie Antoinette, but we have pop stars, reality stars, sports stars, and even actual stars that exist in space (several entities exist to help you brand your own proprietary star in the intergalactic inventory). Announcing "The Celebrity 100"—a list of stars earning $4.5 billion in the past year—in June 2011, *Forbes* put reality star Bethenny Frankel on the cover. Noting that she cross-promotes her Skinnygirl brand on her reality TV show, *Forbes* cited the $100 million sale of her Skinnygirl Margarita, the headliner in a brand portfolio that includes shapewear, nutritional supplements, skin care products, and books. The magazine also gives a shout-out to Lady Gaga, who tops the power list "not just because of the $90 million she earned, but also because of her 32 million Facebook fans and 9.5 million Twitter followers who helped move 1 million digital downloads of [*Born This Way*] in only five days." (By May 2012, Gaga's Twitter fans had swelled to 24.1 million, according to *Forbes*'s "World's Most Powerful Celebrity List.") "They're also happy to buy the MAC makeup, Monster headphones and Virgin Mobile phones she features in her videos."

"In Hollywood, power is more than earnings and followers," *Forbes* notes. "It's also about building a brand and a business." That goes for sports, too. Tennis star Maria Sharapova was ranked number

80 among the *Forbes* Top 100 Moneymakers of 2011—but makes ten times as much from her brand partnerships as from swinging a racquet. She is one of a growing number of celebs who actually earn more from their brands than from whatever it was that made them famous in the first place.

Jillian Michaels, the trainer on a network fitness show, cofounded a company in 2001 that by 2008 exceeded $200 million in sales for products ranging from video games to diet products, as well as lucrative endorsements with beverage, shoe, and other companies, and (of course) books.[3]

The patron saints of this category may well be the Olsen twins, Mary-Kate and Ashley, who launched on-camera careers in the TV sitcom *Full House* at age six months, alternating in on-the-clock work hours in the same role to comply with child-labor laws, and have been on *Forbes*'s "Celebrity 100" list since 2002. Dualstar Consumer Products, founded when the twins were six years old, targeted the now $335 billion tween market of kids from eight to twelve. "The opportunities are endless," said Ashley Olsen, interviewed when she was eighteen years old.[4] Their teen-oriented brand, which mirrored their ages as it evolved, included clothes, books, products, dolls, movies, videos, and posters. In 2005, at age eighteen, the twins took over as copresidents of Dualstar Entertainment Group, focusing on products like fragrances and home décor. Although there was the usual skepticism of young women with Hollywood backgrounds and issues, Ashley was absolutely right. The Olsens followed up with a portfolio of fashion lines, including the exclusive brand the Row. In 2007, *Forbes* ranked the twins as the eleventh richest women in entertainment. In 2011, their fashion brand had an estimated value of $1 billion.[5] The babyhood of the Olsens predated the current capabilities of the Web, but one can only imagine the impact the twins would have had if, as toddlers, they had had their own baby blog and the digital strategies of today's branded stars. Scary!

According to the *Los Angeles Times*, the Kardashians are "a branding machine worth $65 million" and a clear example of how a brand ambassador can actually replace the brand itself. Brand ambassadors—the vehicles through which brands leverage and strengthen their presence—are of paramount importance in today's globalized world, the keys to creating and sustaining an audience for a particular brand. Everyone was under Bollywood's spell before they really discovered India as the superpower nation it is today. And for World Water Day, celebrities like Selena Gomez and Rihanna bottled water from their taps to engage with their stakeholders (or their fan base) and use their brand to draw attention to a global problem. Celebrities even enable several brands to band together: A line of kids' clothing at Target "created" by Disney Channel characters Ci-Ci and Rocky not only adds fuel to that show—it also powers up both Disney and Target. The message has become the medium.

The takeaway for consumers is that there is a new kind of label to read. Now, you are buying an ingredient that's not regulated by government controls, and the only details on the package may be an autograph or a smiling face. Caveat emptor. The takeaway for marketers is that there is a new gateway to opportunity. Twenty or thirty years ago, a Farrah Fawcett might have, and did, lend her brand to a line of hair care products and maybe a fragrance. Today, as a modern superstar Angel, she'd have done a Bethenny and rolled out the cosmetics, the vodka, the workout wear, the videos, the stiletto, the push-up bra, the clothing line (wait—Jaclyn Smith, a true pioneer in this area, *did* do that, very successfully, for Kmart), the bedding collection, the jewelry, and maybe the handgun. Celebrity branding is creating a whole new category of client, with the big change being that the celebrity doesn't even have to be a celebrity. The new category is the celebrity personality, the celebrity who is famous for being famous. That could be anybody. That could be you.

This takes us full circle, bypassing the traditional corporate client roster or, in an alternate route some might choose, avoiding it like the plague. Savvy marketers—be they the Madison Avenue professional, the housewife at her kitchen table, or the teen garage band—are charging through this rent in the fabric of the branding universe to get out there with their own self-created, and often eponymous, brands.

Advertising expert and author Richard Kirshenbaum, cofounder of Kirshenbaum Bond Senecal + Partners and CEO of NSG/SWAT, is not just an Advertising Hall of Famer; he is one of the innovative emerging entrepreneurs bypassing the corporate food chain to seize the new branding opportunities. In addition to his day job advising some of the world's most significant and stalwart companies and brands, Kirshenbaum has become an entrepreneurial evangelist. His book, *Madboy: Beyond Mad Men: Tales from the Mad, Mad World of Advertising*, was a number-one best seller on Kindle. Among the stable of new products that Kirshenbaum and his team have recently created, developed, and launched—which include a branded vodka, rum, and coffee—is the eponymously branded Rabbi Mints, aka "The Chosen Mint," a breakthrough new product in the kosher mint category. Kirshenbaum's partners included not the people who make Altoids, but the very real Rabbi Adam Mintz. The "aha" moment occurred at a Jewish wedding, officiated by Rabbi Mintz and attended by Kirshenbaum and an entrepreneur friend. When the groom leaned in to kiss the bride, Kirshenbaum cracked to his friend, "Just in time for Rabbi Mints."

A new product idea, a top-of-the-line kosher mint "with panache"— and a new business—was born. Chewing gum, lip balm, and other related products will round out the line. Rabbi Mintz had inspired not just a good idea, but a fortuitous name; as the comedian Jackie Mason noted, "He's lucky his name wasn't garlic."[6]

Kirshenbaum's is an interesting scenario because his is not just an integrated model, but a shape-shifter table to morph across both traditional and digital platforms. Like a reverse-branding Superman, Kirshenbaum the caped brand crusader, known for aiding and abetting the traditional big brands and media budgets, has backed out of the (i)phone booth and emerged as a Clark Kent of entrepreneurialism. In a way, he has come full circle from the days when social media equaled the underwear admonishments he created and spray-painted for his client on the sidewalks of New York.

"Creating Rabbi Mints was the ultimate dream for an ad man," says Kirshenbaum, noting that Rabbi Mints is just one in a portfolio of brands he has created, including Blackwell Fine Jamaican Rum in partnership with Island Records founder and Jamaica native Chris Blackwell. "Part of it is having a sense of being a self-starter, a sense of control, and not relying on someone else to say yea or nay. It's been a great balance to my client-side business, traditional fee-based accounts—to work on some things we have equity in, while the fee part of the studio allows us to hire and bring talent to bear on things we have equity in. It's symbiotic. I think that, as marketing profession-als, we'll be relying less on larger companies and brands to steer our future."[7]

# Chapter 2

# BRAVE NEW BRAND WORLD

Branding has always been an important component of marketing, but as the world flattened out, so did the branding canvas. Today there are an unprecedented number of branding opportunities, propelled by technologies including but not limited to the Internet. The egg people created a way to stamp branding on eggs in their shells, fresh from the hen. Intel taught people to look inside the computer and branded the microprocessor. Now, anything—and anyone—can be branded. Platforms once termed "guerilla" media, and considered sort of out there, off-road alternatives to established media, such as print, radio, and TV, have become democratic branding opportunities for all. There are few things that can't function as a delivery system for a brand message—whether it's the sky, the street, the handle of your grocery cart, the back of the bathroom door, your phone, any edifice, your wallet, your abs, or even that cap they give your newborn in the delivery room five seconds after he or she is born. The digital world acts as an amplifier and accelerator. Times infinity. Where branding used to be more about interruption, it's now about connection. If there is a possible connection point, it will be found—and leveraged.

Fourteen years ago, Richard Kirshenbaum, with his partner Jon Bond, wrote *Under the Radar: Talking to Today's Cynical Consumer*, a seminal, predigital book on guerilla branding. Today, the man who once spray-painted lingerie ads on sidewalks says, "When we first went into business and we created guerilla marketing, there was no such thing, and we weren't really living for the most part in a digital age, so we invented street stenciling and advertising on fruit and the pop-up store, and all those things that created a huge amount of tension. They were ideas that lived outside the digital world. Of course today, if you have a great viral video and you get huge pick-up, you can still build your brand through great ideas. But, again it gets back to the idea that if you have a viral video and nobody cares about it, then no one will see it."[1]

In the expanding world of branding options, the corporate "naming rights" phenomenon has proliferated. This allows the entity to purchase the right to name a facility or another entity—or even a person. Stadiums with brand names—for example, the Staples Center in L.A.—are just the beginning. The name of a new species of monkey sold for $650,000. And at least one couple sold the naming rights to their child to a corporation. Google currently lists more than two million entries for the sale of baby-naming rights. If each of these venues is considered a new revenue stream, the opportunities are endless.

Cradle-to-grave lifestyle sponsorship is a reality, and products that simply rely on promoting product features are increasingly being inched out by branding entire chunks of consumers' lifestyles. Gerber Babies have been around since the 1920s, but branding has now firmly permeated the parenting lifestyle. Stroller brands are shaping parents' perceptions of themselves. It's not just about the product feature/function/quality issues, such as, "Will this stroller easily collapse to fit in my car and does it have a drink holder on it?" Stroller brands now define the parent, rather than vice versa. Bugaboos signal adventurous off-roaders, while Maclaren means conservative soccer mom. A website called Thebump.com has decoded mothering styles based on stroller brands—sporty mama, trendy mama, practical mama, and so on. No need for dads to feel left out—another site has a similar analysis for them. Branding sets expectations early. Most new parents have also been exposed to "The Mercedes." Not the car—the crib, with a similar level of postnatal luxury, for parents who are prepared to pamper—and pay. This is a good example of brand "piggybacking"—the halo effect of the renowned luxury car jumps across categories onto the back of something else—in this case, a completely unrelated product or category, transferring decades and millions of dollars' worth of brand equity for free, never actually stating this is based on the car, but allowing consumers to close the loop for themselves.

Education, increasingly starved for funding, is a natural and probably inevitable next step. In the United States, there is no such thing as
public nursery school, so there is a theoretical opening to insert brands
into kids' mindsets and into their backpacks early on. And would this
be a bad thing? In New York City in 2011, there were 28,817 applicants
for 19,834 private preschool seats. The preschool application process has
forced many parents, even those with seemingly unlimited resources,
into panic mode. Some extremists have resorted to planning their preg-
nancies to coincide with an increasingly ruthless application process.[2]
Others are self-creating a flurry of "underground" parent-run preschool
co-ops. In this environment, would a Gerber Preschool, for instance,
be less than welcomed by parents? Or how about an Apple Preschool,
stocked with Apple electronics? (Actually, that sounds great—sign me
up!) For parents, it would be an island of relief, an answer to a wrench-
ing problem. The brand would be heroic. For Gerber, it would be a step
toward extending the brand into an older age bracket, paving the way
for the development of products for older children. Gerber already has
a branded line of life insurance for babies. I have no idea which brand
extension would be more profitable, but certainly there is no argument
that education is a massively more attractive brand extension to a parent than the prospect of a baby's death.

Weddings are inching into branded territory, via Martha Stewart,
Vera Wang, David Tutera (who rolls around in a giant trailer emblazoned with "David Tutera Weddings," a fixture on his reality TV
show), and The Knot. Weddings are now considered the ultimate
opportunity to define not just the bride's style, but the couple's. With
the average cost of a wedding topping $28,000, branded sponsorships
of the "I do's" are being hawked on eBay and beyond. In the old days,
when the bride's parents ran weddings, some couples were offered the
choice between a wedding and a check. And, unless it was a friend or
family member doing the baking, who knew or cared who made the
cake? But today, branding allows savvier couples to have their wedding cake and eat it, too. For instance, one New Jersey couple sold off
branding rights of everything from the flowers to the cake to a list of
sponsors ranging from 1–800 Flowers to a local hotel and Entenmann's
bakery—in return for conducting the ceremony, courtesy of the
Brooklyn Cyclones, at KeySpan Park in Coney Island in front of 5,000

guests—with the sponsors' brand names flashing on the JumboTron. Before long, we may see the sponsor as the third, fourth, and fifth partners in the ceremony. For marketers, this opens an entirely new media opportunity. The wedding as a brand-delivery system is an embryonic form of guerilla marketing. Expect it to grow, especially if the economy doesn't.

Even funerals are ripe for branding. I was part of the ad agency creative team for a coffin account. Branding was key, as marketing in the funeral industry is quite competitive. It is difficult to demonstrate the desirability of your brand to a dead person. In an effort to tackle that thorny issue, one competitor's memorable tag line, admittedly tough to top, was, "New hope for the dead." As the vast boomer generation ages and begins to winnow, competition for funeral services will drive an explosion of Final Branding, so marketers should brace themselves for more brand action in the Netherworld.

The Internet is also driving a surge in funerary branding. In an article called "Branding Your Funeral Home," which ran in a funeral industry publication, a consultant to funeral homes advised the industry: "In today's funeral service marketplace, your competition is no longer just the other funeral home across town or those in the next town. Instead, you compete with the Internet discounter or the warehouse store a couple of blocks away."[3]

I'm not sure which local warehouse stores are offering funerary supplies or services, but clearly, branding has washed up on the shores of the River Styx.

Every inch of the planet is available for branding, actually. Without educated awareness of the power and relentlessness of branding, there will be a veritable monster mash. Brandzillas, not robots, will be the action stars of the future. Like the T. rexes and the stegosauruses that once ruled the earth, these Brandzillas will battle for territory and power, dragging consumers in their wake. Consumers will have choices, but these choices will be among brands that have already been precurated.

## WHO LET THE BRANDS OUT?

We're all familiar with the sneak attack. Martha Stewart's brand crept like a grease fire from the kitchen through American homes and right out the door to the garden. Eddie Bauer moved from the tent to the décor of our cars. The raw food movement has claimed the territory of food that's not even food yet—it's still produce.

Branding is claiming territories never before dreamed of, staking out even the most intimate real estate, below the belt: Brazilian wax, anyone? Sandiego.com reports that before 1990, only strippers went completely bare down there. Today, the Brazilian brand has become synonymous with youth and fitness and is flaunted by mainstream women of all ages past puberty and through grandmotherhood. (If you doubt me, I dare you to go to Wikipedia and click on "Brazilian wax," but first shut the kids out of the room.) The Brazilian even earned a starring role on the hit TV show *Sex and the City*. It probably has an agent and a house in the Hamptons.

Brandzillazation is spreading. But once in the hands of consumers, Brandzillas lack the rulebooks and guidelines that come along with the strategies of corporate marketing. There is, therefore, an ever-present danger of a brand crash—such as the one caused by Kim Kardashian's divorce, eighty-eight days after her Brandzilla wedding, or Tiger Woods's morality implosion, which reportedly resulted in a loss of $17 million in brand value.[4]

Jobs and employment are always a concern, and so, not surprisingly, the lead article on the AOL homepage recently was about how to get work. But it wasn't about polishing your résumé. The article was called "The New Rules of Job Interviewing." A question was posed: "I'm looking for a job—what should I do?" The answer was, "Stop worrying about the 'shoulds' and, instead, focus on your individual branding choices...you've got a brand!" The key consideration for the modern jobseeker is not his or her experience or references, but how his or her personal brand fits with the brand of the potential employer. One brand aligns with another, forming a daisy chain until we are all connected.

## BACK TO BASICS

Branding has become so ubiquitous as to be almost essential. The number of brands is staggering, and if people become their own brands, that adds more than 300 million to the total in the United States alone. A website is devoted to 154 brands of pencils globally,

many of which are so distinct as to have collector value. On this pro-
liferate playing field, how does one brand rise above the other? How
do you beat, much less become, a Brandzilla? The answer may be: To
get more, do less. Throw ninety-five pages of the one-hundred-page
marketing deck out the window and start over. New rules call for new
plans. The good news is, they don't have to break the bank. They don't
even necessarily need to involve a bank.

What do they have to involve? What's the common denominator of success? An idea. As Richard Kirshenbaum emphasizes, "At the
end of the day, just like a great Super Bowl commercial, just like a
great viral video, just like great ads on fruit, or a great pop-up store—
it's really all about the idea. That's the truth. This is all wonderful,
because it gives us so many more options, but really, the best way to
view it is, it greatly expands the colors in the color palette that you can
paint with—that's it. I think it's getting back to basics, getting back to
the idea. The medium is the message, but the message is still the message. Everything is leaning to technology, but it's all still about a great
idea."[5]

# Chapter 3

# ONCE UPON A TIME: SELLING VERSUS STORYTELLING

Today, the average adult is confronted with as many as 3,000 media impressions a day. It's the job of branding to slash through that jungle and make us care about—and remember—the brand. The emotional connection is the key. Emotion transfers the brand's attributes—such as prestige, strength, sentimentality, softness, or scandal—from the actual brand to the target market. Suddenly, the consumer is not just observing and making smart decisions; the consumer is part of the story.

That's where storytelling beats selling. Look on Google: There are 6.3 million entries for corporate storytelling. It's a whole new art, one that's, if not replacing, certainly enhancing the more quantitative science of sales. The numbers don't get you into the bedroom, kitchen, and bathroom, or into somebody's heart. The story does.

One of the conflicts facing the corporate environment today is the gap between the quantitative and qualitative cultures—those of sales and storytelling—although ideally these should operate synergistically. The sales approach is often short-term, with little to no emotional connection, the path papered with pitches, websites, and "one-sheets" that give the facts and just the facts. They may be great facts, but facts alone do not build enduring brands. A brand like Apple has astonishing sales volume, but it is also built on an interwoven model of quality and a culture with a story. The reality for most CMOs is that the drive to make quarterly quotas and feed analysts' projections and expectations has not eradicated—and has often intensified—the border between marketing and sales. Traditional sales techniques are not necessarily synergistic with building a storytelling culture, and the content is often largely quantitatively based, with minimal emotional connection. Perhaps the biggest offender is Microsoft's PowerPoint, aka the template panacea. Ninety-eight percent of organizations today use and share PowerPoint for sales, marketing, and training.[1] Google in fact recommends that only 20 percent of information be put on PowerPoint slides and that the rest of the presentation should be given personally by the presenter.[2] Still, we've all seen our share of slides crammed with barely readable words, facts, and charts. We've probably even created them. Things are bad enough that May has been declared PowerPoint Abuse Awareness Month.

The fact is, to be a proficient marketer today, you have to be a superb storyteller. But not just any story. Anybody can make up a story and paste it onto any product. In 1975, a California ad executive created the Pet Rock, a gray rock packaged in a little cagelike box with a thirty-two-page "care and feeding" instruction manual, including ways to "train" the rock—like pushing it to roll over. The guy made millions on this novelty, and nobody could question its success within its category. One could say the brand even sustained because you can still purchase a USB Pet Rock, the digital version with a cord coming out of it that plugs into your computer. The brand is described thus: "Simply plug the USB cable into a port and let the fun begin.... People will stop by and ask you what your USB Pet Rock does. Each time, you can make up a new story, for no matter what you say, it will be greater than the truth—because these USB Pet Rocks don't do a dang thing. Except make you smile. And confuse your friends and coworkers, which will make you smile even more. So, get your USB Pet Rock today, and help make us rich tomorrow."[3] The problem ensues when brands try to use Pet Rock tactics outside the novelty aisle.

Authenticity and sustainable storytelling that truly connects, engages, and motivates means being an honest storyteller because even if you are a skillful exaggerator, much less a liar, it's not possible to hide anymore. One false or two-faced step brings out the Web harpies, retribution, and reputational suicide. Even if you do everything right, the risk remains. Anybody can say anything about you and put it on Facebook—including Facebook itself, which in 2011 attempted to launch an orchestrated smear campaign against Google. Top PR firm Burson-Marsteller was revealed to have been hired by Facebook to contract an influential blogger to write Google-blasting posts, and Burson was accused of "spreading a whisper campaign" by pressuring the media to write negative stories about Google. When outed for this transgression by *USA Today*, Facebook admitted it, with the rationale that Google was doing some things Facebook didn't particularly care for that "raised privacy concerns," including, potentially, launching its own social networking site competitive to Facebook.[4]

It's pretty much open season out there in Dodge Cybercity, and nobody is running around wearing a badge.

However, obviously stories can be used to illuminate or rehabilitate as well as destroy a reputation online. Elvis Presley, for instance, did not die a gentle death. The official website Elvis.com leapfrogs the issue by pulling out the stuff of legend. Elvis's demise, for instance, is handled indirectly, via a firsthand video story told through the lens of the local florist who handled the floral tributes at his passing, a sweet-looking, grandmotherly type who managed the tsunami of arrangements from Elvis worshipers that flooded the mansion in respectful and loving tribute. Other storytelling videos from those who knew, or tangentially touched, Elvis—found on the Legacy Video Gallery section of the website—include childhood friends, a person who spent the day with Elvis, Elvis's jeweler, and the doorman from the Memphis theater where Elvis went to the movies.

In his book *The Storytelling Animal: How Stories Make Us Human*, Jonathan Gottschall describes how we are hardwired culturally to allow stories to shape our perceptions. Since the rise of TV and other recent media, he notes, research has shown how "fiction *does* mold our minds. Story—whether delivered through films, books, or video games—teaches us facts about the world; influences moral logic; and marks us with fears, hopes and anxieties that alter our behavior, our perceptions, even our personalities. Research shows that story is constantly nibbling and kneading us, shaping our minds without our knowledge or consent. The more deeply we are cast under story's spell, the more potent the influence."[5]

The most iconic brands evolve from a foundation of storytelling. In *How Brands Become Icons: The Principles of Cultural Branding*, Douglas B. Holt notes that brands emerge as various "authors" tell stories that involve the brand. These authors may be companies, culture, industries, intermediaries, such as critics or salespeople, or customers. The relative influence of these authors and stories varies across product categories, and various storylines may result, which merge and intersect in our everyday lives and experiences until their collective aggregate emerges as truths. Stories that consumers find valuable in constructing their own identities, or can project themselves into, tend to grow up socially, outside of corporate confines, and have the greatest stickiness because these brands embody the ideals and values that consumers admire and find aspirational. The most successful of these have the greatest chance of becoming iconic brands. These brands are expressions of and reflect aspirational social values, not just product attributes.[6]

The evolution of media, from print to radio to film to TV to the Web, has made storytelling increasingly accessible, interactive, and impactful. Ray Gaulke, owner of Great Expectations Marketing, has been president of the Public Relations Society of America as well as of two major advertising agencies, Publicis (United States) and Burson-Marsteller. Gaulke was president of Burson when the ad agency created one of the greatest storytelling commercials of all time—the iconic Dannon yogurt commercial that told the story of centenarians in Soviet Georgia eating yogurt—and living longer. "The difference between storytelling and selling is that selling is about the product, and storytelling is about something else," Gaulke says. "There's emotion in storytelling—it's not just fact, it's emotion. The walls are broken down. You are selling the experience.[7]

The storytelling of the future is heading in visual directions. Take Pinterest.com, the virtual pinboard site that lets visitors create, curate, and share visual imagery that reflects their sensibility or a point they wish to illustrate, connecting people and brands through the things they find interesting. Pinterest has grown explosively, growing to 103 million visitors in the United States in February 2012, hitting more than 20 million unique visitors in three months—faster than any other website. Growth slowed from the early supersonic rates but has remained in the double-digits.[8] The spider effect of this form of social networking, powered by visuals and its marketing impact, is capsulized in this post on a LinkedIn marketing professionals board: "Pinterest...is one more place to plant a seed. In a week since I joined, over 150 people were following my pins, and some, even the links to my website and blog, were spread to other people's networks."

Jason Damata of Fabric Media says, "It used to be what they called 'one night stands.' You told a story once, and it was gone. You can still do that, if that's all the situation really requires, or that's all you can really get out of it, but what we like to do is work with companies that have something to offer the media industry in the way of a tool, or content, and work out partnerships whereby both are benefitting because I know what it's like to be on the other side, and at the end of the day, it's an attention economy, it's about how many adults can you reach, how many adults look at your brand."[9]

But speed of connectivity is just the beginning. Charlotte Beers, former CEO of Ogilvy & Mather, Undersecretary of State for Public Diplomacy and Public Affairs, and author of *I'd Rather Be in Charge*, notes, "If you want fast recognition, you can travel like lightning in social media. You can put something up on YouTube and what you'll get out of that is sometimes a shock of recognition, but in order for it to go further than that, you have to build a lot more around it." The relationship that is built along with the story is as critical as the content, Beers explains. "When you open into the broader range of social media, it has the unique advantage of creating the appearance or the reality of a dialogue, and a dialogue is a more real aspect of a relationship. So the user says to the product, 'Here's what I think. Here's what I'd like to see happen,' and so on....Often there's a bit of a gimmick out there where they say, 'Would you rather have this ending or that ending.' It's not really that we need their creative resources. It's just another way to involve [consumers] deeply in explaining how the relationship works."[10]

In *The Dream Society: How the Coming Shift from Information to Imagination Will Transform Your Business*, Rolf Jensen theorizes that we are transitioning "from Information Society to Dream Society,"[11] and that emotions, rather than facts, will dominate the marketplace. Like films, stories will be created and narrated. Jensen has tracked the evolution of the marketplace and its communication delivery systems, from cave paintings created 30,000 years ago through the invention of the printing press, which shifted the dominant media from visual imagery to the written word, and then the invention of TV, which shifted the balance back to visual imagery. When visual imagery dominates, it is easier and more effective to communicate information through emotion—say, a tear or a smile. With the increasing speed of delivery via electronic media, we can view far more images than we could fifty years ago.

"In the very old days when we were hunters and gatherers, it was about obtaining cohesion among the tribes, ensuring our tribe was different from the others," Jensen explains. "Storytelling described how the tribe originated, where it came from, why it existed and why it was better for others. A story marks the beginnings of a brand. When the story has been told to sufficient numbers of consumers for them to remember it, the company in question may claim, 'We now have ourselves a brand.'" A story helps inject the emotion that helps consumers become passionate about a brand. In rejecting New Coke, consumers wrote a new storyline. "It's 'We the people,'" says Jensen. "They are saying, 'The company does not own Coke; we, the consumers, do.'"

"Consumers used to be passive listeners. Now, they are the storytellers. Who is the story-owner when social media comes into play?" As for the corporate or marketing role, "You may still be the director, but you can't control the actors and the actors will not always obey the director." Ten years in the future, he predicts, "branding will belong to the greatest storytellers."

Jensen believes that the iconic storytellers of the future will not be consumer brands. "It will be a complete flip of the paradigm," he says. Already, we see companies trying to inject more passion into storytelling about their brands by sponsoring blogs and creating interactive opportunities to create dialogue around brands as well as real-people-turned-"reality stars" pitching products via their stories. And it's working. For instance, "real housewife" Bethenny Frankel's Skinnygirl Cocktails, acquired by Beam, Inc., the company behind Jim Beam whiskey, for an estimated $100 million in March 2011, was the fastest-growing spirits brand in the United States by April 2012.[12]

Jensen notes that this trend is especially notable in passion scenarios such as socioeconomic stories. Many companies are at an inherent disadvantage. "In Egypt, people are ready to die for democracy or freedom, or to further the prospect of freedom. But I think nobody is prepared to die for Coca-Cola—correct me if I'm wrong. But marketing managers are trying to inject more passion into their brands. That is what they are trying to accomplish. For instance, the largest bank corporation in Denmark is sponsoring the national football team. They are trying to put passion in via other things. But part of the problem is you have a lot of MBA types being taught rational things and then you can't blame them because they weren't taught or trained this way."

The point of differentiation for a brand will not be attitudinal and psychographic, versus features-oriented and quantitative. A prime example of this is Occupy Wall Street. "The rebel instinct is a very powerful storytelling engine," says Jensen. "I buy into this because I am a rebel. You see this also in Occupy Denmark. The idea that there is rebellion against the elite one percent. What's clear is that people don't trust leaders, who they perceive as part of the elite one percent—as much as in the past." Lady Gaga, with her Little Monsters, and Justin Bieber, with his lovelorn teens, also fit this paradigm. Jensen predicts the future—the near future—will bring "Occupy Wall Street × 10."[13]

We've seen the power of the Twitter Revolution in participatory social change. But, from her unique perspective as former Undersecretary of State for Public Diplomacy and Public Affairs, with a special emphasis on the Middle East, as well as one of the world's most eminent experts on branding, Charlotte Beers sees opportunities as well as the cost of missing them. She comments,

When I was the Undersecretary of State in 2003, the Middle East was already ahead of us in social media, and the reason for that is because they didn't have access to very much traditional media. So anybody who had a telephone would be connected in a special way. I remember [sources in the region] making very clumsy videos of somebody blowing up somebody in the United States and putting them out in a viral system just to create the expectation that this could be done. I thought this was daunting to see and yet we had nothing in the U.S.

government that would counter that, and I think now we're all aware that we're engaged in that dialogue. And part of the reason social media was far more important in the Middle East than it is here is because the government had no open dialogue with their people. They didn't know what their people were thinking or doing. The processes where we have those kinds of dialogues all the time were not readily available. So the Arab Spring was, in that sense, very predictable.

I was recently interviewed by Al-Jazeera about that because I had said, in 2003, that I thought if people of the United States could talk to the people of the Middle East instead of just dealing government to government, that we would reach many more points of common understanding. If you go and interview the young men—that's what the game is about in that part of the world, where 70 percent of the population is under 30 years of age and nearly 50 percent is under 20 [The population of the Middle East is experiencing a youth bulge that puts critical mass in the hands of a much younger population. The median age in Yemen, for example, is 16.4; in Uganda, it's 15.1; the median age in the United States is 37.1.[14]]—what emerges is a stunning array of common needs and desires.

Beers notes common values that could be explored and built on via social media. "I used a survey in the government that asked people in all of Europe and the Middle East to rank their number one, two, three value needs—not necessarily political or government values. And what we found was, in the United States, people would put family—meaning many things; then safety and faith; and the third one is education. Well, if you went to the Middle East countries and you interviewed the women in those countries, they put exactly the same three things at the top of their priorities. Social media was made for that kind of shared understanding, if we can continue to keep opening those doors."[15]

Ralph Jensen says,

At some point, they will have to see that the current business model used by most businesses in Europe and the U.S. won't work anymore. They will have to find new visions, new materials. Twenty years from now, talking about money and material things will be looked down upon as old-fashioned, not part of this century, and greedy. The focus will be on emotional versus material things. "Branding" will need a new name, because the term "branding" will be too commercially associated with products. That name may be storytelling. Branding will become storytelling. This will herald the return of the storyteller. I believe Lady Gaga is the harbinger of this. She is identified as a rebel, a plus in making a strong emotional connection. She is identified with speaking for those without a voice, enabled and empowered by social media. Social media is just a delivery system—but it is the best and most powerful delivery system. Within ten years, there will be a complete flip. Branding will belong not to the corporate world, but to the greatest storytellers.[16]

As Jason Damata similarly notes, "People want to sign up for something aspirational, not 'The Mountain Dew Challenge.' It all comes down to emotional ground."[17]

And who will those emotional brand makers be? Jensen believes they could be a pop celebrity, a sports team, or an individual or entity with the power to, as he puts it, "be a focal point" of consumer awareness and put passion into the equation. "I do believe someone like Lady Gaga can lead us there. She's just one example," Jensen notes. He foresees a future where consumers buy not products but a lifestyle that the stories convey, a shift he describes as transformational.

"The role of companies and marketing will become the facilitators," Jensen predicts. "They will facilitate the storytelling, help in new ways, add new features. They will be the channel, not the originators. The point of difference will not be a product difference, but attitudinal."[18]

The Internet today is like the Nile Delta—we are at the beginning of the most fertile ground the world has ever seen for storytelling—and a new kind of brand building and marketing. Or, as futurist Watts Wacker believes, we are paralleling a situation of five centuries past. Wacker, author and coauthor of books including *The 500 Year Delta* and *The Visionary's Handbook: Nine Paradoxes That Will Shape the Future of Your Business*, believes that

> We are in a transitory period. We're living in a time that is absolutely, positively identical to 500 years ago. Five hundred years ago, people went to bed snug as a bug in a rug with the knowledge that the world was flat. And the next day, they woke up and suddenly they were told, the world's no longer flat, it's round. And you could choose to believe it was flat, or you could choose to believe it was round, but either way, great fortunes changed. I have described this as cultural schizophrenia, where the world as it presents itself and the world as we intuit it to be are no longer in synch. And this is why the concept of a perception is so critical. The two most important things to understand are aspirations and perceptions. What are the new aspirations, and where do our perceptions exist that are and are not able to change? A perception is a belief, based on your instincts, and not your intellect. And the hardest thing to change is a perception, period. The world as it presents itself it and the world as it is are not in synch. What happened 500 years ago were three things that became an age of tectonic change—that is not about the rate of change or the cause of change, it's beyond that. It's a conspiring of the economic, technological and social agendas all adjusting at one time.
>
> What did we have 500 years ago? We had the Gutenberg press, which was the unleashing of information that I would call "the Internet 1.0." We had the discovery of the New World. Why was that important? Because the Dutch, the Portuguese, the French, the Italians, the British—everybody who came over [to] the New World found this thing called gold and brought it back to the old world, and we suddenly had enough monetization to create market-based economics. The entire engine of value creation and wealth formation changed from barter to markets. And the word renaissance means renewal of thought. So we had a complete readjustment of the social agenda.[19]

With great change inevitably comes the counterweight of push-back and, in the interim, transitional stagnation. Wacker believes that those in power and institutions try to prohibit change and maintain the status quo.

Something as simple as the Beatles appearing on the music scene with long hair in an era of crew cuts once inspired an entire generation of parents, authorities, and status quo-ers to rise up in arms. I'm old enough to remember school principals doing collar checks to make sure boys' hair cleared their collars—or they were sent home, or worse (and girls being forced to kneel to be sure their skirts touched the ground). That was until those enforcers grew their own hair long and shortened their own skirts. Has anybody checked out Michelle Obama's hem lengths lately? If somebody would give her the kneeling test, she'd probably flunk. Even before the Kennedy assassination, a massive change had begun. The rebranding of an entire generation had been triggered, but some people, particularly those in authority, remained stuck at the end of the previous phase.

The point is, as Wacker says, "We have this terrible conflict of the world moving toward new social norms, and our institutions trying to delay or stop them." Wacker calls this the Epoch of Uncertainty. "It's time for a new story." In fact, Wacker believes that we are at the end, not the beginning, of the last great epoch, which he calls the Information Age. So, much of what we see around us is a holdover effect, the epochal equivalent of the principals doing the collar checks. As we evolve stories relevant to the new age and the social appetite to tell them, the technological channels for this transition are proliferating. This is in turn fueled by a demand for authenticity, a desire to share, and a motivation to counter or backlash against the sweeping crisis of confidence and ethics wrought by socioeconomic crisis with a desire to do good—stories and business models that are centered on goodness, responsibility, and accountability, rather than capitalism and its evil stepsister, greed. And, as Wacker emphasizes, "It's not the equivalent of, say, Disney owning ABC, or GE owning NBC, where you start blending fact and fiction. It's organic—bloggers will find you." It is, however, a matter of "putting the myth in the context of the times in which we live."[20]

"A good story engages, captivates and takes the reader on a fantastic journey," says Todd Semrau, owner of the Urban Eats Consulting Group, which finds creating cohesive and tangible brand stories to be integral to its clients' businesses. "In the end, if magic is present…you have succeeded in creating an epic, game-changing idea. Otherwise you are just dust in the wind."[21]

## Chapter 4

# IF BIEBER WAS A BURGER

By the time this book comes out, Justin Bieber may or may not have seen his moment come and go because he is a brand at a tipping point. Much of his momentum was based on his age—thirteen at the time of his mother's first YouTube postings. None of us can stop the clock, however, and Bieber is now in his later teens. Whether his brand and his fan base will make a successful career and brand transition—like, for instance, Justin Timberlake—or he will become the next male Shirley Temple is yet to be seen. One thing is certain, however—Bieber and his management are keenly aware that, along with puberty, they have hit dangerous brand territory.

One of the maxims of branding is that the less well-known a brand is, the more flexibility there is for change. The more well-known a brand is, however, the more difficult it is to change. Everyone knows what happened to New Coke when they messed with the classic. From the beginning of her career, Lady Gaga has employed certain trademark style elements. The execution may change, but they're there: lingerie, towering heels, boots, Marie Antoinette–inspired hair, outrageous headgear, bold red lipstick, fishnet stockings, second-skin bodysuits, and masklike face gear. At one point early on, executives from Gaga's music label suggested she mix up her look a bit and, say, lose the lingerie, to give the fans some variety. Gaga refused, retorting that she was not well-known enough to do that—she was creating a recognizable silhouette, and they should *back off*! One of the basics of branding is knowing what not to change. The classic Coca-Cola bottle is the second-most recognized symbol in the world (following the crucifix).[1]

Consistency gives stakeholders a foundation for trust—break it at your peril. According to his hairstylist, Justin Bieber ruminated for about six months before making the potentially career-impacting decision to cut his trademark long locks. And he was apparently prescient because the minute the shears hit the salon counter, 80,000 fans unfollowed him on his Twitter account.[2]

Would his 15,200,000 remaining followers still buy his brand portfolio—stretched to include a singing toothbrush and even nail polish (the One Less Lonely Guy Collection by OPI)? Will he remain an icon? One thing remains certain—by the time he was sixteen years old, Bieber had entered Brandzilla territory. And he did it his way, just as, two generations previously, Frank Sinatra did it—with talent and an ironclad relationship with his fans. In Sinatra's day, the conduit was the radio. Today, it's social media. Either way, each fan feels a special relationship with the star. In Frank's case, in addition to his mellow tones, unique phrasing was the basis of his brand and made fans feel he was singing, as if speaking, directly to them. In Bieber's case, as well as Gaga's, they actually *are* speaking directly to them.

"There's a sense of discovery and a sense of ownership," said Bieber's manager, Scooter Braun, a breakthrough hip-hop and recording manager who has worked with Bieber since the beginning of his career. "The kids found him. They didn't find him on the radio; they didn't find him through Def Jam [record label], or even through my recommendation. They found him by us simply letting him introduce himself over the Internet, like any other teenager would. They built his brand through word-of-mouth.... [Justin] continues to tweet often, post YouTube videos, and spends time on Facebook."[3]

At the time of his "discovery" by Scooter Braun, Bieber had 70,000 views on YouTube. He now has 50 million. How did Brand Bieber do it?

First, it failed. Bieber had the good fortune to be rejected out of the gate by the traditional media club. Disney, Nickelodeon, and other kid-oriented media companies turned him down because, unlike Justin Timberlake (*The Mickey Mouse Club*), Christina Aguilera and Britney Spears (ditto), Johnny Depp (*Saved by the Bell*), Michael J. Fox (*Family*

*Ties*), or anyone from *American Idol*, Bieber had never had a hit TV show or other tried-and-true teen success platform. "People didn't want to sign him...they were not interested whatsoever," said Braun, noting that prior TV stardom was the only acceptable path for a teen. The establishment said no, so Team Bieber, which included his mom, went off-road and straight to the source—the fans—and a Brandzilla was conceived. Those 70,000 YouTube viewings gave them a clue—and a path to superstardom that detoured around the traditional corporate marketing machine.

"What we introduced," said Braun, "was a new philosophy showing that if the number one retailer in music is iTunes, then why shouldn't the number one marketing avenue be the Internet?" Instead of veering off into the corporate marketing cookie cutter, Bieber continued as he had begun, communicating directly with his fans. He did it organically. Now, as a superstar, he may have a sophisticated machine around him, but he has been true to his foundation and has not left his fans behind. For instance, on an Australian tour, Bieber chose, over the objections of his label, to meet with two girls who started and ran a fan club of 90,000 followers rather than with a traditional media outlet. The fan clubbers videoed the interview and posted it on their Twitter page. "That was the video all his fans watched," said Braun. "They aren't going to read some dot-com news site. The secret is keeping it organic....When I see people say that Justin is a part of this machine—no, he isn't." There were no expensive production values or highly produced antics involved—no smoke machine, backup dancers, or pyrotechnics to come between Justin and his fans. Scooter Braun commented, "If my one laptop and my camera is a machine, then yes it is. There was no other marketing behind it. It was my laptop, a flip camera, and Justin and his laptop....Justin does it himself and we create our own content."[4]

The delivery system? Social media, which makes consumers not just fans, but partners in success, a conjoined part of the story. Savvy brand building begins with building the relationship. According to Scooter Braun, Bieber makes it a point to talk directly to his fans on social media, one on one, on a daily basis. "We communicated directly with the consumer, with the fans," says Braun. "We let them tell us what they wanted." This personal collaboration is the common language of today's Brandzillas. Marketers can help leverage, but the communication must be direct in order for the connection to take. Lady Gaga worked with a digital media agency, ThinkTank Digital, from 2008, but as cofounder Tynicka Battle says, "She took great pride in engaging directly with her fans across every medium available to her....I would definitely say that that plays a very large role."[5] Gaga also shares her successes with her fans, drawing them in as active members of her team. Her coffee-table book is dedicated to "My Little Monsters," as she calls her fans. When her *Born This Way* album went number 1 four weeks in a row, Gaga hailed her Little Monsters with this tweet from @ladygaga: "BTW's 4th week at #1 on BILLBOARD + World Charts is both a musical+cultural triumph. Monsters it's official. You're Punk Art Pop Phenomenon."[6]

Similarly, the Kardashian sisters launched a fan contest to name their novel and also ran the cover art for their autobiography by fans directly for their opinions, asking online, "Dolls, what do you think of the book cover...can't wait to hear what you guys all think of it." This was clearly meant to be read as a message direct from the source, not a contest run by the publishing company with the Kardashians observing as interested third parties.

Brandzillazation is, somewhat counterintuitively, a highly personal process. You'd think that a major celebrity with a global brand name would be by nature deified, put on a podium, and distanced from the public, but today it is impossible to achieve Brandzilla status without that personal connection. The fans feel they know these Brandzillas. If they are waiting in an endless line at a Gaga concert, they are not surprised when Gaga herself sends out pizzas. Because that's what friends do.

Tynicka Battle notes, "With Bieber and Gaga, their fans feel as if they own the brand. And in a way, they do. They are intimately connected with it, they are extremely accessible. I couldn't even count the amount of fan pages and profiles on Justin Bieber, and they really don't feel they are outside his world, they feel they are in his world, they feel they are helping him out. And Justin Bieber's manager is also extremely savvy in that way in that he invited girls in from the very beginning—making sure that communicating with and inviting in the fans is always in the forefront. The content itself was key," Battle stresses.

Battle continues,

Gaga has unique talent and she made that accessible in the form
of content. We had access to an incredible amount of content
directly from Lady Gaga, from her team—from photos, to videos, to direct access to her. There was media access, which is
hard to come by today with her incredible schedule—so all of
that really helped to make it the monumental campaign that it
was. This isn't something that happened overnight, although
it looked like it did. It was really a matter of the fact that she
had the talent and she was incredibly resonant in touching on a
base that didn't have a voice. So her imagery was so new and so
fresh, and people identified with it because they had not seen
anything like it before. That innovation is key.

Also critical is timing to the market, notes Battle. "Justin Bieber—
incredibly talented, but he came into a space where nobody was there—
the young, cute kid who can really sing. And that moment, when there
was nobody else, makes a huge difference. *NSYNC and Backstreet
Boys were wildly successful, but those fans were now in their 40s, the
Jonas Brothers were getting married."[7]

There is one caveat: authenticity. In order to resonate, the brand
and what it stands for must be authentic. As Bieber's manager said,
"He has something special that cannot be taught."[8]

"The first part is always the talent," notes Dan Schawbel, author of
*Me 2.0* and a personal branding authority. "If they don't have talent,
nobody's going to care."[9]

Doug Hall, founder and CEO of Eureka! Ranch International,
an innovation think tank, and author of *Jump Start Your Marketing
Brain*, says,

Pop culture has caught interest. You can't override the whims of
teens. But that doesn't make it a reproducible model. Someone
has to win the lottery. It's like the black swan model. When
they're hot, everyone thinks these people are geniuses. But if
10,000 people try to be a singer, only a couple will succeed.
Studying the one that won is like saying, when I won the lottery I was standing on one foot, so if you stand on one foot, you

will win the lottery. We want to give a cause and effect—but what if it's random? The odds for stickiness increase dramatically however if you have something meaningful.

What's meaningful? Music. "Music is the conduit," says Hall. Today, more than ever, music is a link to the emotional connection that binds the brand and creates the rent in the fabric of our consciousness that lets a brand break through.[10]

Fabric Media's Jason Damata agrees: "To me it depends on the level to which they have emotionally affected that consumer. Apple people are staying for life. Lady Gaga has probably touched enough people that she is the soundtrack of those people's lives. To be the soundtrack of people's lives is very effective. It's like time travel when you listen to music you heard 20 years ago. So the emotional connection of music is a powerful thing, and I think new media crosses that quite a bit."[11]

Then again, a new kind of Brandzilla, based on authenticity—aka "reality"—is emerging.

"As much as they get bashed, the Kardashians absolutely leveraged their notoriety to make money," says Battle.

In general, they've done everything they need as a brand, and they've done it better than most. The fact that people say they don't have talent is not fair. There are people who can't sing and they can't invent the iPad, but they still have something to offer and it's probably celebrity, some kind of socialite persona. There's something there that is essentially a talent, but because people can't associate it with something they can sell or respect, they bash it. But clearly there is something there. Just being in that whole in crowd kind of thing, that in crowd status, is an actual skill.[12]

Social media has created an opportunity that did not previously exist to leverage a persona into a brand. "It's made the Internet accessible for everyone [and] it's given people the opportunity to become someone for no reason," says Leandra Medine, a twenty-three-year-old whose quirky, highly personal blog, the *Man Repeller*, is considered the leading fashion blog and attracts one million visitors a month, 400,000 of them uniques.[13]

On the other side of the coin are the wannabes who are attempting to reach Brandzilladom by following the social media recipe for success. One burger restaurant now expanding as a national chain seems to have taken a page from the Bieber Book of Branding. Twitter, Facebook, YouTube? Check, check, and check. The burger chain is firing on all cylinders. The company states on its home page that it is "building a community of like-minded people," turning the eating of burgers and the personal choice of condiment selection into a global communal experience. Customers are urged to send in their videos, photos—of burgers or otherwise—and tweet their experiences, and the company mans its Twitter page seemingly 24/7. There is an urgent effort to create "branding in a box," to form an instant culture out of thin air by squeezing every ounce of interactivity out of the situation. Whether emphasizing culinary empowerment by customizing the burger with a choice of more than three hundred possible combinations or inviting customers to send in photos of themselves in logo T-shirts, this burgeoning brand attempts to go beyond the burger and inflate the brand like a Macy's balloon, to channel the Biebs by cloning the social media template. Except—beyond the bun, there's no there there. As Wendy's once said, "Where's the beef" in this scenario? The authenticity aspect rings hollow, a boldfaced attempt to pilotfish along with the sharks. Let's face it—a burger is just not a Bieber. The fact is, some things don't go down so well, even with a side of fries.

Even when click-through nirvana is achieved, brand resonance is not guaranteed. "There is no proof that having millions of fans on a Facebook page or a social media site moves sales," points out Milton Pedraza, founder and CEO of the Luxury Institute and a world-class customer relations management practitioner. "To me the litmus test is, does the consumer have an extraordinary experience—because in doing that, the word will spread. Viral marketing in and of itself is nothing—create an extraordinary experience, then people will flock."[14]

## I'LL HAVE WHAT THEY'RE HAVING

Where does that leave corporate marketers? Scrambling to catch up. Certainly Brandzillas were born and built centuries before the Internet. They did it one step at a time, one brick at a time, one unit and footstep at a time, with the original social media—human beings. Back in the day, word of mouth was spread by actual mouths—belonging to minstrels, ministers, portrait painters, town criers, and neighbors. Speedy spreading of a message involved a fast runner or a string of fresh horses. Marie Antoinette's brand launch, her initial progress from her native Austria at age fifteen to the home of her bridegroom, the Dauphin of France, Louis August de Bourbon, involved 376 horses. Shortly after her arrival, a ball was held at which she was viewed by four thousand people, at which point she was proclaimed charming, the portrait painters broke out their brushes, and her brand was born. (Only decades later would bad brand association by marriage, the Bourbon brand's tarnish, lead to her demise and violent death.[15])

The first advertising messages were print—on walls of caves and, centuries later, buildings. Political messages have been unearthed, frozen in time, on the walls of Pompeii, and the ancient Egyptians scratched out messages on papyrus. But scalability changed everything—first, in the form of mass media, such as newspapers, and then electric power and radio waves gave instant access to information and were quickly harnessed by marketers. The 1920s in radio and the 1950s in commercial television marked the beginning of the rule of corporate brand building. And since that's all the brand history most of us can remember, many people assume or take for granted that's the way it has always been. The role of branding has traditionally been to generate use and consumption of—or belief in—products, services, people, or doctrines by creating and leveraging beliefs about them.

Branding is a means to connect with consumer belief systems to impact how they feel about, or respond to, the entity involved, whether it be dishwater detergent or a presidential candidate. Brands are about an emotional connection, not just a logo. That is why one-to-one communication between a brand and a consumer is the gold standard. The *really* old-fashioned way is still the best way. Once the consumer communicates back, the brand is mainlining into his or her emotional core. That is the advantage that Lady Gaga has over Marie Antoinette. Marie Antoinette, isolated in the French court, increasingly lost touch with her subjects, retreating to a fanciful make-believe farm with shampooed sheep—and it cost her her head.

Steven Hess, chairman of Weapon7, a division of Omnicom Group, a digital agency based in London with clients including Mercedes-Benz, sees the correlations:

If it's just a click and you can get a lot of people to do it, then you can very easily become famous. But by the same token that fame can be taken away. If we look at one of the greatest brands in businesses at the moment, which is Apple, when the iPhone 4 was launched there was a huge public backlash against it because it kept dropping telephone calls. And instead of that driving down the iPhone 4, the sales continued to grow. Why? Because Apple really cared about the problems they had with the phone. They were honest. They were straightforward. There was nothing to hide. And people continued to respect that. I think that talks about a level of depth and integrity to the brand, which a lot of manufactured brands like, for example, Paris Hilton, people brands like that. They come and go. There's no doubt. It doesn't matter whether they're here or there. There's no story behind them. There's no equity within them.

In many ways the 21st century brands that are being built through social media networks, which enable people to communicate with each other on a one-to-one basis peer-to-peer, are no different than the ones originally conceived that were also built on a peer-to-peer basis. I think we've just moved into a much more efficient peer-to-peer networking brand-building world, which is actually very similar to how it was done historically. The reliance on brands to be able to convince people to buy into their story, their proposition, go buy their product, simply by talking at them is no longer going to be possible. So actually, if any of the brand-building skills should be looked at, they are the skills that we should learn that Marie Antoinette utilized, revisited for today. So I think that doing a comparison between the medieval world or the renaissance world or the Versailles world and the world of today kind of just prior to printing press is a much more interesting way of beginning to understand how brands developed. Why? Because both worlds are peer-to-peer. One is just extremely fast.[16]

Consumer power flexed its muscles in a dramatic way in 1985. The Coca-Cola Company slipped, hit its head, and momentarily lost touch with its consumers' hearts. It almost cost Coke its execs' heads, too. But, in heeding an early warning that no brand is too big to fail when the consumer is in the driver's seat, the company showed true grit, turned lemons into lemonade, and became an early adopter of embracing consumer leadership. At the time that New Coke was developed, the original brand was caught in a battle for market share with a smorgasbord of diet drinks and was counting on new product development to produce a trump card. Focusing on the formula, executives underestimated and discounted the century of emotional attachment and loyalty consumers had built up around original Coke, including a strong Southern contingent that considered the Atlanta-based brand integral to their regional identity. The taste of the new formula was preferred in tests by consumers, but that mattered little in the face of tampering with "their" Coke.

Laurie Ashcraft, president of Ashcraft Research and an expert in consumer dynamics, points out, "In the research that the company conducted, the point was a side-by-side blind label taste test, not a branded taste test. The New Coke formula was preferred, but the brand connection was not factored in. They did not do the kind of focus group research that would have probed around the brand."[17]

One would have thought that the company, having spent the better part of a century and untold millions of dollars building strong emotions around the brand, would have realized the loyalty it engendered. Original Coke's loyal consumers took the formula switch personally and hit the eject button; they not only boycotted the brand, they held the company responsible, addressing complaint letters to the CEO as "Chief Dodo" and calling him "one of the dumbest executives in American business history." Leveraging snail mail, the phone, and the pre–social media media, these dissenters complained loudly and visibly to everyone from the company switchboard operators to the maintenance crew—and the media.[18]

What this marketing debacle accomplished, however, was to put consumers back in touch with the brand. In a kind of twisted reversal of fortune or move of marketing genius, depending on how you looked at it, the Coca-Cola Company ended up breaking new ground in communicating with consumers. Two-way communication was established. Calls to the company hotline (1–800-COKE) surged, rising from 400 a day before the change to 1,500 a day. Protest groups cropped up, but the net result was not so much a put-down of New Coke as a tsunami of love for original Coke. People started hoarding original Coke like it was gold from the last mine on earth. One desperate drinker was found with 900 bottles in his basement, as if soft drink Armageddon had arrived. Songs were written; legends were born. "Suddenly," says the history on the company's corporate website, "everyone was talking about Coke and realizing what an important role it had in their life." The original formula, renamed Coca-Cola Classic, was brought back. Within two days, the company received more than 31,000 calls on the hotline. "Coca-Cola was obviously more than just a soft drink," says the company website, an understatement.

## THE NEW PARTNERSHIP

That "more than" is the key, the essential DNA of a Brandzilla. Instead of setting the marketing strategy in concrete and disseminating it to the target audience via advertising, savvy marketers have broken down the borders and barriers and invited that audience to join them as partners. The resulting content is organic, participatory, and antididactic. It precipitates an integrated strategy that includes traditional advertising globally, but it also explores a wide variety of avenues to connect and tap into an emotional nerve that will open the door to the brand partnership.

The shift in generational dynamics is also driving this. "Interruption marketing is still active," says Jason Damata. "You've got all these consumers who grew up being interrupted, and they know how to tune it out, so it has to be something different—there has to be a different kind of value proposition between a brand and a consumer."[19]

Instead of sending messages about the brand, the Brandzilla Effect fuses the brand as part of a story that matters and adds value in some way to the audience. The more it matters, the bigger the potential for the brand. "It becomes the era of 'capture,'" says Damata, who worked on the first twenty-four-hour television network for the Web. "It was really interesting. We talked to advertisers and they realized that banner ads really didn't work, but they didn't know what to do. And so they went back to the old days of Jack Paar and 'branded entertainment.' They would get these million-dollar contracts to go back to the olden days. They want to capture you."

In Portugal, Coca-Cola planted a wallet in a shopping mall with a hidden camera. A ticket to a soccer match visibly stuck out of the wallet, and two hundred dollars was tucked inside. Ninety-five percent of the people who found the wallet checked inside, found the money and the ticket, and turned in the wallet, complete with the soccer ticket and the cash. As a reward, Coke gave the good Samaritans their own tickets to the game and sat them all in a special section. At halftime, the hidden camera video ran on the stadium JumboTrons, turning the group into instant ethical heroes. The videos are also in Portuguese on YouTube, where more than 200,000 people have viewed them to date.[20]

On the Coca-Cola website, consumers can register to join its Facebook page—which was started not by the company, but by two fans, and now has more than a million fans—and connect with others who love Coke. Once more than a million Coke-lovers had assembled virtually on this page, Facebook informed the Coca-Cola Company that the page needed to be run by the company, which it now is—with the original fans as consultants. On YouTube, Coke videos have been viewed 33.5 million times, and the brand has 500,000 Twitter followers.[21] The Coca-Cola organization makes sure that there is a plethora of opportunities for consumers to dive into Coke, from an interactive promotion that invites fans to send in their own videos or photos of Coke cans or bottles in settings from all over the world to a promotion allowing fans to share in the effort to protect polar bears in the Arctic.

Today, you better believe the Coca-Cola Company listens to consumers. Although, as Wendy Clark, Coke's senior vice president of integrated communications and capabilities, noted, "The days of controlling all the variables of your brand are over ... [consumers'] truth is what is relevant." Coca-Cola has 36 million Facebook friends, and 800 million people source the brand on Facebook—the equivalent of the third-largest country in the world. Fifteen hundred people a day mention Coca-Cola brands on Twitter—and the company answers every tweet. For advice on this strategy, the company is turning to ____. Time for a pop quiz:

A. Harvard
B. The London School of Economics
C. Bill Gates
D. See below

"We are looking at Gaga and Bieber," says Wendy Clark. The company met with the stars' managers to see how they drive their Facebook pages, to "share lessons learned." Instead of driving the strategy, the company now "allows fans to react and plan the strategy."[22]

Don't you somehow wish you could jump into a time machine, flash back to the 1980s, zip into Coke's Atlanta headquarters, and prophesy that, a few decades hence, the world's largest soft drink manufacturer would be taking its marketing cues from a teenager barely old enough to drive and a twenty-something college dropout in ripped fishnet hose and a dress made of meat?

They're also taking cues from things that don't seem like advertising at all but that often have greater impact. For example, if you pick up a banana or a kiwi in the produce case and it has a message on it, you can thank Richard Kirshenbaum and his agency for putting advertising on fruit. Kirshenbaum and his team also got out there first with pop-up stores and branded TV shows for pets, including the first show targeting cats as the viewing audience, Meow TV. None of this seemingly antic stuff is accidental; all of it is highly and brilliantly strategic. "The Internet has democratized the conversation," Kirshenbaum says, "and also the art of marketing. Any time you have a radical shift in media, people confuse the media with the message.[23]

In other words, for a brand to sustain, whether you're a Bieber or a burger, the product still has to deliver the goods.

# Chapter 5

# "OH THIS IS GOING TO BE ADDICTIVE"

The title of this chapter is actually the verbatim text of one of the first tweets ever, made by one of the inventors of Twitter, and, in retrospect, you'd have to say it was prophetic.[1] But it wasn't casual. Twitter was in fact a strategic concept, generated by board members in an in-house brainstorming session for a San Francisco podcasting company in need of a reboot. But it quickly became clear to the inventors that 140-character electronic communication was "going to change the world with this thing that nobody understood."

As John Lennon sang, "Well, you know, we all want to change the world." These guys actually did it. Literally—if you count the Twitter Revolution in Egypt, which, if history books can count Paul Revere's contribution to the American Revolution as game changing, seems fair. While the rest of the podcasting company hedged their bets by focusing on business as usual, Jack Dorsey and a four-person team evolved a closed-system technology for small groups to a private shorthanded communications system. The project was code-named twttr. That name sounded like the word "Twitter," which, when they looked it up, meant "a short burst of inconsequential information" and "chirps from birds." "And that's exactly what the product was," according to Dorsey.[2]

Seven months later, Dorsey and his group spun out of the podcasting company and bought the assets, including Twitter. By 2009,

Twitter was the third-ranking social network, with tweets emanating at blinding speed. During the 2011 FIFA Women's World Cup Final between Japan and the United States, for instance, 7,196 tweets per second were published.[3]

This kind of speed puts Twitter, one of the prime Brandzilla engines of the twenty-first century, smack into Brandzilla territory itself. Today, Brandzillas spawn Brandzillas.

Behind all these tweets and postings, of course, are human beings. They are increasingly tweeting and posting instead of other things— such as watching TV, reading, or having actual face-to-face interactivity. The average American spent thirty-two hours a month on the Internet in 2010. The demographic that spent the most time online? Surprisingly, not teenagers. It was adults aged forty-five to fifty-four, who averaged more than 39 hours per month online, while young people aged twelve to seventeen averaged a mere 22.3 hours per month, and those aged eighteen to twenty-four averaged 32.2 hours per month.[4]

The Internet has lapped TV in the amount of time spent a week, with young people aged thirteen to twenty-four spending an average of 13.6 hours a week watching TV versus 16.7 hours online. Meanwhile, young readership of magazines and newspapers has crashed into the basement—the number of eight- to eighteen-year-olds who read a newspaper or magazine in a typical day dropped from 42 percent in 1999 to 23 percent in 2009.[5]

The seductiveness of the Internet is hard for young people who have been raised largely in the virtual world, to resist. Today's Eve is not an apple, but an Apple. Stan Tatkin, an assistant clinical professor at the University of California, Los Angeles, notes, "When we tweet and have lots of friends follow us, we get surges of dopamine and other neurochemicals that make us feel excited. These reward circuits activate, and we want to do it again." In extreme cases, the result can be social media addiction. Those most vulnerable, according to a paper in the *International Journal of Environmental Research and Public Health,* include two types: egocentricists, who gain pleasure from the positive feedback they receive from presenting themselves positively; and people with low self-esteem, who find the virtual world easier to navigate than the real one.[6]

How many teens must fit these profiles?

The amount of time and intensity applied to Internet activities is also veering toward obsessive, to the extent that the scenario has spawned a sociophysical disability called Facebook/Twitter Addiction Disorder (FTAD). Shall we unplug our kids? We may have reached the point of no return. Research reveals that four in five students suffered "cold-turkey" withdrawal-type symptoms ranging from significant mental and physical distress to depression, anxiety, and panic when forced to disengage from technology for the entire day; the term "crackberry" isn't too far off base.[7] College students have been shown to be especially vulnerable to Internet addiction. In an experiment with 1,000 college students asked to go without the Internet for twenty-four hours, many couldn't face life without Facebook. "I sat in bed and stared blankly," said one. "I had nothing to do." "Media is my drug," said another. "How could I survive 24 hours without it?"[8]

The implications for young people—and, therefore, the future—is particularly staggering, as rising Generation Y, 105 million strong and equal in heft and influence to the Baby Boomers, will forever alter the brand landscape and how marketers deal with it.

A massive, technology-driven behavioral shift, bordering on disorder, is also fueling a shift in consumer behavior. When Baby Boomers were growing up, parents became concerned that their kids were watching too much TV. Since then it has not been uncommon for parents to limit how much TV their children watch. However, nobody has ever had to put conscious limits on how much advertising their kids consumed—most people, of any age, avoid advertising like the plague. It takes billions of dollars of creativity for advertisers to successfully snag consumers to watch commercials intended to sell products. But the Internet has opiatelike qualities that are only beginning to be recognized for their ability to pull participants in like an undertow, one into which they swim, even to a point of drowning, willingly.

Internet addiction has become a serious global health concern, with cases documented in Italy, Pakistan, Germany, Iran, China, Korea, and Taiwan, among other places. The Center for Internet Recovery, the first of its kind in America, offers treatment programs such as Digital Detox Rehab, while South Korea has set up an Internet addiction prevention clinic in the form of a children's camp to theoretically head off addictive behaviors before they become set in stone. But while thousands may seek help for this perceived disorder, many millions consider it a lifestyle. So, add compulsive behavioral tendencies to the group of accelerators of Web communication.

A national study conducted out of Stanford University's School of Medicine revealed that nearly one in eight Americans suffers from at least one sign of problematical Internet behavior.[9] It is estimated that 5 to 10 percent of Internet users are actually addicted to the Internet.[10]

Internet addiction, according to the Institute for Internet Addiction, takes over people's lives in the form of a compulsive behavior. The Institute has identified the signs of compulsion as:

1. Feeling preoccupied with the Internet.
2. Feeling the need to use the Internet with increasing amounts of time in order to achieve satisfaction.
3. Repeatedly making unsuccessful efforts to control, cut back, or stop Internet use.
4. Feeling restless, moody, depressed, or irritable when attempting to cut down or stop Internet use.
5. Staying online longer than originally intended.
6. Jeopardizing or risking the loss of a significant relationship, educational opportunity, or job because of the Internet.
7. Lying to family members and others to hide the extent of Internet activity.
8. Using the Internet as an escape from problems.
9. Gaining weight, an additional side effect, among others.

Disorders such as Internet addiction are classified by experts as impulse control disorders. In other words, many people feel compelled to participate in the Internet, some to the level of an actual disorder, others to a less than disorder level but still with some level of intensity. This aligns with and is fed by the interactive nature of the Web. One click, and you've got a relationship—with something or someone. It's like a shot of heroin. Keep clicking, and you're a user. More clicks, you're an addict. And when you're an addict, or have addictive tendencies, or other complementary social disorders, you and millions like you are joining the infinity loop of cyberspace and social media. No traditional advertising on the planet ever had this level of intensity behind it. No corporate strategy could have spawned it, no marketing budget could have bought it, and no ad agency execution could have delivered it.

"To a large extent, we live in a saturated culture, where you can't even get away from digital technology," says Dr. Kimberly S. Young, founder of the Center for Internet Addiction. She continues:

> People use it as an escape mechanism, they're in an immersive environment that is not necessarily healthy for them and have disconnected from relationships. With blogging, people are addicted to blogging but they can't talk to people about it, they need to blog out to strangers. It's an easy, passive sort of thing to create an online character. But that doesn't represent who they are in real life. You can have a shy, withdrawn 24-year-old man who represents a strong, rugged, hard-core gamer who plays all the time online and is popular online—people can get stuck online. They can't take those skills and transfer them to real life. There's an enticement aspect to it. There are those who say that the gaming industry makes these games addictive. There may be a game that gives you 8 hours to complete a task, so they want you to play, and then you have to spend more money to buy the virtual equipment you need to execute different levels of the game.[11]

Now add to this a bankroll to rival Fort Knox. Millennials, the most avid Internet users, will shortly wield massive and unprecedented purchasing power as the beneficiaries of the largest generational wealth transfer in history.

It has been predicted that the combined net worth of Generations X and Y will triple by 2018 to $28 trillion. It's estimated that an additional $18 trillion in generational wealth will transfer to Gen Y from their parents from 2017 to 2052.[12]

And where will you find these empowered consumers with their fat wallets? Forget the mall—they'll be hanging out in cyberspace. According to a 2010 study released by Kaiser Family Foundation, the amount of time 8- to 18-year-olds spent with media increased by an hour and 17 minutes a day over the past six years, from 6:21 hours in 2004 to 7:38 in 2010, and in the same time frame, the amount of media consumed during that period increased from 8:33 to 10:45. This jump was mainly driven by increased use of mobile media, such as cellphones and iPods. Meaning, media-to-go gives kids a 24/7 opportunity to push out messages, endorsements, and interactive communication.[13]

Word of mouth becomes word of millions of mouths, in an ongoing, 360-degree, global Greek chorus to infinity—a reach that is far beyond that of a mere TV show, magazine, or any other traditional media born of bricks and mortar. Looking under the hood of the social media vehicle, this engine is propelling today's Brandzillas. And it's only going to get more powerful.

What happens to a media platform that is based on advertisers paying to reach "eyeballs" by basically wrapping a commercial message with a candy coating of content? The hope was always that the candy was sweet enough to lure in the market. The bigger the lure, the more people watched, the higher the ratings, the more expensive the commercial time. Programmers needed an ongoing supply of winning formulas, big name stars, or breakthrough "must-see" shows to achieve the prime-time nirvana of "appointment viewing," meaning a show viewers literally marked on their calendars to watch at its particular time slot. One example would be *Saturday Night Live*, in its John Belushi heyday, which at the time had the power to pull young people out of bars and parties and back to their TV sets on a Saturday night, a notion that now seems almost quaint. Another would be any successful soap opera in the days when a critical mass of women could be found at home during that part of the day. In fact, soap operas, with their crazy plots and home-grown stars, were so successful at luring the adult female demographic that Proctor & Gamble (P&G) actually produced them, in addition to producing actual soap. P&G sponsored the first radio soap operas in the 1930s and moved on with technology to sponsor—and produce—most of the soap operas on television in the 1970s. In January 2012, with the sudsy warhorse *As the World Turns* off the air, P&G announced the end of the P&G Productions "Soap Era."

Not to be left behind by technology, however, the company announced that Tide and Future Friendly were cosponsoring the Tide Coldwater #washcold Twitter Party, hosted by the online community

SheSpeaks. "The groups invited participants to meet online in the 'Twitter-sphere' to talk about easy ways to lower their energy bills and reduce waste at home."[14] Now, you may not be particularly inspired to rave it up on the #washcold Twitter Party, but it's clear P&G is covering its bases—this is just one of numerous Internet plays it was fielding at the time this book was being researched. This is a strategic move on the part of P&G. Tide is no Internet start-up, but the venerable company clearly recognizes and is trying to put into play the first rule of staying power on the Web: reinvention. Doug Hall, a man who knows a thing or two about reinvention, gives kudos to Tide for this capability. "Tide has done 61 innovations in 61 years," he notes. "That's great. The first principle in getting someone to take action is novelty, the second is meaningfulness. Novelty creates awareness, but it doesn't stick. Reinvention is a form of serial novelty." Hall cites Madonna as a patron saint: "One could argue about her level of meaningfulness, but that is why she has managed to remain relevant for such a long time. You have to be able to do that. Or you're dead today."[15]

The hunt for meaningful content has brought out a paradoxical group of consumers—those who reject the traditional plug-and-play content delivery systems and are playing it by ear, creating their own menu. They don't like TV, where the content is locked, loaded, and ready-made—but they're desperately seeking another kind of solution. There is a notable and growing group of about 56 million consumers whom media experts call the Off-the-Grid segment. Off-the-Gridders are not sitting around taking in TV shows—or the accompanying commercials. In fact, they're turned off by intrusive ads and have a declining—or no—interest in watching TV of any sort. About a fifth of them don't even own a TV. But it's not that they are averse to content; they consume a lot of it—just not on TV. About 40 percent of them own mobile devices like smartphones or iPads, and their focus is video content. Those without TVs consume twenty-some hours of video content a week, half of which is consumed online. All in all, Off-the-Gridders join Internet embracers in wanting content, but they want it on their own terms.[16]

As Jason Damata points out, "The playing field got changed. The new breed is not ordained by some executive at NBC, they're ordained by their knowledge and ability to communicate. The consumer is saying, 'Educate me and satisfy my desire for knowledge.' It's about empowerment—back to the people."[17]

Continuing mobile device proliferation will only magnify this impact. It took nearly ten years for households to have more than a single PC or cellphone. But it is estimated that by 2014, one in three online consumers will be using a tablet, and within three years of the introduction of the iPad, multitablet ownership was on the rise.[18]

These on-demand consumers—current and future—are not going to be sitting ducks for network programming lineups targeted at "women 18 to 54" or some other demographic or psychographic bloc. Instead, consumers are composing their own anthologies, one fragmented slice of cherry-picked, customized content at a time. The stakes are immense, but the game will be waged in a Prufrockian fashion, teaspoon by teaspoon. There will be no declared winner of the media war because consumers will be—and, increasingly, already are—working with a customized dashboard populated with a plethora of devices and delivery systems, not a *TV Guide*.

"Forward-thinking brands will embrace these new behaviors and give customers the experiences they want, however, they choose to shop," says Erin Nelson, chief marketing officer of Bazaarvoice, specialists in leveraging social media and data to build brands. But there will be a reward. "In return, they will gather a tremendously valuable trail of customer data to help them improve their businesses and boost profits in the long term."[19]

Before his death, Steve Jobs was said to be steering his company in search of the one touchscreen system that mastered all these devices and programs in one place—a kind of content central. He foresaw it, brilliant minds are working on it, it's out there, and it's imminent. In the Twitter Smackdown, nobody wins—but everybody plays.

# Chapter 6

# BURY ME BRANDED

Those guys walking around wearing sandwich boards were always the brunt of a lot of jokes, losers who were stranded on a street corner who looked like escapees from a vaudeville time warp. Who wanted to be them? Well, the joke's on us—we've all become them. In retrospect, we can recognize that the sandwich-boarders were innovators and visionaries—a bit on the primitive side, maybe, but definitely first-movers. From every Chanel purse that flies off the shelf to the tune of several thousand dollars to every backward baseball cap with a logo, a debt is owed to those brave pioneers who paved the way for the human being as a living, breathing, walkabout brand platform. Where once brands paid to reach consumers, the paradigm has flipped, and the consumers are now paying the brands. Lifestyle marketing, where a brand embeds itself within the perimeter of a consumer's personal space, is, for marketers, probably both the least and most challenging form of branding. The act of getting someone to attach the brand to themselves or their life is simple—once the affinity for the brand is there. Getting and keeping it there is another story, requiring strategic and at times heroic acts of relevance and endurance that must be constantly reinforced and reinvented.

One of the best ways to get a brand in the game is to be there from the start, literally. Today, there is an infinitely scalable benefit to this because the Web allows immediate and incalculable access to a person's life. Branding starts immediately, when Dad, or whoever is the family chronicler, whips out the video camera or the iPhone and records before baby's first breath. As this is being written, a commercial for Optimum is running, in which a new parent announces, "She was on Facebook before she was born." Once the video is uploaded onto Facebook's Timeline, a virtual brand is born—and broadcast to the ages.

What kind of branding can a newborn with a theoretically blank slate have? Plenty, for those who know how to create a touchpoint. Homerun to Beth Israel Hospital in Boston, which proudly announced its new delivery—as official hospital of the Boston Red Sox, when its website officially proclaimed, "Our newborns are all Red Sox babies!":

> From our compassionate nurses to our extraordinary expertise and leading-edge technology, there are many benefits to having your baby at Beth Israel Deaconess Medical Center (BIDMC). As the official hospital of the Boston Red Sox, one more great benefit has been added to the list: your baby will be a Red Sox Baby!

Families of every baby delivered at the hospital receive a baby cap and canvas bag adorned with the BIDMC and the Red Sox logos. The hospital website features a virtual photo gallery of the adorable "Red Sox Babies" in their tiny logo caps.

OK, let's grant that that's cute. Especially if you're a Red Sox fan. But let's look closer. You, yourself, are now not just a Red Sox fan. You are immediately a Red Sox Family. Red Sox Baby, Red Sox Mom, Red Sox Dad, Red Sox Grandpa—etc. Logo merchandise for everyone! There are forty-three types of Red Sox baby clothes on the Major League Baseball (MLB) merchandise site. A three-piece starter set is available including logoed bib, bottle, and pacifier. Don't forget the Red Sox diaper bag for Mom and, of course, the logoed stroller blanket. Baby hasn't gotten his first tooth, but he's off to a great start as a brand ambassador for the Boston Red Sox.

I'd like to think that as an experienced marketer I have been immune to immersive branding tactics as a parent. Full disclosure: At six months, my son could recognize the Golden Arches from the highway; and when he saw the picture of Big Bird on his plastic baby bottle, he not only grabbed for it, he went berserk trying to pull the picture off. Twenty years later, Big Bird hasn't figured out a way to keep him in the fold—although I'm sure the Yellow One has ensured a place cribside when my son has his own children one day—but he still pulls over like Pavlov's dog at the first glimpse of the Golden Arches.

In a world of a myriad of prismed and splintered segmentations, affinities with commercial brands create a two-way street by helping consumers define who they are and what they stand for. Defining personal brands has never been more important, especially for those with aspirations to be employed. "A lot of companies now are paying more attention to what the online world says about you," says personal branding guru Dan Schawbel, who publishes *Personal Branding* magazine and is the author of the international best seller, *Me 2.0: 4 Steps to Building Your Future*. Schawbel says,

> There's no going back at this point, because, if you look at any social profile online, the picture's right there, the name's there, whatever you publish, how you represent yourself—there's no going back from that. You are you, and what we're going to start seeing now and in the future is that your personal and professional lives are just going to become one. Your entire life is going to be documented on the Web, forever. As you get older, it's all going to be there. It's like your online diary. If you're not telling your personal story, or you can't do it, then no one's going to really care or listen to you. It's really important for you to process and hone it and make it something that's intriguing.[1]

According to Schawbel, personal branding is especially important in start-up companies. "Start-up companies don't look at résumés for the most part," he states. "They don't look to see if you went to Harvard and your grade point average, they just see what your LinkedIn profile is, or they read your blog and make a decision based on that. Jobseekers have to think of it as a story, and they have to always treat their experience as something that's more powerful and important to a company than education."

It's estimated that about 20 percent of all businesses in the United States are start-up businesses.[2] If Dan Schawbel is right, 20 percent of the U.S. workforce is thus being judged largely by its personal e-brand. The controllable aspects of this are both positive and negative. While jobseekers undoubtedly like being able to control their brand, brand equals reputation—and outsiders can anonymously impact, interfere with, or even sabotage a personal brand online by seeding reputational content. Additionally, one of the solid maxims of marketing is that the more audiences know about a brand, the more likely they will have an opinion, and the harder it is to change that opinion. With the Internet, a lot can be known very quickly about a corporate product brand or personal brand. And once that information is out there, right or wrong, changing the mindset it evokes is going to be more challenging. Opinions will be formed before people are known, and transparency does not necessarily equate with validity.

Moving along, it's now possible to cover the full arc of the branded continuum in a lifetime. Let's say a consumer was born too late to make the branded baby brigade. There's still the chance to say, "Bury me branded." Successfully covering the cradle-to-grave bases, the Boston Red Sox have licensed their brand to a coffin manufacturer. The MLB team logo is featured on the coffin lining and pillow, as well as on the exterior, "so the world can know the deceased's true Red Sox dedication."

"It's really a beautiful thing," commented one Massachusetts funeral home director. Die-hard fans would theoretically agree.[3]

The funeral industry, which for a century remained unchanged and relied almost solely on generational connections for marketing as the businesses changed hands from father to son and, more recently, to daughter, is increasingly moving into branded territory. "Ninety percent of funeral homes are family-owned, up to five, six, or even seven generations," says Christine Pepper, CEO of the National Funeral Directors Association. "Consumers think they know a funeral home because a grandparent used it twenty years ago. But so much has changed regarding personalizing a funeral and making it meaningful to the families—and communicating that to the market." There is a growing trend, she notes, to "brand the end of life process."[4]

Supporting that goal, the funeral industry holds the world's largest annual trade show, the International Funeral Fair, a one-stop show that spans the market with funeral directors, manufacturers, cremation exhibitors, and autopsy services. There, enthusiasts can find products from Eternal Image, a funerary services and products company that has exclusive licensing deals to present "memorial products from the world's finest brands," including Star Trek, Kiss, Precious

Moments, MLB, and the Vatican. The range includes caskets, urns, headstone engravings, and wall coverings that allow a consumer to "respectfully celebrate the passion that your loved one had in life." The Eternal Image website is designed to serve consumers as well as industry professionals and includes links to an e-newsletter, Facebook, and Twitter—as well as an online grief columnist, "Dear Maddy."

Pepper stresses that the funeral business is dedicated to responding to the needs of the community. Some of this response is based on meaningful contributions in community advocacy, such as sponsoring local bike helmet giveaways or, on a more micro level, individual funeral homes creating unique applications such as providing a trained "grief dog" to offer solace and help relax bereaved visitors. Though subtle, these kinds of services dig deep emotionally and help differentiate a funeral home's brand as much as a logo can differentiate a coffin.

The online bereavement community has extended the reach of end-of-life branding in the same way the Internet has amplified every other kind of communication. At the time this book was written, there were almost 5 million online bereavement sites searchable on Google, with numerous segmentations. Loss is a common experience for which the Web can uniquely offer emotional connectivity as well as private solace. In her book *Resilience: Reflections on the Burdens and Gifts of Facing Life's Adversities*, the late Elizabeth Edwards, a public figure seeking social connection in a private setting, reached out to the online grief community to come to grips with her crushing feelings about the death of the Edwardses' teenage son, Wade. "Grief is a long process of untangling ourselves from the physical reality of the person and from our expectations of our future with them," she wrote. "In the moments when I felt at loose ends...I turned...to my fellow travelers, those struggling with the same kinds of moments, trying to keep their balance now that the world around them was so disarranged. I turned to the Internet. It is hard to overstate what the online grief community meant to me."[5]

Twelve years ago, I examined the emergence of online communities based on such emotional benchmarks as birth, illness, and bereavement for my book *The Change Agents*. After studying dozens of such sites and interviewing industry experts across the spectrum, it became clear that the unique intersection of intimacy and anonymity with the environment of a wider, borderless community was creating an unmistakable impact. The emotional interchange that was happening on the Web had begun to eclipse in-person communications in certain ways, such as a rise of anonymous intimacy. I wrote then: "In the future, it is clear that the keyboard will become as critical as the telephone as an avenue of human connection…a place where, at any hour of the day or night, someone, somewhere, is there."

Interactive platforms like bulletin boards and blogs provide opportunities for authentic connectivity that are spawning a new kind of brand voice. In the past, the editorial "voice of authority" might have been modeled on Edward R. Murrow or the TV anchors who followed him, such as Walter Cronkite, Dan Rather, or Diane Sawyer. It might have come from a spiritual leader like Mother Teresa, the Pope, or L. Ron Hubbard—or Martha Stewart, Dr. Spock, Dr. Oz, or Revlon. Today, the "voice of authority" is more like the "shoulder of empathy."

Richard Kirshenbaum identifies what he sees as two major shifts: first, the ability via Twitter and Facebook to interact and touch people in a different way; and second, the reversal of the "one-way brand street" to a scenario where consumers now have their own conversation, talking to brands and each other. "There's been a democratic shift in information—major magazines and newspapers vs. major blogs," notes Kirshenbaum. "It's the reality of a grubstreet.com vs. a slick culinary magazine. Compare the circulation of traditional magazines like *GQ* or *Us Weekly* with blogs—some of the blogs have more reach. And the bloggers are the people who are in the forefront in many ways. Some of these blogs will do well, and some will not—but it shows you how powerful connecting people is. Until now, you had to be chosen to be in a magazine, or if you might be interviewed by a great newspaper."[6]

Chad Jackson, cofounder of The 88, an award-winning, bleeding-edge digital marketing agency, notes, "Right now the brands we're working with create a kind of authentic and interesting voice." In this endeavor, Jackson notes, smaller brands can have an advantage. He notes,

It's nice to have a clean slate and being smaller and to have the personality and entrepreneurs behind the brand which, a lot of times, embody the characteristics, by nature, of the brand. When an entrepreneur is building something, he has some passion behind it, so we're able to capture and encapsulate that. And express that authentic and interesting voice through Internet channels.

We work a lot with bloggers here. Tier one bloggers are bloggers that get over a million page views a month, and these are independent people who are just tapped into a really engaged audience... they are the purest form of endorsement because a blogger is based on endorsement. I mean, people come to a blogger because this woman or man expresses a point of view and people appreciate that point of view, and, if you can authentically connect the brand with that point of view then you're getting a really direct connection with that audience, and so the challenge is obviously finding brands, making that connection, understanding that, and evangelically working with the bloggers to create content that doesn't reek of endorsement. That would turn the consumer off. It has to feel natural, and not misleading. [Consumers] have to think, "That makes sense."

We also have to give more back to the blogger's audience. For example, if a blogger doesn't shoot video, and you can basically create a video with that blogger and offer their audience more of them. Then bloggers become excited to accept the newest sponsored-by brand, because they're getting more of what they already want. So it's giving added value to the experience via content, and then the blogger pulls the brand right through the channel. They're basically their own media channel. If you work with a blogger, you're guaranteed to get a million authentic, engaged impressions. So we've done a lot of those kind of brand collaborations with people with built-in audiences that have already been found by consumers. So that involves excelling the process, that ebb and flow of the active community that is looking to talk and engage with the thing.

Harry Bernstein, a cofounder of The 88, adds, "And so, we really try to leverage the types of bloggers out there by their reach and exposure.

Some of them can have a small audience themselves, but that audience can be very influential, and it's about understanding the networks out there, and the network effect of how information flows. It's like a river, the source and destination, and which way gravity is going to take it, and so, with an understanding of who you are working with and of the brand, you can be incredibly influential."[7]

Intuitive marketers like The 88 are leveraging the intersection of content, emotion, and authenticity as emerging, accelerating brand opportunities. The delivery system for the ability to imprint a brand at the exact moment of the keystone events of the human life experience, with real-life and real-time commentary and visibility, is one that is uniquely the province of the Web. In fact, the Internet is probably the only venue that consumers born in the past twenty years will proactively seek out as a content venue that is not only crucial to, but embedded in, their lifestyle. The connective tissue of brands with birth, death, weddings, and everything in between is not ads, and not even marketing at all, but the human connection.

There is nothing more powerful.

# Chapter 7

# A TALE OF THREE KINGS

Today's supermodels and fashionistas, teetering around on sky-high Christian Louboutin trophy shoes with their "trademark" red soles, might be shocked to learn that they're not such trendsetters after all—Louis XIV got there first, more than three hundred years ago. During his reign, only aristocrats of the court—and *male* aristocrats, at that—had the right to wear shoes with red soles. "It's all about the walkaway" is how one Louboutin-loving lady put it at the recent Paris collections, echoing the sentiments of Jennifer Lopez's hit pop song, "Louboutins," which extols the power a woman has when she walks away from a relationship. Louis would have heartily endorsed the message of the power of the branded shoe sole. In his time, a glimpse of a scarlet sole immediately made a statement about class: This was a person of the ruling class with some serious coin in his pocket. Today, the woman who shows her red soles along with her backside is likewise sending a branding message about her status and stature that goes beyond the sexy stiletto: *I'm powerful, right down to the soles of the shoes that you probably can't afford.*

But the Sun King was the originator. His was an era when it was ultrachic to wear your wealth—the more glitter, the better, as long as you didn't outshine *le roi*, which, considering he owned Versailles, was virtually impossible to do. The branding of the French nobility was literally from the ground up, starting with the soles of their shoes. These crimson soles showed that the wearer was an important individual who never dirtied his shoes. Louis's proclamation aside, nobody but the wealthy could actually afford red-soled shoes. They were costly not because some designer declared they were "in," but because red dye—once rumored to be made of dragons' blood—was expensive; the process to create it involved crushing the dried bodies of a specific insect that had to be imported from Mexico. Red soles—and, ultimately, heels as well—became a symbol of the monarchy throughout Europe. The fad ended with the French Revolution, when bling could get your head cut off, only to reemerge two and a half centuries later on the feet of Carrie Bradshaw in *Sex and the City* as a symbol of femme fashion and empowerment. The color red has, in fact, had a long and significant journey in becoming a symbol of power. A 1675 portrait of Charles II of England shows him wearing red-soled shoes. And when today's women in politics or on the red carpet appear in the color, it is a power mnemonic—as women who wear red to address Congress or to report the prime time news—understand.

But for Louis XIV, the shoes were just the beginning. Proclaiming the sun as his personal emblem in 1662, Louis embraced the logo like the swoosh on Nike. He spent a lifetime as a living mnemonic of the brand. In a nonstop stream of prominent court performances and ballets, he often strategically played the role of the sun. There is a portrait of Louis at age fourteen dancing the role of Apollo, the god of the sun, in a royal ballet, sunburst emblems radiating from his ankles, wrists, waist, and neck, and wearing, around his head, a massive sunburst crown—lest anyone miss the point. In his *Mémoires*, the king explained that the sun did good to everywhere, stood for fairness because it shone light equally all over the earth, and for authority because it dominated all other heavenly bodies.[1] The image of *le soleil* was stamped over *le Tout-Paris*. Louis's personal home and the center of his court, the palace of Versailles, and much of its garden architecture, devised in 1664, is organized around the theme of the sun and the planets that orbit it. The elements of the palace were organized to reflect the home of a sun king; the orientations of the building and the landscaping were organized around the symmetry of the sun's journey across the sky, rising and setting in water. In seventeenth-century France, domes, windows, ceilings, murals, tapestries, statues, sculptures, fountains, lamps, bridges, and urban plans all featured the sun as their emblem and theme, spreading the mnemonic of the monarchy. Versailles and the legend of the Sun King sparkled through the long reign of Louis XIV and for a hundred years, until the Revolution, including a grain riot at Versailles in 1740 and the storming of the palace in October 1789, which precipitated the flight and ultimately the overthrow of the royal family. Even today, a visitor to Paris strolling over those enduringly glorious bridges of the Seine can see the Sun King's logo, still shining on and marking his territory after three and a half centuries. L'état, c'est moi.

Now that's branding. For modern corporate brands, longevity is often cited as a key attribute of success. Brands such as Coca-Cola, Wells Fargo, Rothschild, Coutts, and Cadbury are examples of enduring brands that have dominated their markets for the last century. Monarchies, however, are measured in centuries, plural. Monarchial brands start life as a reflection for the monarch, but in time the brand takes on its own life beyond the individual.

The key to the enduring branding success of Louis XIV, and most monarchs—including corporate monarchs—starts with the caveat that the leader not be superficial. Louis XIV actually cared passionately about the values that the sun symbol stood for during his reign— innovation, the arts, culture, progress, and the dawning of a new era for France. He did not show his support halfway, inconsistently, or as a mere figurehead or ribbon-cutter—he consistently pulled out all the stops. Contemporary portraiture of the king depicts him as a triple threat—arts patron, military leader, and religious supporter. From busts to bas-relief, the visual imagery was on-brand. One display among eight rooms devoted to dance and music of the period in a recent exhibit at Versailles included an image of Louis at age fifteen, dressed as le Roi Soleil, his hair arranged in golden beams to match his sunburst shoes.[2] But Louis did not just trot out his sun costume for show—he personified the sun and all it stood for by demonstrating total commitment to support of the arts. Over his lifetime, he performed eighty recorded roles portraying the sun, the sun god, or other regal leads in forty major ballets, the rough equivalent today of the career body of work of a professional dancer. Today we might call this quality authenticity, the watchword of the Web.

The model of the Sun King is still in use today. Case in point: the Sun King of Cupertino—aka Steve Jobs. A former colleague, Jeff

Raskin, has been quoted as saying that Jobs would have made an excellent king of France.[3] In many ways, Louis and Jobs could not have been more opposite, with one being a master of beautiful excess and the other a genius of functional restraint, but in their understanding of their market and the sensibilities of their time, they were closely aligned. Each, for instance, brought a breakthrough tour de force of branding that combined functionality and beauty of design to his respective era, a blend of form and function that set the standard for the century and beyond.

Equally important, both had incomparable skills at identifying and partnering with artists and technicians who could bring their vision to life. The role of the visionary vis-à-vis the necessary partners in making the brand vision a reality is critical, no matter what the product, delivery system, or century. At Versailles, Louis XIV relied on the great architect Louis Le Vau and master gardener André Le Nôtre to create the palace and 19,800 acres of gardens with twenty-seven miles of trellises that marked a testament to his rule; at Apple, Jobs worked with industrial designer Jonathan Ive to physically transform the standard-issue computer in battleship neutrals to a tool as beautiful to look at as it was technically proficient. The partnership between innovative visionary and technician is one that distinguishes these and other great brand stories. Louis intended for his incomparable garden, which has never been equaled in the Western world, to be the embodiment of his rule, the immortality of his brand, a living mnemonic that has diminished in size over the centuries to merely being about double the size of New York City's Central Park, but it remains an enduring monument to the Sun King's brand. Steve Jobs, in contrast, was a brilliant aggregator, enlisting precisely those individuals who had the talents and tools to execute his innovative vision, like a painter with his palette. His end result, like Louis's, was so consistently distinctive that no one could ever mistake an Apple product for anything else. The products themselves are their own mnemonics, reflective as much of their monarchial visionaries as the brands they created.

Postscript: In the 1990s, the national museum at Versailles decided that after more than three hundred years, it was time to refresh the official logo of the site. It conducted a design competition for a new emblem for the palaces and estate that would have instant international recognition. The winner: a stylized emblem of the god Apollo as the sun, culled from one of forty images of the Sun King found throughout the palace. "We thought we could escape the traditional image of the Sun King," said the designers, "but it was not possible."[4]

## ELVIS HAS NOT LEFT THE BUILDING

This is a bit of a personal tangent, but I'm going to go there anyway because it's not easy to cite something everyone hasn't read dozens if not hundreds, of times about Elvis Presley. After all, he was, and still is, the King of Rock 'n' Roll. My godmother, Gloria Lovell, was Frank Sinatra's private secretary in the sixties and as such she dealt on a daily basis with most of the big celebrities of the time. When I was quite young and mostly unappreciative, she gave me a personalized autograph from Elvis—and taped onto the page was a lock of his hair that she had personally cut. I have no idea how she accomplished this; Elvis must have been really tight with Frank. I recently sold this at a rock 'n' roll auction. How did the dealer know it was authentic? I certainly hadn't asked Lisa Marie for a DNA sample. The dealer, a world leader in celebrity memorabilia, told me he was confident it was authentic because, along with the provenance, he had the lock of hair examined and found it had been dyed black, then oxidized over time, and it was known that Elvis dyed his naturally light brown hair black from very early in his career. No PR agent or brand manager told Elvis to dye his hair. He certainly didn't need any help in the looks department—he was dazzlingly handsome as a young man. He hadn't yet gone gray. He wasn't copying another star on a video or a fashion shoot. Elvis probably dyed his hair because he instinctively understood the brooding brand identity he wanted to project—if dark hair was better for that image than light, he was fine with dying it. It was likely a strategic, not a vanity, choice. And so, most likely, nobody would have approved more of what his brand has become than Elvis himself, if he were alive and in his seventies today. He also might be a bit amused at his newly wholesome-ized image, but he would have certainly given it the thumbs-up, as he was always big on family.

How do you go from a shack in Tupelo, Mississippi, to being the ultimate monarch of music? How do you create one of the world's most successful branding empires—and do it mostly after you're dead? When someone today mentions "The King," they are probably not referring to the King of Spain or any other country. The King is the undisputed brand of one person, the King of Rock 'n' Roll, Elvis Presley. Presley died in 1977, but he still has more than 500 active fan clubs in the United States alone.

The fact is that now, forty-some years after his death, the Elvis brand shines brighter than ever—even more brightly than when he died. Elvis's brand is an example of a zigzag of spectacular highs and equally spectacular lows, to the point where, in future generations, and with the afterburner effect of the Internet, there is a good possibility that the real Elvis will be completely obscured by his monster brand presence. This process of brand reinvention occurred postmortem—as it did for his contemporary, John F. Kennedy—with afterburners supplied by the digital community. Elvis is perhaps the supreme role model of not just branding, not just brand reinvention, but modern brand building for the ages. It started with the basics: him, his talent, and his music. But that was just the foundation for the bigger brand story—the story of a true and gargantuan Brandzilla.

From almost the beginning of his career, Elvis was one of those one-name celebrities, maybe the first and most iconic of all. His first name alone conjured up swagger, rebelliousness, and sexiness. This was remarkable in a time of clean-cut, sanitized teen entertainment, and also largely because of the fact that nobody had ever seen—or heard—anything like Elvis Presley.

Elvis had an ultramodern approach for his time, but he broke through the old-fashioned way—with a unique selling proposition. Carl Perkins was in the musical territory, but Elvis took it to the next level and had the talent plus the brand. This wasn't Grandma's Caruso warbling operatically or Mom's Sinatra serenading the ladies over a jigger of gin. This was a guy who TV cameras cut off at the waist because what was happening below seemed unfit for prime time and who could make a hit of a song about a hound dog. In fact, Elvis actually serenaded a basset hound on a popular TV show of the time and even managed to have that stunt boost, as opposed to end, his career.

Here was a guy who grabbed the emerging superpower teen culture by the hips as well as the throat. Leonard Bernstein, no slouch in the music culture department, called Elvis "the greatest cultural force in the United States." No one could ever dispute that Elvis's name, image, and voice spurred a social revolution, impacting music—not to mention selling more than one billion records—more than any single recording artist.

It would be easy to say, and has been said, that Elvis was a pawn in his own success, a phenomenal country-boy, aw-shucks talent who was manipulated by his canny manager, Col. Tom Parker. Although there were legal battles and, at one point, villification of Parker, he clearly played a key role in Elvis's success. Jack Soden, CEO of Elvis Presley Enterprises, said, "Colonel Tom Parker managed Elvis Presley's career from 1955 to 1977. Theirs was probably the most unique artist-manager relationship ever in show business, clearly one of the most successful. The world's music and pop culture changed forever when the greatest performer of them all joined forces with the man who wrote the book on promotion. Elvis and Colonel Parker made history together."[5]

It's interesting to speculate that Elvis was never as unsophisticated as his early "yes ma'am," naive country boy branding suggested—at least as far as his own image, if not his finances, was concerned. High school classmates reported that in school plays, Elvis played lead roles in Shakespeare productions. He seemed to have a definite and distinct strategy to create and cultivate a sexy, rebel image almost from his first steps on stage. He was responsible for his own image as his career evolved—for better or worse. His performances were meticulous. His motto was "Taking Care of Business," with a lightning bolt—not "Good Times," with a musical note. Nobody forced Elvis into those Las Vegas jumpsuits and sequined capes. It makes sense that by the Vegas years, he certainly had the confidence of a person who knew he could pull the genie out of the paper bag. Even at the end of his career, the man could always just open his mouth and sing like nobody else, and he knew it.

In spite of his phenomenal success and talent, this was just the beginning. In fact, although Elvis's music was consistently at the top of the charts, the Elvis brand didn't really take off until his death. Elvis didn't die pretty, and he died after a decade of what was not exactly gold-standard brand stewardship that milked his brand—but the brand survived and, without Elvis's actual physical dissipation to drain it further or his live genius to enhance it, made a comeback equal to any of his own. There was rock 'n' roll Elvis, then military Elvis, then comeback Elvis, then jumpsuit Elvis, then the fat Elvis who had recently lost the contest to be the face on a U.S. postage stamp, to thin Elvis, and now immortal Elvis.

From the start, the Elvis brand was a successful, revenue-generating commodity. As early as 1956, Parker had made a deal for seventy-two different Elvis-themed products, which generated $22 million in sales within six months.[6]

Following his superstar start, Elvis was drafted into the army as a regular private in 1958. From his release from military service in 1960 to 1969, he starred in a series of Hollywood films, most of them vehicles for his songs—and, in fact, he preferred at that time to focus on acting. He returned to TV in 1968 and then to live performing in 1969 with smash-hit concerts that restored luster to his brand. Most of the 1970s were spent touring and living the peanut butter, banana, and burned bacon sandwich lifestyle, with a side of drugs. While he never lost his remarkable talent, his health and image declined, until he died in his bathroom at Graceland in 1977. His cause of death is still being discussed, but the autopsy revealed fourteen drugs in his system at the time of his death, including:

Morphine
Demerol
Chlorpheniramine, an antihistamine
Placidyl
Valium
Codeine
Ethinamate, largely prescribed at the time as a "sleeping pill"
Quaaludes[7]

That was in 1977. Elvis's brand took a torpedo and with it its value to the estate and its trust for his sole heir, his daughter, Lisa Marie.

Enter Priscilla Presley, who stepped in after a decade of brand doldrums, if not outright erosion, to take back control for her daughter,

Elvis's only child, turn back the tide, and reshape her ex-husband's image for the ages. Unlike Jackie, Priscilla's contributions were of an immediate business nature. Brand iconicity and messaging were carefully controlled, an approved list of artists and photographers was created, Graceland was reborn as a revenue-generating tourist venue, and brand management was employed. This was especially challenging as the music recordings were no longer a part of the estate, as Elvis and Parker, his manager, sold the master recordings of his music to Sony in the early 1970s—but Elvis Presley Enterprises assiduously stewards the brand.

Fast forward to today. Elvis has never been bigger. Twitter @ElvisPresley gives ongoing updates. Elvis's Facebook page is approaching 6 million fans. The Elvis brand has 200 licensees selling products in more than 120 countries. More than 1 billion Elvis records have been sold worldwide—more than those of any other solo artist in history.[8]

The principals in the posthumous Elvis Presley industry have made more money from his brand than Elvis himself ever did in his lifetime.[9]

Scott Williams, vice president of digital marketing for Elvis Presley Enterprises, points out that Elvis had one of the earliest entertainment sites: "We very much embrace new media." Elvis is represented on Facebook Pinterest, Foursquare, and all other social media, and the Presley marketing team does not shy away from new or innovative digital initiatives, allotting a portion of the marketing budget each year to try out new media frontiers.[10]

Tynicka Battle, cofounder and CEO of ThinkTank Digital, who was involved in Lady Gaga's landmark digital program, notes that Elvis Presley Enterprises was looked to by marketers as a benchmark of digital success almost from the inception of Internet marketing. "They harnessed one of the largest online bases, a long time before anybody thought to do so. They were the first that really pulled together their fan base and started talking to them, as soon as they could," she confirms.

Williams says,

We think of it just like, in the fifties, when Elvis was first exposed to people watching live performances, or watching television and listening to the radio, it created instant fans. . . . A lot of people who were first exposed to Elvis back then today share memories of how they suddenly became a fan. Thanks to the Internet, people from every walk of life, every corner of the world can now be exposed to his music and his imagery, and that also creates fans just like it did back in the fifties. Additionally, it gives people an opportunity to celebrate their affinity with Elvis Presley, and with Graceland it also creates an opportunity for other people who share that same love and create great relationships. I just talked to a lady last week who met four other fans on our message board five years ago, and they all flew to Memphis from their various cities to meet up, and now they've all become the best of friends. So the digital opportunities are to both expose people to Elvis and also introduce them to each other. Elvis's Facebook page gives us a chance to post something online, and then people can take that and share it on their own pages as a badge of honor. So they're able to shout out their affinity for the brand in a very simple and easy to use way.[11]

The Graceland mansion and its thirteen-acre grounds, the former home of Elvis and the site of his death and memorial, is a delivery system of Elvis Presley in itself—a kind of Memphis Versailles, a mnemonic reminder of Elvis's life, music, and brand. The fact that Graceland is still wholly owned by Lisa Marie Presley further strengthens the brand connection. It is now a tourist site attracting 600,000 visitors a year.[12] In the contemporary world, just the name "Graceland" invokes a cascade of emotional imagery attached to Elvis, his style, his life, and his legacy. Regardless of the status of Graceland as an attraction, its existence and its link to Elvis and his family imbue an emotional halo effect to the brand that impacts instant and timeless connectivity, a kind of social media nirvana. You can log onto the Graceland widget and see a real-time, live video of Graceland, courtesy of the Graceland cam. Try it yourself at http://www.elvis.com/graceland/graceland_cam.aspx.

Scott Williams notes,

The brand of Graceland is the rock 'n' roll pilgrimage....It has nearly 100 percent awareness all over the world, which is remarkable. If you ask just about anybody, visiting Graceland is on their bucket list. And a lot of people want to bring their children or grandchildren. From Paul Simon's song *Graceland*, to all the thousands of mentions of Graceland that take place in pop culture every week, it's transcended a tourist attraction and become something greater that's relating to music and yet it's different. People are often surprised, when they go through Graceland, of the emotion that it generated, and the whole feeling of a Shakespearean tale.[13]

Then there are the Elvis impersonators. True, they're just impersonators, but they add an element of living, breathing vitality to the Elvis brand and a man who isn't here to do it himself. The Elvis silhouette—instantly recognizable at any stage of his life or career, even without the accompaniment of his brilliant music—is the ultimate mnemonic, the sui generis human being who is recognizable in a line drawing even in deconstructed elements of just his hair, his collar, or his posture, thirty-five years after his death. More than 640,000 listings for Elvis impersonators are found on the Web, embodying all stages of his career—young Elvis, military Elvis, Las Vegas Elvis, and so on—cropping up as everything from "The Reigning Elvis Presley of the Philippines" to the Flying Elvi—quasi clones of the King who parachute in precision formation—to Elvis Herselvis, a female variation. It could be argued that any Elvis impersonator, even a baby in a sequin cape—I actually found one of a newborn doing an Elvis impersonation to the tune of "Since My Baby Left Me," and if the kid is bald, no problem, there are Elvis wigs for toddlers—has a better than average chance to go viral.

Elvis is evergreen, and people can never seem to get enough of him—or his doppelgängers. The number of Elvis impersonators at his death in 1977 was estimated to be a few hundred. By the year 2000, there were said to be 85,000 working Elvis impersonators. Based on the metrics this pattern implied, statisticians calculated that a third of the world's population would be Elvis impersonators by the year 2019.[14]

Talk about brand proliferation. In Elvis's case, social media involves numbers that equate with the populations of cities or even countries not just talking about, but *being* the brand.

Elvis's brand has been totally rehabilitated and more. Today, the Elvis Presley brand resonates with G-rated, family wholesomeness. Graceland has become a phenomenally successful global tourist destination. The mansion is preserved as a monument in a bell jar, frozen as it was when Elvis was in residence. OK, he's left the building, but he's actually still in residence, buried on-site, and you can pay your respects. In 2012, Elvis Week, a week dedicated to celebrating Presley's life but scheduled around the anniversary of his death, attracted 75,000 people for its Candlelight Vigil, in which fans light candles and file past the driveway of the Graceland mansion.[15] Can't make it to Memphis with the kids? Check out the Elvis.com website. There's a special tab for kids that reads: "A visit to see the King of Rock 'n' Roll's home is a fun and educational experience for kids. This site is a great way to get your kids ready for their upcoming visit." On the site, a twelve-year-old takes kids on a virtual tour of Graceland, with a history lesson about the mansion and a bunch of fun facts. There's a downloadable Graceland activity coloring book. The brand torch is being passed as the next generation of Elvis fans is being teed up.

On the 2012 Scout Day at Graceland, 1,100 Boy Scouts and Girl Scouts attended a special event. Video is posted on the Elvis Presley Enterprises site, where a group of preadolescent Girl Scouts can be heard chanting the lyrics to "Jailhouse Rock"—"The warden threw a party in the county jail." The kids were entertained with visits to the exhibits of Elvis memorabilia, art projects where they colored in pictures of guitars, and a live hound dog they could pet. It was a total edutainment experience, offering the scouts an opportunity to earn credits toward badges in art, music, citizenship, American heritage, journalism, and forestry. "We frequently experience young people who are children or teenagers who themselves are fans of Elvis," says Scott Williams. "Their parents may or may not have been fans, but the kids are, and so they bring their parents to Graceland."

What if the Internet had been available during the rise of Elvis Presley? Williams thinks that if Elvis were alive and performing today, he would have been an eager early adopter of digital technologies. "He loved technology, he loved newness, things other people were afraid to try. He embraced change and this would have come through." Williams thinks Presley might have achieved international fame more quickly if the Internet had been available, but he also sees the impact of the original social networks on spreading Elvis's fame. "People didn't have digital social networks back then, but they certainly had social networks. There were fan magazines, people listened to radio shows—and the media then and now had a love affair with the work of Elvis."[16]

If you phone Elvis Presley Enterprises, the music you hear when calls are being transferred or put on hold is one of the greatest hits of the King. Williams talks about picking up the phone and having people beg to be put back on hold. In the end, the Presley brand, for all the bells and whistles, survives and thrives due to the music of the King of Rock 'n' Roll. "It's all about exposing people to the actual work, to the actual music," says Williams. "We in marketing are guilty of loving to throw the term 'brand' around a lot, which is a way for us to communicate with each other, but at the end of the day, it truly is Elvis Presley performing, using his God-given skill. People are exposed to this and instantly become a fan of his work. The work is what creates the fans. As long as we don't screw it up by trying to get too clever."[17]

Following an acquisition in 2010 by CKx, the entertainment content and intellectual property company owned by Bob Sillerman, the majority rights to the Elvis Presley brand were acquired by the same ownership group as the *American Idol* franchise, Apollo Global Management. *Idol* subsequently featured a show built around performances of the Presley songbook, and in May 2012 Lisa Marie Presley performed her new single on the show.

In May 2011, *Idol* launched Facebook voting. *Billboard* reported, "The move by *American Idol* will ramp up the show's producers' direct access to many of its most-engaged fans." *American Idol*'s Facebook page already has more than 4.7 million "friends."[18]

Elvis + *Idol* + Facebook—now, there's a brand equation.

All genuflect: The next generation will now kiss the ring of the King.

## DON'T LET IT BE FORGOT

At the time of their funerals, the entire civilized world knew what Louis XIV—and Elvis—stood for; their brands were clearly established and have remained cemented in place. However, when his motorcade entered Dealey Plaza, JFK's brand—what he would stand for in the ages—was still an open question. That question was to be answered definitively not during Kennedy's presidency or even his state funeral, unforgettable as it was, but a week later, in Hyannis Port, Massachusetts. That was when author Theodore H. White, a former classmate, Kennedy insider, and author of a best-selling chronicle of the Kennedy-Nixon campaign, *The Making of the President 1960*, was summoned to the Kennedy compound by Jackie Kennedy, who wove a modern parable of just knights, fair ladies, and an incomparable king and queen.

It was a rain-lashed night when Jackie, sitting alone with White, poured out her perspective on her husband's presidency. The urgency of the meeting, which took place on the Saturday night after Thanksgiving, was such that White had taken a limousine from New York to Cape Cod because the weather had grounded air traffic. Jackie Kennedy felt sensitive to the timing because, she noted, already, within mere days of Kennedy's death, writers—and, more to her disliking, "historians"—were assessing the Kennedy presidency. This concerned Mrs. Kennedy, she said, because she did not want her husband's legacy left to the "dusty" historians. And so now she painted the image she preferred to portray, something more personal, more romantic than political—but which, ultimately, turned out to have great, if unintended, impact on the brand perceptions of political ideologies and activities in the years and decades to come.

Jackie summed it up to White: "When Jack quoted something, it was usually classical, but... all I keep thinking of is this line from a musical comedy. At night, before we'd go to sleep, Jack liked to play some records, and the song he loved most came at the end of this record." The lines he loved to hear ended: "... *for one brief shining moment that was known as Camelot.*" The lyrics came from the 1960 Broadway musical, *Camelot*, which at the time had been a hit show with lyrics by Alan Jay Lerner, followed by a popular record album.

The deeper idea of Camelot, however, was a centuries-old and much-romanticized story, the heroic legend of King Arthur and his knights, the subject of myth, oral tales, poetry, and books since the sixth century. Jackie Kennedy was no stranger to the power of poetry and storytelling and was a known lover of poetry, as her daughter,

Caroline, has since reconfirmed, publishing a collection of Jackie's best-loved poems after her death. As early as 1953, Jackie had written and given her husband a version of a classical poem about the myth of Jason and the Golden Fleece, which extolled him as an Argonaut of Massachusetts: *"He would find love He would never find peace/ For he must go seeking The Golden Fleece/ All of the things he was going to be/ All of the things in the wind and the sea."*[19]

White adjourned to a guest room and immediately typed up his notes, and at 2:00 A.M., he phoned in his story to the waiting editors of *Life* magazine. The presses were being held on an issue that would be sent to a circulation of more than 7 million and by a commemorative issue to several million more; *Life* was a media giant of the times. At least one of the editors at the other end of the line thought that the Camelot analogy was a bit heavy handed and suggested it be cut back or dropped. Jackie, standing there firmly shaking her head, disagreed. Camelot stayed. And a myth—and an iconic brand—entered history.[20]

John Fitzgerald Kennedy, the thirty-fifth president of the United States, had hardly been in office one thousand days when he was cut down by an assassin's bullet in an open limousine motorcade in Dallas, Texas—the sixth-briefest term of any U.S. president. Yet compared to other relatively brief presidencies, his brand is gargantuan. Who beyond the most avid history buff, for instance, has clarity about the Millard Fillmore or James Garfield brands—other than their lack of clarity? Garfield, like Kennedy, was assassinated in office. His presidency lasted two hundred days, during which, among other things, he was known for political reform and his advocacy of civil rights. But who today cares—or even recalls—what Garfield stood for? Yet the initials JFK alone conjure up an immediate image of all Kennedy embodied, his shimmering brand. And one word sums it up. Jackie Kennedy's word: *Camelot*.

The Kennedy presidency certainly had the media advantage. It has been called the first TV presidency and was the first to leverage TV to shape the image of America's chief executive. In 1950, when Harry S. Truman was president, 11 percent of American households had a TV. By 1960, that number was 88 percent. The Nixon-Kennedy debates were viewed by more than 70 million Americans—and almost as many viewed Kennedy's inauguration. Kennedy's stunning visual advantage over Nixon in the debates, which caused even Nixon's running mate, Henry Cabot Lodge, to remark, when comparing Nixon's overall impression to JFK's, "That son of a bitch just lost us the election," is well documented.[21]

Kennedy's inaugural address was viewed in person by an audience of 20,000, but by 77 million on TV. One of the first and best brand image masters, Kennedy, a genius at presenting a youthful, healthy media image, appeared outdoors in twenty-degree cold looking tanned and fit without a topcoat or hat—in fact, history has shown he was an unhealthy individual, suffering from Addison's disease that had once nearly killed him, a chronic bad back that involved surgery that also almost killed him, and other ailments requiring a maintenance program of ongoing medications and a stiff corset under his clothing to even maintain an upright posture. Although JFK was a habitual womanizer outside of his marriage, he, Jackie, and their children presented the JFK brand as the picture of the ideal American family, with a barrage of official photos showing the family at play, at church, and in idealized circumstances. Tragedy only intensified these images, which were replayed until JFK was not only branded, but seared indelibly into the public consciousness. In life, he had been a superstar. In death, he became a Brandzilla.

Kennedy's assassination catapulted him into a new level of the public consciousness not only due to the fact of the assassination itself, but also due to the aftermath. The three days of coverage of the funeral, modeled, at Jackie Kennedy's specific direction, after Abraham Lincoln's, featured a coffin on a caisson followed by a riderless black horse, boots reversed in the stirrups, muffled drums, ruffles and flourishes, the veiled widow, and John-John's salute—a gesture impossible to preprogram and for that reason all the more gut-wrenchingly impactful. Every instant was broadcast to the largest TV audience ever at the time, elevating and embossing a presidency that was cut down before a critical mass of real substance could emerge.

Louis XIV left the cultural legacy of Versailles. Elvis died at age forty-two after a twenty-year career, but he left the legacy of Graceland—including a body of musical work that is still unsurpassed and still performed globally—and his innovations changed the musical landscape forever. Both of these kings were historic game changers in their respective venues and times. Conversely, Kennedy did not have the gift of time to cement his legacy and align it with reality. As Kennedy expert and historian James Piereson notes, "Kennedy had not really been president long enough to accomplish what, for instance, Lincoln had achieved when he was assassinated. At the time of his death, Kennedy had no real brand."[22]

When he accepted his party's nomination for the presidency in 1960, Kennedy announced the "New Frontier," an era which pledged to address space, technology, poverty, peace, and forward progress. The term was ultimately adopted by his administration and attached to legislation and programs of the time. But the New Frontier and what it stood for has since been superceded by Camelot, which was undeniably a posthumous creation. In this respect, Bobby Kennedy, who stepped in to carry the fallen president's agenda forward, in fact "may have been the only true son of Camelot," Piereson says.

Following the assassination, however, the "New Frontier" morphed into Camelot and Kennedy into a modern-day King Arthur.[23]

Piereson points out some unvarnished facts: "Kennedy was a practical, pragmatic Democrat who won the election with a very narrow margin and was not yet proved. The liberals of the Democratic party didn't trust him because he'd never been a spokesperson for liberal causes while he was in the House and Senate. He was not known to take any risks. The liberals of the Democratic party at the time of the election were supporting Adlai Stevenson."

"Jackie Kennedy came up with the concept of Camelot," notes Piereson.

This was almost all Jackie—and almost all Jackie, the week and weekend after Kennedy was shot. The concept of Camelot does not appear to have been made up before that. It was not a factor in anything Kennedy thought or did. It was something Jackie developed, right in those days immediately after he was killed, the moments leading up to the funeral and the week after.

I think that Jackie Kennedy had a very imaginative turn of mind. She hated the cynical world of politics. When Kennedy

died, her immediate thought was to try and ennoble this whole
thing, in terms of the kind of myth that people would remember him by. What she jumped to was the Broadway play,
*Camelot.* . . . The musical was based on a novel by T. H. White,
*The Once and Future King*, which was a mythical retelling of
the King Arthur legend, but in modern times, so that King
Arthur becomes a peacemaker. At the end, the kingdom has
come apart, the dream is over. Arthur tells a young follower
to take a candle and light it from the bonfire that has been lit
before the final battle to represent his ideals and spread his
story forward, so this society could be reborn at some future
time. This section of the book is called "Candle in the Wind,"
and my speculation is that the eternal flame at Kennedy's grave
is the candle in the wind.

White published "For President Kennedy: An Epilogue" in *Life*
magazine on December 6, 2003. "White was very taken with this idea,"
Piereson says. "That was where Camelot came from, and it stuck. That
all happened within a week after the assassination."[24]

Although the culture of the Kennedy administration had certainly
been known for its patina of glitter, glamour, style, and wit prior to
the assassination, Jackie had in fact identified more with Louis XIV
than Arthur, and her references were to style rather than substance—
although, in the end, she succeeded in making style substance. The
British prime minister Harold Macmillan said at the time of the
Kennedy administration, "They certainly have acquired something
we have lost—a casual sort of grandeur about their evenings, always
at the end of the day's business. The promise of parties, and pretty
women, and music and beautiful clothes, champagne, and all that. I
must say there is something very 18th century [about JFK], an aristo-
cratic touch."[25]

Jackie told Oleg Cassini, her official dress designer, that she wanted
to bring Versailles to the White House. She brought in a French gourmet chef and wore French designs. She was famously wearing a Chanel-
inspired pink suit on the day of the assassination.

Piereson adds, "All this had nothing to do with Kennedy. He didn't
think in terms of King Arthur and Camelot." There were also political

implications, Piereson contends. "Jackie also wanted her husband to be remembered as a martyr to peace and civil rights, which would make him an Arthurian kind of figure. The idea was that the eternal flame was carrying forward these ideals of peace and justice. The Camelot legend is totally abstract and detached from the real events that happened. It was a double myth, actually. So Kennedy's assassination totally transformed him. But it was a brand that was in a way disconnected to the way he was in life."[26]

In *Camelot and the Cultural Revolution*, Piereson makes the case that the Kennedy Camelot myth that grew up after his death for the most part flies in the face of the reality of the man, his policies, and his presidency. Myth: Kennedy was a liberal idealist, a martyr for civil rights who had gone into politics intent on the problems of the world. Reality: Kennedy was a pragmatic politician, "reluctant to get too far ahead of public opinion, especially in the area of civil rights, wherein his hand was eventually forced by developments beyond his control."[27]

"When Kennedy was shot, they looked at it in the context of civil rights, because there was a lot of civil rights violence in that period. But his legislative agenda at the time he was elected was still bottled up in the Congress. If he was a monument to anything, it was to the Cold War, not civil rights," Piereson noted in an interview for this book. "Kennedy waited until June of 1963 before he supported a civil rights bill. But this was not how Jackie Kennedy wanted him to be remembered. She did brand him. So Kennedy became branded as an idealist for peace, justice, and racial equality, a martyr to that cause. That was the idea that came out—that the Kennedy administration was kind of a modern Camelot, a magical period that has now been destroyed, and we can never get it back."[28]

Piereson opines that the negative concept of "lost Camelot," combined with the implication that a conspiracy of socio-politically motivated elements, blurring the responsibility into the broad stroke of Americans in general, was somehow responsible for throwing us out of paradise (as Jackie Kennedy, refusing to change out of her blood-stained suit, said, "Let them see what they have done"). This then had a profound impact beyond the assassination itself on American politics and culture. According to Piereson, Americans rationally knew that

Lee Harvey Oswald killed Kennedy, but Oswald did not kill Camelot. What killed Camelot was, rather, "the idea that JFK was brought down in a climate of hate that had overtaken the nation. Thus they placed Kennedy's assassination within a context of violence against civil rights activists…when in fact an anti-American Communist killed Kennedy."[29]

The nostalgia for the Kennedy years, guided by Jackie and the lyrics from a Broadway musical, began immediately. Piereson argues that this perception of the end of an era was largely a posthumously invented mirage, the result of the branding of Camelot, and that this marked the reinvention of American liberalism into a dark and accusatory form that was unrecognizable in the actual days of Camelot—the end of optimism in American liberalism.[30] As if Americans were ever after seeking not a happy ending but a social target to blame—for the assassination, for civil unrest, you name it—sidestepping what really killed Kennedy, if you believe the evidence to date—which was Oswald, a registered communist. Piereson theorizes that Jackie Kennedy's Camelot brand perception of Kennedy and his era changed attitudes to the point of altering American political perspectives, which in turn changed history. Beyond the impact of the assassination of the president, it resulted in the assassination of a belief system that, once buoyant and optimistic, took on darker tones.

"So Kennedy's assassination totally transformed him. But it was a brand that was in a way disconnected to the way he was in life," Piereson says. He adds that the brands of most monarchs or national leaders reflect more of the reality of the situation than Camelot has for Kennedy. For instance, at the time of his assassination, at the end of the Civil War and emancipation, Lincoln had accomplished most of his mission. Queen Victoria successfully branded herself as a family person to restore the monarchy following the dissipation of her grandfather and predecessor, George III. Queen Elizabeth I lived well into old age as the Virgin Queen. Kennedy's Camelot brand "only could have happened in the modern media era."

If left to history, the Kennedy presidency would undoubtedly have emerged with another kind of brand, but not Camelot. In fact, Kennedy's contemporary and closest colleagues never bought into the Camelot myth. Larry O'Brien, Kennedy's liaison with Congress, felt that hard work, more than anything else, characterized the Kennedy White House. He added, "If at any time Camelot existed, it eluded me....I never saw or felt it."[31]

Theodore White later said the Camelot myth was created as a kindness to a distraught widow of a fallen president, and that he regretted his role in popularizing the Camelot image to the public. He said in his memoir, "Quite inadvertently, I was her instrument in labeling the myth."[32]

Kennedy's longtime secretary, Evelyn Lincoln, commented that the Camelot myth was a total fantasy. She claimed that she never heard Kennedy play the *Camelot* record in the White House, and that his favorite song was "Bill Bailey, Won't You Please Come Home."[33] It didn't matter. The Camelot brand has become much greater than a brand, evolving into an iconic collective cultural memory—more *Brigadoon*, in fact, than *Camelot*.

As a young woman, Jacqueline Bouvier alluded to herself in her essay for *Vogue*'s Prix de Paris contest (which she won) as aspiring to be "a sort of Overall Art Director of the Twentieth Century, watching everything from a chair hanging in space."[34]

As a new widow, Jackie Kennedy told Theodore White that she did not want her husband's legacy to be "left to the historians."

She succeeded on both counts.

In the decades since Kennedy's death, revelations about his personal life have abounded, yet the Camelot brand remains almost impervious. In *After Camelot: A Personal History of the Kennedy Family, 1968 to the Present*, J. Randy Taraborrelli says, "Lost in Jackie's romantic view of her husband's presidency is how badly the actual Camelot story played out—with infidelities, betrayals, murders, and even the death of King Arthur himself."[35]

Piereson says, "Jackie may have been surprised by the long-lasting power of the Camelot myth. Teddy White thought it was slightly ridiculous when he put it into that essay, and so did his editors for *Life* magazine. But, here we are 50 years later, still talking about it. Camelot created the ultimate brand from out of nothing. The Camelot myth just goes on."[36]

Camelot is the quintessential modern myth. As opposed to the allusion itself, the more accurate parallel might be the ancient minstrels who created odes of greatness in honor of their liege, the wandering Theodore Whites of their time who sang tales of greatness that were embellished and layered until the truth disappeared somewhere into the mists of time. The JFK–Camelot legend is one of the most significant examples of the power of storytelling to build a brand in modern history.

# Chapter 8

# FROM BOATERS TO BLOGGERS

Fashion is fickle. But as centuries turn, the winds of change are often driven by the afterburners of technology. The leading and, ultimately, sustaining women's fashion brands, however, have often come not from the arbiters and experts, but from women who are out there in the crosscurrents of life. This makes sense. It takes a lockstep emotional connection with consumers to sustain a brand in today's fifteen-minutes-of-fame environment, much less for a century. We are currently in the midst of a reality revival. This is presumably partly reflecting a desire to grip on to something authentic in the face of a faceless technology tsunami. Fashion brands that resonate with consumers reflect the voices and faces of real women, not exalted designers. And sometimes, real women, like Stella McCartney, become exalted designers and build global brands. But the successful ones never lose their realness. Reality is the new luxury.

McCartney had a rock pedigree, but she built her brand not on the rave stage, but the runway. She rocketed out with her graduation show at Central Saint Martins College of Art and Design in 1995, which was stacked with McCartney's famous model-friends (to be fair, that's her reality), and her designs were purchased immediately by at least three major fashion retailers, including Joseph and Neiman Marcus. Within two years she had replaced the iconic Karl Lagerfeld as creative director at Chloé. Next stop was her own brand, of which she sold a 50 percent stake to Gucci Group (now the PPR Luxury Group) in 2001. The brand pushed into the black ink in 2006, when it posted a 14 percent growth in profits, to £2.1 billion, and sales continue to rise, with the Stella McCartney brand one of the core growth drivers of the parent company. In this journey, McCartney maintained her core brand attributes, which reflected her own personality and values, whether designing Madonna's wedding gown; designing for the needs of women on the red carpet or the nursery carpet; being honored for her work fighting breast cancer; espousing vegetarianism; or refusing to work with leather, fur, skins, or, as she calls it, "every dead animal."[1]

It's likely that Stella McCartney is a Brandzilla in the making.

McCartney is a link in the chain of fashion brand evolution that routinely leaves "it" brands scattered in its wake like so much roadkill in lipstick. But these shifts in power also reveal commonalities and shared sensibilities that are keys to success and survival. This can be seen by comparing two women who, a century apart, created unique brand platforms that shifted paradigms by reflecting the changing world around them. One is an iconic household name synonymous with women and luxury. The other is a largely unknown, bleeding-edge twenty-three-year-old blogger who, until her summer 2012 wedding, lived at home with her parents and is neither a designer nor a fashion retailer or editor. Nonetheless, she stiletto-tracked over Lady Gaga, Anna Wintour, Michelle Obama, and Kate Middleton to lead *Ad Week*'s Fashion Power 25 list in September 2011.

## THE FEMANCIPATOR

A century ago, fashionable women were prisoners of their clothes, bound by boa constrictor corsets, floor-sweeping skirts, and hats that were like gigantic confectionary shops with beekeeper nets perched on their heads. Then a young Frenchwoman, raised in a monastic convent/orphanage and recently a quasi-courtesan of the demimonde, opened a simple hat shop in Deauville, a seaside vacation retreat for the wealthy. Financed by her lovers, she introduced millinery such as she herself wore—straw boaters, similar to those worn by orphans in her school and by local fishermen, trimmed with simple decorations like grosgrain ribbon or an architectural feather. Coming off a wartime discomfort with opulence, the fashionable women she now mingled with noticed and embraced the style. Within two years, Gabrielle "Coco" Chanel opened her second shop in Paris, Chanel Modes, and within a year, she opened the doors of what would become her flagship on Rue Cambon, still standing today, and now the symbolic epicenter of a $6 billion global brand.

At the time Coco Chanel introduced her little boater hats, technology was changing everything. The introduction of the automobile made women mobile in a way that the horse and carriage obviously could not, and the introduction of fashion journalism and photographs in magazines of fashionable women not staged in the studio, but attending exciting, aspirational events in dazzling locations, brought fresh images to new eyeballs. It was the birth of modern fashion PR. Coco Chanel, entering the world of fashion from an outsider's vantage point, a woman's vantage point, took aim and struck gold. "It was grotesque. How could a brain function normally under all that?" was her comment on the hat styles of the day, which she referred to as "enormous deep-dish pies."[2] Promenading along the seaside at Nice or at the Paris racetrack, and often accompanied by her beautiful sister, who served as her model, Chanel was escorted by her wealthy investor beaux, who had a vested interest in displaying her wares in high-profile circumstances. By 1912, Chanel, who got her nickname from a ditty she had once sung as an unsuccessful music hall performer, was also the milliner to the female stars of some of the most fashionable productions of the day, on and off the stage. *Les Modes*, the top French fashion magazine of the day, announced that a new hat designer had arrived in an article that featured full-page illustrations of the most beautiful red carpet celebrities of the day wearing her hats. From here, it was an easy step for Chanel to suggest clothing styles that expanded on the lifestyle lessons of the hats themselves.

Women recognized and embraced Coco Chanel as "one of us." Unlike the male designers who preceded her, she did not squeeze them into hourglass shapes, plop turbans on their heads, or immerse them in clouds of net and plumes. Inspired by Chanel's own wardrobe of corsetless boy-tailoring, humble fabrics like jersey and tweed—formerly seen only in underwear and in the proximity of horses and guns—and basic colors like black, stylish women of the day stepped from the pages of the fashion magazines, stage, and gossip columns, and into Chanel's atelier for a makeover that was as much social as style. World War I had provided women with a new personal freedom, allowing them to circulate unchaperoned, alone if they wished, on foot, in cars, and even as passengers on motorcycles, and Chanel's style symbolized this new unfettered, emancipated lifestyle.

In fact, Chanel's trademark simplicity was organic and consistent because Gabrielle's vision was born not of articulated opulence and luxury, but of the sparseness and strictness of the convent where she was brought up as an abandoned child. Discipline of mind, body, and line all converged to manifest in the brand identity that became Chanel. The themes of that early, monastic existence in a stripped-down convent resonated throughout the life and work of the girl who grew up to be Coco Chanel.

In 1921, Chanel introduced her first fragrance, No. 5, in a bottle as spare and pared as her clothing styles. The proprietor of Galéries Lafayette, where she had first purchased the straw boaters that she trimmed and sold, introduced her to Pierre Wertheimer, owner of one of the largest cosmetics companies in France. In order to step up production and achieve scale, she sold 90 percent of her fragrance business (a split she would come to regret) to these two partners. Her brand template was already set, and she had the instinct and genius to stick to it. Every morning, before she entered her Rue Cambon premises, an assistant would spray the doorway with Chanel No. 5. In her apartment across the street at the Ritz, she sprinkled the perfume on the hot coals of her fires. The brand was reinforced at every level.[3]

In the 1920s, Chanel took another step when she innovated the concept of sportswear, another reflection of the evolving needs of the modern woman's lifestyle. The combination of luxury, active freedom, and comfort was thus taken to another level. By the 1930s, Chanel had a workforce of 4,000. After World War II, following a rather open wartime romance with a Nazi officer that would have demolished any other brand, Chanel retired to Switzerland. She herself may have felt her brand was dead. Yet she saw an opportunity rise following World War II, as she had in the wake of World War I. Again, she reacted to what she perceived as a constricting trend. Chanel reopened in her original location in 1954, amid the wasp waists and flouncy skirts of the New Look and criticism that her brand of modern simplicity had seen its day.

The critics were wrong. By the mid-1960s, the Chanel brand was a staple of women ranging from Marilyn Monroe, who famously claimed to sleep clad only in Chanel No. 5, to Jackie Kennedy, who was wearing a Chanel-inspired pink suit when her husband was assassinated. Coco Chanel continued to build her brand until her death in 1971, by which time she was a legend that shows no sign of fading. Tended by the artistic likes of Karl Lagerfeld and propelled by the profits of the indomitable flagship fragrance, the brand retains its burnish as others come and go. It remains a Brandzilla because it is a brand with which consumers have a relationship beyond the purchase. A fourteen-year-old girl who buys a Chanel lipstick may never have heard of Coco Chanel, but she is buying all that Chanel stood for.

"The Chanel No. 5 fragrance is arguably the most coveted consumer luxury product of the twentieth and twenty-first centuries," writes Tilar J. Mazzeo in *The Secret of Chanel No. 5: The Intimate History of the World's Most Famous Perfume*. "But it hasn't changed in any of the essentials; rather, decade after decade, we have reinvented it in our minds.... All along, we have been willing participants in the production and reproduction of its legend. Indeed, we have been the principal agents of it.... Chanel No. 5 has been about the stories we tell of ourselves from the beginning, and that includes all the people who have shaped its history... and, of course, no one was as tightly bound to the fragrance as Coco Chanel. It was part of her history and her story."[4]

Today, the entwined double Cs, camellia flower, and simple tailoring of Chanel have survived shredding, piercing, shrinking, and every other style trend to maintain the brand integrity that Coco Chanel introduced with a simple straw hat. The little straw boater was the engine that fueled the fashion empire that today is synonymous with luxury branding and the modern woman—a symbiotic relationship that leverages women themselves as walking delivery systems of the brand statement that has only proliferated. Coco Chanel the superstar designer and the Chanel brand may together be the first both created and sustained by that reality.

# THE MAN REPELLER

Today, a century after Coco's modest straw chapeaux, one of the newest and most breakthrough fashion brands started completely outside the industry, an entrepreneurial effort launched at home in a college student blogger's parents' apartment—which was less than a year ago as of this writing. She's not a designer, she has never sewn a stitch, she has never opened a shop or worked in one, and she's not even an aggregator of other people's viewpoints, like so many on the Web. She's the Man Repeller.

"I started my business the way that most college students who are writers start their business," says Leandra Medine, aka the Man Repeller. "I basically wanted a forum to be able to write without seeing my work, without getting so editorialized. I was used to pitching publications and getting my work published, but I thought, 'Gosh, all the funny, quirky, sarcastic things that I thought strung this piece together, the editors just took out, and I thought—Why?' I really wanted in this forum to be able to write what I wanted to say, curse when I wanted to, and not have to worry about having to go through five different tiers of editors."[5]

Medine defines being a Man Repeller as "outfitting oneself in a sartorially offensive way that will result in repelling members of the opposite sex. Such garments include but are not limited to harem pants, boyfriend jeans, shoulder pads, full length jumpsuits, jewelry that resembles violent weaponry and clogs."[6]

A fellow fashion blogger writes:

She founded the *Man Repeller* blog in 2010 on the belief that women should dress in a way that makes them happy, not simply to attract men. And while Medine writes about clothes in tones ranging from overwhelmingly reverent to hilariously sarcastic to shamelessly personal, her underlying message is celebrated for liberating women from dressing according to the constraints of what men consider "sexy." Her funny, edgy, pushing-the-limits-of-acceptable style has won over casual fashion fans and seasoned industry insiders alike, making her the coolest thing to hit the scene since the parachute pant.[7]

"Man Repelling is about a process of elimination," Medine explains. "Men that are repelled are far too driven by the female exterior. The ones that hang around are the ones who care about intellect and what goes on underneath the turban. I get a lot of e-mails from women with boyfriends, or who are in relationships. Married women e-mail me all the time, too."[8]

Man Repelling is a process that involves Leandra herself demonstrating a lot of creative accessorizing with focus on footwear, scarves, bags, bracelets, and the like. There she is in clearly journeyman photos with funky captions on the Web (bracelets become an "arm party," a phrase she has legally trademarked); now she's live, walking a fashion show or trying on Louboutins in the window of Saks Fifth Avenue. Increasingly, Medine herself is part—make that the star—of the story. And that's just the way her readers want it.

Medine describes her (brief) journey from zero to warp speed brand velocity. "I'd been posting photos from other sites, and then one time I posted a picture of a new pair of shoes I'd just gotten, and I noticed that my page views were like 65% higher that day, and I was like, 'Gosh, the Internet is such a voyeuristic place.' And so I did a social experiment and posted a few more pictures of myself. And that's when it started growing and growing and growing. I realized then that if I wanted this to become something, I needed to put myself out there. And I did." She became her own best model and the face of the brand.[9]

Then "*Harper's Bazaar* had reached out to me about writing a story for their December 2010 issue. It was the first time a magazine reached out to me and my first payment. I didn't start making consistent income, charging for ad space, until March or April 2010. I began being paid to style look books or make appearances at stores."[10]

Medine is well aware of the realities common to bloggers of monetizing a site, and she has featured items and charged revenue per click to online retailers, but she is careful to keep a balance that maintains her brand integrity. Medine insists,

One thing I will never, ever do is take money for a blog post. If you're trying to make a name for yourself as a writer on the Internet, the most important thing is to earn integrity, and even more difficult, to maintain it, so it's really important that that is the first thing on your mind, always. It's not about parties or free swag. I will have a bucket for sponsored posts, a single bucket on the website. I'm working on a book and a newsletter. There are a lot of things that are happening. But the reason I've been able to brand myself this well and not give off this money-hungry, 21st century vibe is that I've been so adamant about making sure that what I do is true to the brand that I haven't thought as much about the money.

I cover New York Fashion Week and I mobilely cover the other fashion weeks. I don't necessarily do the appearances for payments that might be attached. It's just a really good way to get into the psyche of my readers. It's always just really nice to meet them, to hear what they want to see more of, and what kind of clothes do they love—that's really good for me because it's really important that I connect to whoever's reading the blog, and that's hard to do. All my readers come over to me all the time and say, "I feel like I totally know you," and I totally get it. I am one of them. I feel like that about Alexa Chung, that I want to go over and hug her, because I've followed her career since she was on MTV. I think that's what's endearing about a blogger—we are girls, just like everyone else, but just kind of are an example of uncertified genius. We just started doing something and got totally lucky with the way that things meant.

I think the first time I realized I was building a brand based on myself was when my workload started getting so much and I thought about getting someone to help me—but I simply could not delegate the work because I needed to be involved in everything that happened. Every transaction, every conversation that is happening, I needed to be in the middle of it, because there is no brand without me.[11]

What makes the *Man Repeller* stand out from the other 200 million blogs that swarm cyberspace? Her unique point of view has struck a chord. The fact that she's not a fashion insider is relatable—she's talking about fashion and luxury—but, hey, she's just like us! She's pressing her nose up against the glass of fashion, coming at it from the outside in. Even Medine's wacky poses, which are almost cartoony take-offs on traditional high fashion model stances, are more derivative of the way women vamp in the mirror or for each other than actual fashion pages. Interestingly, there are early pictures of Coco Chanel, on the beach or at picnics with friends, similarly vamping playfully in an era when most women, even actresses, posed stiffly and formally for the camera. Medine wears clothes and accessories, talks about them, and gets excited about them the way real women do. There's a naturalness and joy—a sincere emotion—and the audience responds.

Designer Rebecca Minkoff has stated that she sees Medine as a kind of modern version of Katharine Hepburn. While Medine refuses to consider putting herself in that category, she understands the comparison with a woman who changed fashion by playing to comfort and lifestyle rather than to men, as did Coco Chanel. "Katharine Hepburn and Coco Chanel are such style benchmarks. It's very hard for me to say that I'm 'revolutionizing fashion,'" she insists, noting, "There is still a stigma attached to blogging. I'll see editors at fashion shows looking at me and I know they're thinking, 'Why is she in the front row?' I can't say as I'm revolutionizing anything."[12]

What she *is* doing is resonating being herself. Leandra Medine = the Man Repeller. It's Leandra on the SoHo streets. It's Leandra in her bedroom or on the balcony of her parents' apartment. At a party. Wearing the "arm party" of bracelets that she wants you to consider for yourself. She's one-on-one, and the definition of the "Man Repeller" term is elastic enough to encompass her recent engagement—the one thing she does not feature on her blog. There are no pictures of her fiancé on her site; he's not even named. If she's wearing her engagement ring, it's turned backward. This is how she carves out her own personal space and a piece of privacy. Says Medine,

I'm just so happy that my brand is resonating this way and that people who have a knowledgeable idea about what the industry is and where it is going recognize it. I think the way in which I've tried to represent myself is that I am a regular girl who is always on the periphery of fashion, who has always loved fashion and all of a sudden just became a part of it in a big way—sitting front row in shows, walking in shows, hosting events, making videos with people like Michael Kors and Simon Doonan. It's so easy to become jaded and think everything is normal in this industry, and I've made an effort to represent the woman who is still on the periphery, who still loves it, but can be a part of it. Because I think that this generation is all about everything becoming attainable. Fashion is not just this abstract, chic world of only editors and women who can afford snakeskin coats and Manolo Blahnik—that's not the world we live in anymore. Everyone should have a piece of fashion. It's a democracy. There's no hierarchy anymore. So I try to be the woman who is proof that everyone is normal, on the periphery, and every now and then you can start penetrating the industry and become very much a part of it. I'm like the opposite of Anna Wintour. I'm at the opposite end of that spectrum. That's not to say I don't admire her, and whatever dynasty she's built and the way she's branded herself. She's become the fashion celebrity. She spearheaded the entire notion of the fashion celebrity. But that's just not me. People always ask why I'm not featured in *Vogue*, and I always say, because I'm not *Vogue*—I'm crass, I'm funny, I don't take myself seriously.[13]

Will the Man Repeller, or Ms. Medine, become an enduring brand? The more relevant point may be that this emerging brand has demonstrated how to rip the rug out from under the rules. Or, maybe, how spinning the dial backward is moving it forward.

Is the Web propelling fashion brands into a throwback phase to the sensibility of Coco Chanel (before she was "Coco Chanel" of the double Cs) where the everyday woman was the icon, as opposed to a Jean Shrimpton, Twiggy, Christie Brinkley, Cindy Crawford, or those supermodels who were quoted as not being willing to get out of bed for less than six figures? Do the facts that Tina Fey "anti-starred" in a hair commercial, although she is far better known and appreciated for her wit than her locks, and that Leandra Medine, an everyday girl, can have a top fashion blog based from her bedroom in her parents' apartment and reach 400,000 unique visitors a month and have 60,000 Twitter followers signal a new order?

"Who the hell am I?" she asks. "I'm no one."[14]

*"I'm nobody! / Who are you? / Are you nobody, too?"* These words were written by a young woman who would become a famous poet from her bedroom in her parents' house—Emily Dickinson. A lot of people out there are "nobodies." Nobodies and nobodyism are back—largely because the Internet has given them a place to go. Before her death, the great comedienne Gilda Radner wrote in her book about her experiences with cancer, *It's Always Something*, that she had been unable to get publishers interested in her proposed book of humorous essays about her day-to-day life at home. It took a life-and-death story of cancer—which ended up being published posthumously—for even a top star to get a forum. Today, Tina Fey's book of observations about her everyday life, *Bossypants*, topped best-seller lists, and every Real Anybody has a memoir. If nobody's publishing it, they'll self-publish online. That's not to say that the world of Web content is not evolving and institutionalizing. There is a burgeoning of agents for bloggers and self-publishers and distributors for authors and other content providers, but those are service industries trying to harness and profit from the source.

"I'm just a girl who wanted to blog," says Leandra Medine. "But because of Twitter and Facebook, I was able to connect with PR people at huge brands and different publications." An editor at *Harper's Bazaar*, several major fashion designers, and the *New York Times* all found Medine directly on Twitter or were referred by stylish women who followed Twitter. "Everything that's happened has pretty much been from people finding me through Twitter," she says. "Twitter has been the foundation for *everything*."[15]

Brands may need to increasingly align themselves with real women to resonate with today's cynical, knowledgeable consumer—and the Web is the means to that end—with this paradigm, it's a full circle. The start of the loop is also the end of the loop. Case in point: As Leandra Medine, admittedly "not a model!", walked the runway in a designer show, she videoed blog posts from her phone.

This new order is much closer to Coco Chanel's straw boater than it is to a current *Vogue* cover. The Web has democratized fashion by giving women access that was formerly the sole provenance of "insiders." Anyone can virtually be at the front row of a fashion show. And if she can't, a blogger will surely be there to report in—directly to her, not to, say, Diana Vreeland or Anna Wintour. To keep up, icon brands, like *Vogue*, are employing their own bloggers and digital channels, scouring Twitter and Facebook, further blurring the boundaries. Looking at *Vogue*'s blog, however, is like staring into the pages of the magazine. You sense the stylist, standing just out of frame, and the editor, directing the attitude of the model. Looking at the *Man Repeller*, or other "civilian" fashion blogs, in contrast, is like looking at real life. There's no separation between what is seen on the page and the reader; the connection is direct. It's about connection, not interruption. The Web has enabled reality to become the fantasy, leveraging and amplifying Coco Chanel's hat trick of a hundred years ago.

"The Internet is my generation," says the Man Repeller. "We have access to Facebook to Tumblr, to Pinterest. We are all so well-versed digitally. Who's better at the Internet than the people of my generation? This is our time. That's why this is the age of the entrepreneur."[16]

# Chapter 9

# DIAMOND DUST: LUXURY GOES DIGITAL

Picture the scene: Two young girls, not more than nineteen or twenty, giggling as, arm in arm, they exit Tiffany's flagship store on Fifth Avenue and 57th Street in Manhattan. It's a beautiful spring day, the sun is shining, and a light wind whips their long hair. The view down and across Fifth Avenue is exciting, full of possibilities, bustling business people, and energetic tourists.

One of the girls stops in front of the store and, posing right next to the Tiffany & Co. sign, hands her phone to her friend, urging her to take a photo. Smiling, the girl clutches Tiffany's signature robin's-egg blue bag in her hand, making sure it figures prominently in the photo.

"Your turn now," she calls and switches places with her friend, exchanging phones along the way so she can snap the friend in the same pose.

You can guess what comes next, can't you? Those "we were at Tiffany" pictures will be e-mailed or texted by the girls to their friends and families. They'll probably be uploaded to their Facebook pages. And if they haven't yet Liked Tiffany's Facebook page (unless, of course, they're part of the community that regularly follows Tiffany on Facebook, and barring a terrible experience at the store), they're sure to Like it. Most important to Tiffany: They're not engaged—yet—but, when they are, these girls will flash back on this day, check out everything Tiffany has to offer in the virtual world, such as, say, the mobile engagement ring app, and then drag their fiancés straight into the store. They may or may not buy an engagement ring at that point— but if not, there's always the "push present" for the first baby or the Eternity Ring for future anniversaries. The Tiffany brand is locked, loaded, and embedded.

How did these girls make the leap to those robin's-egg blue bags? Did they receive a Tiffany baby rattle in a blue box when they were born? Or a Tiffany charm bracelet for their sweet sixteen? Are they classic movie buffs who idolize Audrey Hepburn and are channeling Holly Golightly? Did they have a legacy connection to Tiffany, one handed down from their mothers and grandmothers? Or was theirs a digital connection, one that came about through clicking on the Tiffany website, visiting its Facebook page, or downloading Tiffany's iPhone app? Maybe they started out as fans of one of the hot artists whose film or music is featured on Tiffany's romance app. There are many paths that would have taken them to the front of the store this day, posing with their shopping bags. Tiffany & Co. has made sure of that.

In the luxury category since 1873, Tiffany has been one of the most successful brands at reinventing itself and doing so in a way that enables it to forge the digital connections to tap into a completely new clientele while maintaining its identity. After a few wobbles in which the brand ruffled its hard-core luxury base by focusing on mass affluent offerings that opened those robin's-egg blue, security-guarded gates, Tiffany seems to have found its equilibrium.

"Tiffany has maintained its focus on high quality and remained true to its core brand values of consistency, persistence, and restraint as it's reinvented itself online, and it has never shown itself to be unwilling to join the conversation or to not want be a part of the social networks," says Susan Gunelius, president and CEO of KeySplash Creative, who blogs about luxury brands for a number of marketing websites.[1]

To a certain extent, luxury brands can still rely on a dedicated customer base to carry them forward. But if Tiffany wants to expand its customer base and bring in new business, especially to the next generations, they have no choice but to connect digitally with a new set of people who may not be walking through the doors of one of their bricks-and-mortar stores.

The challenge is being able to do this without compromising an elite brand image and reputation. Luxury brands have been built around the premise of exclusivity with an aspirational overlay—which is the antithesis of what the Internet and social media in particular are about. It's not easy to maintain that veneer that qualifies a brand as luxury to begin with while parlaying it into the new medium—especially for those luxury brands that do not sell their products online (e.g., Chanel). But this delicate balance is the only way forward for luxury brands.

While Tiffany may be one of the first names to come up in a generic Google search on diamond engagement rings (a search that averages 23,300,000 results), it still has to have an online presence that sets it apart from the cacophony of brands and companies that also sell diamond rings. For an audience that has a plethora of choices from which to purchase diamond engagement rings and that increasingly does so online, Tiffany not only has to contend with luxury jewelers like Cartier, De Beers, and Harry Winston, but it also needs to distinguish itself from retailers like Zales and Jewelry Exchange, not to mention the bargain shopping meccas like Overstock.com that are more and more popular for everything from rugs to rings. True, nobody's romanticizing about *Breakfast at Zales'*, but in challenging economic times, price can look almost as good as Audrey Hepburn. A luxury brand like Tiffany has more to contend with than ever.

So how has Tiffany cultivated brand loyalty online and racked up more than 2,100,000 Likes on its Facebook page and more than 150,000 Twitter followers?[2] Tiffany relies on an extremely agile and category-innovative use of social media—Facebook, Twitter, and YouTube—with the awareness of the growing importance of cultivating a large and noncore audience for the future.

Tiffany's Facebook page tells the brand's story and creates an intimate behind-the-scenes look into the brand, as well as the people working to make Tiffany what it is. But Tiffany has been careful to keep the conversation interactive, rather than simply showcasing itself and its products. Tiffany has also walked the celebrity tightrope well, maintaining its aura of exclusivity and excellence by not going overboard on the celebrity front, by also picking and choosing its partners with care, from Angelina Jolie to the teenaged Emma Roberts to indie filmmaker Ed Burns.

Tiffany's iPhone apps and digital campaigns appeal to a broad audience and counter the impersonality of technology with the emotion that powers a fine jewelry purchase. For instance, where Burberry offers "The Art of the Trench," celebrating the iconic trench coat, Tiffany's whatmakeslovetrue.com, which positions itself as "The go-to resource for romantics everywhere," offers "The Art of Romance"—stories, films, and even a playlist of "timeless" musical selections that are a celebration of and a guide to love, a platform through which anyone can share their love stories and give and even get relationship advice.[3] "Luxury brands have to be very careful to not be seen as promoting themselves," Gunelius says. "They've got to find ways to appeal by adding value to the conversation rather than being at the center of it."[4]

In the "What Makes Love True" campaign, love, not Tiffany, occupies center stage. But Tiffany is still curating Cupid. For instance, rather than Tiffany pushing out a commercial, Garance Doré, a top French fashion photographer and blogger, presents a digital film in the "True Love" series under the Tiffany imprimatur.

The Tiffany Engagement Ring Finder app is a guide to virtually finding the perfect ring by browsing styles, viewing actual carat weights, determining ring size, and learning about Tiffany diamonds. To boot, consumers can then share their choice on Facebook.

"The new iPhone engagement app provides another access point to Tiffany's expertise and knowledge," said Carson Glover, director of media relations at Tiffany & Co., New York. "Today more and more people are getting their information through mobile devices." The app isn't commerce enabled; customers still have to go into the store to buy a ring. However, the application includes an expert consultation feature, which provides the option to schedule a phone consultation. Customers can fill out a short form with their personal information and send it to a Tiffany's representative, who will contact them within forty-eight hours.[5]

Some might rightly say that nothing can replace an actual visit to Tiffany—that there's no way to know and feel the luxury, reputation, and quality of the brand except by walking around the Fifth Avenue building, holding diamond rings of varying sizes, watching the light shine through the sparkling stones, and then trying them on your ring finger.

The luxury market, however, no longer has the luxury of relying on one point of contact, no matter how sumptuously rewarding. The new platform is about integrating as many touchpoints as possible into the consumer experience—and keeping the level of quality and the brand personality totally consistent. Before she has even entered a store to select her diamond ring, the Tiffany's bride will have gone through a myriad of portals that will lead her to the door of the store. Tiffany's breadcrumbs are diamond dust, setting a virtual trail back to the core retail experience.

## TALK TO ME, HARRY WINSTON

"Talk to me, Harry Winston. Tell me all about it!" cooed Marilyn Monroe as she shimmied through the movie *Gentlemen Prefer Blondes*, decked out like a Christmas tree draped with glittering gems. Nobody who heard Marilyn sing those lyrics ever forgot the name Harry Winston—even if they couldn't afford those sparklers, and few of us could. Because, when it comes to jewelry, Winston is no ordinary Tom, Dick, or Harry. Or even Tiffany. Harry Winston, Inc., is the brand name of one of the world's most prestigious luxury jewelers. Today, no red carpet is complete without the major stars sporting millions of dollars' worth of jewels by Harry Winston—a trend started, in fact, by Harry Winston himself in the 1940s when he came up with the concept of lending jewels to stars for high-profile events, thus cementing the association of his brand with drop-dead glamour. In 1944, Jennifer Jones was wearing Winston when she collected her Oscar for the title role in *The Song of Bernadette*. The talk that night was as much about Ms. Jones's "rocks" as she collected her award amidst the flashbulbs of the media, and a new promotional venue was born. Since then, Academy Award presenters, nominees, and winners have dazzled in diamonds the size of swimming pools, intricately set and of the finest quality. At the 2012 Oscars, best actress presenter and former winner Natalie Portman channeled Jones as she glowed in a diamond necklace and earrings from Harry Winston.

Harry Winston has long been considered synonymous with the world's most spectacular diamond jewelry, with innovative and exquisitely crafted settings. The brand has kept pace with modern styles, employing fabled designers who continue to innovate trends. But the Winston brand name is equally, if not more, famous for the trail of legendary diamonds it has owned: the Crown of Charlemagne, 37.05 carats, sky blue; the Anastasia, cut from a rough crystal weighing more than 307 carats; the Hope Diamond, 45.5 carats, donated by Harry Winston to the Smithsonian, where it now resides; the Blue Heart, 40.82 carats, blue and heart-shaped; the Jonker, discovered as a 726-carat rough crystal; and, for those to whom business is romance, the Deal Sweetener, a 181-carat stone, literally tossed on the table by the head of De Beers mines when Winston—having just made a $24 million purchase, at that time (1974) the largest individual sale of diamonds in history—asked for something to "sweeten the deal." There is a picture of the child star Shirley Temple holding the Jonker before it was cut. The diamond is roughly the size of a kitten. Winston cut the stone into seventeen smaller stones—small being relative, when you consider that one of those was a 71.73-carat flawless emerald-cut diamond and another was the 40.2-carat ice rink that was Aristotle Onassis's engagement ring on his betrothal to Jacqueline Kennedy.

The list of iconic gems owned by Harry Winston is historic and goes on for pages, reeking with the kinds of stories the greatest fiction or screenwriters could never invent—stones stolen from sultans and smuggled out to pawn shops; stones worn by royalty; stones taken into exile by deposed despots; stones with curses (such as the one owned by a man who was subsequently attacked and devoured by wild dogs); stories that swagger through centuries of love, greed, and heartbreak. *Breakfast at Tiffany's* this ain't. In fact, although the company has worked hard and successfully in recent years to democratize its face to the public, one media account tells of a shopper with a $35,000 budget for earrings who was advised to try Tiffany.[6]

This brand is built on reality of the old-fashioned kind, not hype. There really was a Harry Winston, and he really was a genius at gems. The son of a jeweler, the legend goes that young Harry was twelve years old when he spotted a two-carat emerald in a tray of junk jewelry as he passed by a pawnshop window. He bought it for a quarter and sold it two days later for eight hundred dollars. In 1916, at age nineteen, he started his own company. He was so young that he was mistaken for a messenger when he went to the bank and applied for a loan—whereupon he hired a distinguished-looking older man to stand in as a front. In 1932, he launched Harry Winston, Inc., in order to produce his own line and designs. Although Winston later hired some of the greatest artisans and designers in the business, it was his own innovations that set the business apart early on. His settings allowed the stone, rather than the metal surrounding it, to shine, and his use of platinum to offset the purity of cut and color of gemstones was, and perhaps remains, unsurpassed. Having passed to Harry Winston's sons, the firm is now owned by Harry Winston Diamond Corporation, a diamond enterprise with assets in the mining and retailing areas of the diamond industry. It is an elite operation, with eight stores in the United States, twenty-one stores worldwide, and a growing presence in Asia.

Robert Scott, chief financial officer of Harry Winston, Inc., has been with the company for more than twenty years, and he has witnessed the evolution of the luxury market and customer first hand. He notes that jewelry from Harry Winston is of the highest quality and artistry, and the price is reflective of that. "Because our price points are so expensive, we use the Internet to drive clients into our stores," he says. Winston continues to have great success with the celebrity platform. Stars like Blake Lively and Ed Westwick from the TV show *Gossip Girl*, along with Chinese pop star Jay Chou, who in spring 2012 appeared at the grand opening of Winston's retail store in Shanghai, generate the kind of media coverage, press photos, and buzz that even a $50,000 ad placement cannot, Scott says, noting that the world loves glamour.

"We communicate the happenings of Harry Winston on the Web as part of our program—openings, new product launches, philanthropic partnerships—and we lend out jewelry for appropriate events, such as the Oscars. It's all about getting the name out there," says Scott. "And building awareness for future generations, and introducing them to Harry Winston. We want them to be customers for life."[7]

This often starts with the engagement ring.

Harry Winston's website gets more than 100,000 hits per month, but, for this company, the Web is not a venue of choice to actually make the sale. Rather, it is used to educate customers so they can be savvy about their choices. "E-commerce? We're not there yet," states Scott. "Our direct sales over the net are insignificant. But there are big benefits in driving customers into our stores and building awareness, and using the Web as a tool to reach millions of people. With only eight stores in the U.S., for instance, the coverage and outreach to people is limited in person. With the Internet, it grows exponentially."

Scott points to Blue Nile, the largest online retailer of certified diamonds and fine jewelry, as an example of a jeweler that is doing a brisk and successful e-commerce business. "They allow you to build your own ring, pick the diamond, pick the budget. And if you don't like it, you can return it. They sell quite a few diamonds that cost between $30,000 and $40,000," says Scott. "They do volume. And the reason why someone would spend $30,000 to $40,000 on a diamond over the Web is that they are trusted."

Scott notes that brand is not as important in this kind of purchase, and "this is not our customer"—this person who is not as interested in flashing the name of the brand as well as the stone. Winston sells only D, E, and F colorless diamonds, while others with lower price points sell G, H, or I color diamonds. By comparison of level of stone overall and price point, Tiffany is a gift shop. "They sell a lot of silver, china, etc.," says Scott. Not Winston.[8]

"The big value of the Web for us is education," says Scott. Harry Winston Brilliant Futures is a signature event in the company's charitable program, with a mission to provide cultural and artistic enrichment and a platform reflecting its belief that "education is the key to creating brilliant futures" for young people.[9]

Scott points out that Harry Winston, the man, had a history of giving back. "It's in our blood, our DNA," he says. "People like to feel they are giving back when they do business with a brand.... The power of the Internet is the ability to reach many people at relatively inexpensive cost. We never had that before. A lot of the barriers are coming down."

Still, as Scott points out, "We don't have anything below $3,000. Today, selling high-end luxury is about the customer experience, about the pampering and attentiveness you don't get in making a purchase over the Internet. This customer wants privacy, discretion. It's a very personal situation when you are talking about sales above a certain price point. It would be very difficult to translate that sales experience over the Web. The one-on-one relationship is still very important in what we do." Scott feels that the Internet commoditizes certain products. "You lose something," he says.

"Tiffany's little blue box? They spent tens of millions to build up that concept, and if you took a poll among young women and asked what was that brand, many would say Tiffany. Tiffany does a volume business. But selling a $1 million, 15-carat solitaire over the Internet? I don't see that happening."[10]

## DRIVING LUXURY OFF-ROAD

The luxury vehicle market has sped into the digital age at full speed. Where carmakers once strictly touted hard features and miles per gallon, now they are strategically embedding cars into a new level of digital participation and interaction with culturally minded consumers who respond to the quality and artistry of the brand and the product. BMW, a pioneer in making the connection among the automotive, art, and digital categories, is a perfect illustration of how a luxury car manufacturer has connected the brand to culture, creating associations, provoking discussion, and attracting audiences that enrich the brand multidimensionally. Via partnerships with cultural institutions, including the Guggenheim and Tate Modern in London, BMW is building a cultural heritage for the digital age that also puts big stakes in the actual ground. This spanning and integration is one of the core keys to keeping a luxury brand, literally, grounded with its core consumers while expanding to new audiences virtually.

The *BMW Tate Live: Performance Room* digitally broadcasts live performances of selected partner artists from a dedicated studio space to audiences internationally. The performances run live on the Tate's online channel format, giving participants a chance to cross-participate in live discussions of the work. "I am delighted that we will partner with BMW on this important new initiative," said Chris Dercon, director of the Tate Modern. "The development of technology has transformed people's approach to art. Audiences today expect more interaction, participation and personalisation than ever before.

BMW Tate Live will answer this need. BMW Tate Live will bring live art performance directly to people on the Web, wherever they are in the world."[11]

The BMW Guggenheim Lab, meanwhile, is an ambitious and innovative combination of think tank, public forum, and community center, focused on exploring and raising awareness of the challenges to today's urban culture and environments—something automakers must intimately and increasingly address—within a custom-designed mobile structure that travels globally. Launched in Manhattan's East Village in 2011, moving to Berlin in 2012, and from there to Mumbai, the Lab plans to run a six-year tour, traveling to nine cities in three successive cycles. The first confronts the issue of how people can feel more comfortable in urban environments. A key component is a group game played on-site and online, in which participants become involved in role-playing scenarios for city transformation as they build a city that matches needs ranging from education, sustainability, and health care to a wide range of critical issues. The website bmwguggenheim-lab.org offers ways to participate virtually, while visitors or observers can stay connected via dedicated communities on Twitter, Facebook, YouTube, Flickr, and Foursquare. Not surprisingly, the project turns up on coolhunting cultural sites and other virtual venues spidered to young, innovative, and diverse program creators, taking the message far off the traditionally traveled luxury car road.[12]

## THE CONSUMER COLOSSEUM

In ancient Rome, the thumb was a popular form of social media. When the gladiators battled in the Colosseum, 50,000 spectators passed judgment on the fate of the fighters. Thumbs up meant a warrior had earned the mercy or even respect of the crowd and would be spared. Thumbs down meant death. Then everybody got to witness the thrill of victory or the agony of defeat. The Web has created a consumer colosseum where the click is the new thumb signal. Enough clicks, your brand lives. No clicks, prepare to die—in front of everyone's eyes. The Web has turned branding into a blood sport, and no segment is more impacted than the luxury market. The evolution of "affordable luxury" has democratized the segment, bringing more consumers into the category—but also increasing the size of the jury pool in a world of instantaneous judgment.

The luxury market evolved as a service for those who could actually afford and demand luxury brands—the rich. In the 1800s, for instance, Hermès began as a saddle shop that made quality harnesses and carriage fittings for the wealthy beau monde and royalty, including the French Emperor Napoleon III and Empress Eugénie. It is rumored that coronations were postponed for years until Hermès could create the requisite unique design for the royal carriage accoutrements.[13]

The horse and carriage remains the brand logo today, and some customers will still be forced to wait for the goods—the wait is likely to be up to six years for a Birkin bag costing five figures. By visiting a store, it is certainly possible to touch, feel, and appreciate the quality of a Hermès product—one Birkin can take eighteen to twenty-five hours to make—but the perception of the brand and its quality will increasingly be formed by means other than the products themselves. Perhaps that is why there are 528,000 sites on Google with videos of how to spot a real versus a fake Birkin bag. Are there 528,000 women who can even afford this bag? Regardless, there is a vast audience of fashionistas and luxuryites waiting to pass judgment should a fatal flaw occur. And that thumbs down could mean instant death, no matter how many artisans are honing their craft for your handbag.

Hermès is a case in which a luxury brand with a previously impeccable reputation was flung into the arena, teetered, and lived to tell the tale. In 2005, Oprah Winfrey was denied entrance to the company's flagship store in Paris fifteen minutes after closing, although people were still clearly milling about inside. She was told by store representatives that a private event was being held, provided with a card, and told to return the next day. The *New York Post* subsequently reported that she was turned away because the store was "having a problem with North Africans lately." Both Oprah and Hermès denied that that specific language was used, but the damage was done the minute she was denied access to the store. The Web went wild, as indignant blog postings flooded in. Winfrey contacted the U.S. CEO of Hermès, and her production company announced that this incident was "Oprah's Crash Moment," referring to a film in which racism unfolds in subtle ways. It was announced that Oprah would talk about this incident on her show when it resumed taping after the summer hiatus. On this subsequent show, Oprah did discuss the incident on air with the CEO of Hermès USA, whom she had invited as a guest. Meanwhile, the debate rages on the Web, where nothing ever dies. According to the *Washington Post*, "The public probably will never know precisely what transpired in the case of Winfrey versus Hermès. The story has been taken over by the Internet, a forum not known for its subtlety and accuracy. (One posting had Winfrey going to Hermès to 'get her hair done.')"[14]

Milton Pedraza, CEO of the Luxury Institute, notes that in today's digital marketplace, "You can ravel and unravel pretty quickly. You can accelerate in both directions, in your growth and your demise, all in one shot. It's not just the product, it's also the in-store experience. The needs of humanity don't change. With this alleged Hermès incident, if Oprah Winfrey had gone to her constituents and said, 'I was wronged. This happened to me and I think we should boycott Hermès for a month,' it would have had an impact. If Hermès would have said, 'We're not going to lose any sales because people love our product too much,' I think that would have backfired on them big time. Or, if they had seen an effect of ten percent down in sales, they would have *really* apologized. But Oprah didn't want to escalate it further and it didn't become the debacle it could have been."[15]

## VIGILANTE LUXURY

The democratizing power of the Web and the "mass affluent" accessibility and diffusion of the luxury market means that luxury brands that hop onto sites like Facebook or YouTube are, more or less, open season. Rue St.-Honoré it's not. The brand has literally flung its doors open in the middle of the global marketplace, and nobody is there to tell Oprah, you, me, or anybody else that they can't come in.

Burberry's 2009 site, "Art of the Trench," broke ground as it tried to bridge the gap and provide ring-fenced mass access by offering a curated capsule view of how people were wearing their Burberry trench coats, showing influential people sporting their Burberry trenches with their individualized fashion twists in real settings all over the globe. The site reached 1 million visits around more than 150 countries, and, although anyone could drop in for a look-see, only vetted

Burberry customers could post. Burberry well understood the power of partnering with social media, and that, as opposed to hundreds of people seeing a star in his or her Burberry trench on the street, or thousands in a magazine, now millions could be regularly exposed to the world of Burberry as interpreted by a tastemaker.[16]

This kind of tastemaker access has become an expanded way for the once-closed luxury market to connect with its consumers. LVMH Moët Hennessy Louis Vuitton, the world's largest luxury company, won a Webby Award in 2011 for its digital magazine, *NOWNESS*. *McKinsey Quarterly* reports: "Many luxury-goods companies, for example, have built editorial teams to 'socialize' their brands: they are transforming the customer relationship by producing blogs, digital magazines, and other content that can dramatically intensify both the frequency and depth of interactions."[17]

But luxury brands are equally aware of the inherent risks. And style is just the tip of the iceberg. The entire customer experience is on the table, ready for dissection by the consumer scalpel, because, as Milton Pedraza emphasizes, "Life isn't either/or, it's this *and* that." And that total experience is only getting more comprehensive. If Louis XIV were alive today, Pedraza adds, "he would be having a relation-ship with a personal shopper, getting his deliveries packaged better and delivered faster, going to the website," and generally immersing himself in the 360-degree consumer experience. And if the brand didn't deliver—well, as for Louis, when he didn't like what one of his ministers was doing with Versailles, he asserted his divine right, threw the offender into prison, and basically let him rot there for the rest of his life.

Today, the luxury vigilante on his or her iPad, blogging away while sipping a latte at Starbucks, moves even more swiftly than the mon-arch of old. "I can go to my Facebook page and I can tell my friends that there is something wonderful out there and they should try it, or I can tell my friends that I was just wronged and I need your help to give them payback time," warns Pedraza. He says,

And both of those can happen in an instant these days. Facebook and Twitter are both means to an end. There is a world effect of, one, transparency and two, retribution that can be very swift—or success can be very swift. Retribution is not new, but, before, I was an individual. And as an individual, I could not really gain traction. But today I can go online and put up a YouTube video, or a social media site, or a site like change.org, and I can tell my story, and not only will individuals pick it up, but the news media will pick it up. And all of a sudden I've amplified and magnified my message to the point where action takes place and results are gained, whether it's damaging the reputation of a brand or enhancing the reputation of a brand, forcing a brand to take action it would never have considered, or rolling back a step they took because it is too untenable because of that opinion effect and the potential risk of lost revenue and lost reputation. Those are the kinds of things that are happening today that didn't used to happen before with as much traction, with as much speed and as much magnitude. I see that happening *everywhere*, the luxury market is not immune.[18]

In Hong Kong, Dolce & Gabbana (D&G) incited a demonstration when local citizens were banned from taking photos of the stores from the street, while others from China and foreign countries were not. The virtual community swiftly blogged and Facebooked thumbs-down, while, in front of the bricks-and-mortar Kowloon location, more than 1,000 protesters massed, forcing the store to close early. An apology from the brand was viewed with derision. "We are not idiots," was one comment on the D&G Facebook page. "We fully understand the purpose of your 'apology.' You don't really care about people. You just don't want to lose the turnover from the mainland tourist during the Lunar New Year holiday."[19]

Pedraza notes, "These are small skirmishes, but they matter. They get spread around globally and whether that happens or not, in the Hong Kong market, the reputation of Dolce & Gabbana was tainted. So that's where I see a tremendous amount of activism."

As a result of this activism in the luxury market, now no brand, no matter how seemingly elite or untouchable, is exempt from being rated by its consumers, and these ratings, in whatever form, are instantaneous and on the Web for all to see. "I was just speaking to a group of wealth advisers," Pedraza reports, "And I told them, 'You can be rated, too.' Anyone can be rated, and will be rated. Whether that's fair or not, I don't know. Unfortunately ratings have for a large degree been co-opted by the entities that are being rated, so there's a lot of false rating today, and there's no way that you can police for that completely. I think that companies, when they see ratings, tend to tout only the positive ones, but to a larger degree these ratings are helpful. These ratings are largely on the Web, they're not going to be statistically valid or reliable, but they give you a good sense of that brand. The majority of ratings sites or sites where ratings occur do give you a sense of what the brand is, and I think these will get better. You can rate the good and the bad ones. I would say this: I think when a provider is overwhelmingly bad, there is no way they're going to be able to put in enough fake ratings to overwhelm what is the preponderance of truthful and honest ratings."[20]

The future likely holds an even more expanded arena for ratings in the digital colosseum. With sites such as rankings.com, even the websites themselves are rated, and cyberlessons are available on how to rate websites. Meanwhile, entities such as the Five Star Alliance, an organization for luxury hotels, promote ways that members can increase their online ratings.

Marketers are flexing their not-inconsiderable muscle—although increasingly it seems to take more brains than brawn. Mercedes-Benz, for instance, utilized mobile scanning as it literally sent consumers scampering into the streets in a kind of virtual *Where's Waldo?* In the Singapore Mercedes-Benz QR Code Race, consumers were challenged to find five Mercedes-Benz models that had QR codes stenciled onto the cars. The first to find all five won a pair of grandstand tickets to the Singapore Night Race and a weekend test drive with Mercedes-Benz.[21]

Here, the traditional luxury paradigm has dramatically flipped. Instead of the almost or actual out-of-reach, longingly aspirational qualities of the ultimate luxury car experience of the past (and still, often, the present), not infrequently positioned as an "investment" or social badge to which one almost felt the need to earn entitlement, like admission to an exclusive club, Mercedes-Benz has created a scenario where consumers are actually chasing after their cars in city streets, like greyhounds after bait. Who's in the driver's seat here? This shows that marketers are catching on to digital power—and using it.

As Milton Pedraza says, it can go either way.

Marketers would do well to remember what the gladiators said to the crowd as they entered the ring: *"Ave, Imperator, morituri te salutant"* ("We who are about to die salute you"). And the response to this line from Claudius Suetonius to the Emperor Claudius as they faced off in a war game: *"Aut non"* ("Or not").

# Chapter 10

# THE VIRTUAL GOLD RUSH

All classes of citizens seem to be under the influence of this extraordinary mania...what will this overwhelming spirit of emigration lead to? Will it be the beginning of a new empire in the West, a revolution in the commercial highways of the world, a depopulation of the old States for the new republic on the shores of the Pacific?
—*New York Herald*, January 11, 1848

By 1854, more than 300,000 people—one in every ninety people living in America at the time—had made the then-arduous journey to California (15,000 miles by ship or 2,200 miles over land) to try their luck at making their fortune. Thus began one of the most massive migrations in human history.[1] They were mainly young and ambitious, with a risk-taking exuberance, and they called themselves "The Argonauts," after the mythical adventurers who traveled with Jason in search of the golden fleece.

And they did establish "a new republic on the shores of the Pacific." The 1850 census found that 73 percent of California's population was between the ages of twenty and forty, establishing a new way of life, creating the rules as they went along in a society where there were none. A new arrival wrote, "Here there are no parents' eyes to guide, no wife to warn, no sister to entreat."[2]

No boundaries, no rules. No capital and little experience required.

As it turned out, actual gold was the least of it. Although massive fortunes were indeed made, most of them were made not by miners, but by those in support businesses—clothing, transportation, and dry goods. Brilliant PR was at play when the first Gold Rush millionaire, Samuel Brannan, a shop owner who founded the *California Star* newspaper and ran a store that sold miners' necessities in San Francisco, cornered the market on the supplies the miners needed. After first buying every shovel that existed in the town, as well as most of the picks, axes, and supporting supplies, Brannan purchased some gold dust, poured it into a bottle, and ran through the streets waving the gold-filled bottle screaming, "Gold! Gold! They've found gold!" Everybody raced out into the fields to look for more gold. But first, they needed that shovel. Brannan immediately jumped his prices tenfold.[3]

It didn't take long for him to become California's first millionaire—in the days when a million really was a million, and a loaf of bread sold for four cents in New York City (and seventy-five cents in San Francisco, to give you some idea of Brannanomics). By 1856, Brannan owned one-fifth of the city of San Francisco. Yet when he died in 1889, his holdings barely covered the cost of his funeral.

For some, like Brannan, the Gold Rush proved to be everything they had dreamed of and more. Levi Strauss, for instance, made the journey to California with the intention of selling dry goods. But by the time he arrived at his destination, he had run out of the provisions he intended to sell. All he had left was a bit of canvas, but he struck gold of a different kind when he fashioned the fabric into a pair of sturdy work pants for a miner. In just a year, Levi Strauss had become the biggest manufacturer of pants in California and eventually one of the largest and most legendary brands in the world.[4]

Then there was John Studebaker, who made wheelbarrows during the Gold Rush and whose family went on to become part of American automobile history, or his neighbor, Phillip Armour, operator of a meat market who parlayed his fortune into a Midwestern meatpacking plant. But such entrepreneurs were a Gold Rush minority. There were also millions of others who thought they would be guaranteed fame and fortune but ended up worse off than before. Nonetheless, the California Gold Rush forever changed America's view of the relationship between wealth and labor, expectations and values, and a different kind of vision—one of the potential to go somewhere with fewer rules, to pull up stakes, stake a claim, and get rich quick—emerged from the gold dust.

More than a century later, between the late 1990s and 2001, many of those who rushed onto the Internet with their brands and businesses during the Internet Gold Rush ended up equally empty handed, while a few ended up with founders' shares of the brands that rule cyberspace.

That was the epoch of pioneers like Amazon, eBay, and Yahoo. But it was also the era of ventures like pets.com, which went from a Macy's Thanksgiving Day Parade balloon to that great dot-com doghouse in the sky in just two years. Backed by venture capitalists and Internet "prospectors," who flung cash at them, many Internet start-ups, often headed by leaders with little or no experience, burned through billions of sunk dollars and countless failed brands.

As a marketing consultant, I remember the unique experience of being barraged by business cards of Internet entrepreneurs in the elevator of a New York City loft building where several had taken office space—all literally begging for marketing advice. A year later, I returned to the same building, and those elevator doors opened on floors of empty spaces with cords hanging out of bare walls—the skeletons of brands gone off the rails.

That crazy, heady time came to a crashing end in 2001. Internet stocks tanked, and the money was gone. But the heart of the Internet was still beating. It is like deep space, where we still boldly go into a vast and untapped void, waiting for the next entrepreneur with the next big idea.

Internet real estate was slow to catch on. From the launch of the first dot-com domain-name online launch on March 15, 1985, it took more than two years for the first hundred sites to go online. Before domain names, there was a series of coded numbers—and who could remember those? The domain-name concept changed everything. The total number of domain names registered as of the third quarter of 2011 was around 220 million.[5]

The Internet promises to become even bigger and more lucrative with the extension of domain names that the Internet Corporation for Assigned Names and Numbers (ICANN), the organization charged with managing the domain-name system, has undertaken. Critics have said that the expansion of top-level domain (TLD) names beyond dot-com, dot-org, dot-net, and so on, of which there are currently twenty-two, will make companies and other entities already on the Internet that much more vulnerable to cybercrimes, such as cybersquatting, cyberterrorism, commercial fraud, and consumer confusion.[6]

Others welcome the extension of generic top-level domains (gTLDs), as they're known in Internet parlance. Having a greater number of domain names can only spur creativity and innovation and enhance economic activity on the Web, these supporters say—and this is also ICANN's intent.

"At ICANN, we believe that new gTLDs are a platform of innovation," Scott Pinzon, the agency's director of marketing and outreach, wrote on his blog. "No one can predict what smart people will do with them. Lots of new business models will be invented. Some will work. Some won't...but we can't predict the future to tell you what kinds of new products and services might be developed."[7]

What would this bigger, broader Internet mean for brands? Two years ago, Toys"R"Us spent $5 million to secure the domain toys.com to promote its brand. But what if the company could have secured the gLTD dot-toys instead? It could have divvyed it up any way it wanted to showcase every aspect of what it sells—into mini domains with names like www.christmastoys or www.toddlerstoys. This—and it could still happen if Toys"R"Us has applied for that name and if ICANN approves it—would also cost Toys"R"Us far less than the $5 million it spent for toys.com, noted Afilias, one of the world's most experienced registry providers, in a survey entitled "Envisioning Your Dot-BRAND New World: A Field Guide for Brand Builders."

The $185,000 application fee for a new and unique gTLD is a drop in the ocean for large, established corporations—and, indeed, a minimal investment for any brand that wants to hone its presence further on the Internet, says Vance Hedderel, a spokesperson for Afilias. No one knows yet which companies, governmental entities, or agencies have actually applied and which ones ICANN will finally approve, but in essence, whoever gets their own dot-brand will have the opportunity to really personalize that brand on the Internet and differentiate it from others.

Imagine the possibilities that a dot-coffee or a dot-music offer. What about a dot-Pepsi? Imagine a dot-Kardashian, instead of an http://kimkardashian.celebuzz.com/ and a khole.kardashian.tumblr.com.

The process is not without stumbles. ICANN's software suffered a glitch in early April 2012, delaying the first stage of the submission/approval process. And there are also many specifics and legalities involved with respect to trademark and copyright and other issues regarding what actually would constitute a generic top-level domain name.

But directionally, at least, it's clear that the new gTLDs will give brands the opportunity to interact more directly with consumers, Hedderel says. By carving out an entire piece of the Internet for themselves, they'll be able to refine their brands and make themselves that much more visible in a virtual world.[8]

Imagine the brand reinforcement opportunities. gTLD owners would be in total control of their space. Imagine the viral possibilities of an army of fans with blogs, e-mail addresses, or websites all promoting a particular dot-brand. Luxury brands like BMW could launch new services tying a dot-BMW e-mail address to a new vehicle purchase and communicating service updates directly to the car.[9]

But just because a dot-Pepsi may be more visible does not mean that the big brands would dominate the Internet. Studies have also shown that it will take consumers a long time to get used to new domain names, given their familiarity with the dot-coms and the dot-nets. And Hedderel emphasizes the fact that these new gTLDs are only at the very top level of the domain ladder, which means they would initially have to constitute new, broad categories like the dot-coms and the dot-nets. As they filter down, though, into the secondary and tertiary levels, the opportunities opened up for many, many other brands and companies would be endless.[10]

Pair that vision with the outlook for e-commerce, which market-research firm Forrester projects will soar in coming years. In 2010, Forrester's five-year e-commerce forecast predicted that online retail sales would skyrocket to a whopping $250 billion in the United States by 2014 (e-commerce sales topped $200 billion in 2011), and that sales in Europe—which has been slower to adopt online shopping—will also rise significantly. In a February 2012 report, Forrester announced that it expects online sales to grow from 7 percent of overall retail sales to close to 9 percent by 2016, as consumers become more comfortable with mobile and tablet devices, innovative new shopping models that divert spending away from physical stores (such as flash sales and subscription models), online loyalty programs, and aggressive promotional offers from Web retailers.[11]

Perhaps if pets.com had launched at this stage of the Internet's development, it would have been more successful. Like many other start-ups of the time, it failed because of an over exuberant marketing effort, that spent a plethora of seed money on advertising efforts. Perhaps you remember 2000, the year when all those dot-com Super Bowl commercials debuted. That year, the pets.com Super Bowl commercial cost $1.2 million in media time. With the advent of social media, however, brands can now leverage their customer bases on more cost-effective platforms like Facebook and Twitter. They can discuss, engage, and learn what people like about them and what they don't. They can crowd source when they want to test new products. Their visibility is greater, and they can grow their business models more organically and economically.

But given that advantage, and the broadening of the Internet, the greatest challenge that brands face is that innovation is "notoriously hard to predict," ICANN's Pinzon blogged. "Nobody knows what new gTLDs will bring."[12]

Are any great ideas left? No matter how much of a Gold Rush opportunity the Internet continues to offer, becoming the next Levi Strauss or Mark Zuckerberg is by no means a given.

In the privacy of her New Jersey bedroom, a busy woman unrolls her yoga mat. She lies down on her back and stretches her legs. She flips around onto her stomach and arches into cobra position, loosening the muscles in her back. Then she reaches for her iPad, positioning it where she can see the screen clearly, clicks onto the website www.balletbeautiful.com, and enters a SoHo, New York, exercise class she signed up for online earlier that morning by clicking "Take Live Class" on the website. And just like that, she's there, but virtually. It wouldn't matter where she actually was. This is not your mama's Jane Fonda video—this woman can see the instructor in real time, and the instructor can see, and give feedback, to her. It's the new frontier of fitness—an Internet exercise class done in real time with face-to-face interaction.

Mary Helen Bowers, a former dancer with the New York City Ballet and founder of Ballet Beautiful, is best known for training actress Natalie Portman for her Oscar-winning turn in the 2010 movie *Black Swan*. But really, she should be hailed for staking her claim on the Web through a unique brand of online fitness that owns its place in the virtual world that uses social media to its advantage and leverages technology to fuel its growth and reach a broader audience across the globe.

You can be anywhere in the world and do this workout: New York, Los Angeles, Tokyo, or Buenos Aires. You could be at your office, in your kitchen (if it's large enough and the floor isn't too cold and hard), or in a hotel room. All you need is a webcam-enabled device and Skype to connect with Mary Helen and a group of others like yourself, who have eschewed the gym, thrown out the dusty collection of fitness DVDs they've had lying around for ages, and signed onto Jane Fonda for the twenty-first century.

Fonda (whose workout method is still available on Amazon) was happy to tell you to feel the burn, and maybe you did. But when you're on live with Bowers, sweating it out in a Ballet Beautiful class, she *knows* when you're not feeling the burn. She can see that your leg isn't lifted high enough or that you're not scooping in your abs to the extent that you should be. That is one feat that even Jane could not pull off.

This is the new frontier for fitness, possible only because of what the Internet offers.

Bowers actually launched Ballet Beautiful in the real world, as a high-end, in-home fitness training company. Its online component happened quite by accident, more as a solution to maintaining her client base in New York—which comprised numerous supermodels and celebrities—while she trained Portman for *Black Swan*. But it quickly became a calculated move to bring fitness into the digital world.

"I needed to be with Natalie wherever she was in the world—in Los Angeles and Belfast, where she was based for a few months, when I traveled with her to Paris and Israel," she says. "The only solution for me to keep my clients in New York was to look at technology."[13]

Bowers began on a simple level, using Skype and iChat, but soon outgrew them. In order to grow her brand more efficiently, she sought a technology partner that made videoconferencing software that would account for movement and action.

That was hard to find, so ultimately Bowers commissioned her own software for Ballet Beautiful, giving her even greater control over her brand's growth and destiny, its look and feel. Working with technical developers who understood the esthetic side of Ballet Beautiful, which straddled the worlds of fitness, fashion, and beauty, Bowers created a brand deeply reliant on technology—yet extremely user friendly and unintimidating—like someone who wears tons of makeup but who applies it so skillfully you'd think they were born that way.

The result: a state-of-the-art at-home workout model that enables users to take live classes taught by Bowers from her SoHo studio, download streaming videos to any kind of device that connects to the Internet, and do it at their convenience any time of the day or night. Ballet Beautiful has since extended into e-commerce, selling merchandise and DVDs on the site.

The Internet is a packed place, busy and happening all the time. Any brand hoping to make it on the Net needs to find its niche and claim it. Not everyone will apply for a new gTLD, and not everyone will be able to create unique technology. But the formula for brands seeking to define their online space, personalize it, and fold in an e-commerce revenue model is totally accessible.

A burgeoning brand like Ballet Beautiful could never afford—nor would it want—a million-dollar TV commercial. For a new brand growing in the digital space, social media is a natural and cost-effective part of the course. In fact, new brands find social media much easier to use and understand than older brands do. For a brand like Ballet Beautiful, born of a digital-age branding model and without the bricks-and-mortar baggage to transition from, social media is a perfect tool to form a community of users, whose feedback then fuels future brand growth.

The kindling of this fuel is often self-generated. "We tweet photos from the studio or from a trip I took, what I am eating for breakfast today, or maybe even a photo of a really beautiful bouquet of flowers I saw and that inspired my day," Bowers says. "People share their reactions, share their stories, tell us how we're doing things, how we could do things, what they would like to see, what they like and don't like. I am building my brand with my customer base."[14]

It's a perpetual motion machine. No ad agency, creative director, production team, sock puppet, or shovel required.[15]

# Chapter 11

# BRAND ALCHEMY: TURNING LEAD INTO GOLD

It has been estimated that 80 percent of a brand's value is in its name. For instance, if Coca-Cola lost its brand name tomorrow, it would theoretically lose $64.2 billion of its $79.6 billion in 2010 value. According to Aswath Damodaran, professor of finance at New York University's Stern School of Business, a brand's value is measured by the extent to which it can sell its goods and services at a premium price.[1]

Coca-Cola is an example of something that has minimal intrinsic value but a desirable brand that gives it phenomenal value. Branding giant Interbrand estimates that today, the majority of business value is derived from intangibles. This is not a new thought. In 1900, John Stuart, then chairman of Quaker Oats, said, "If this business were split up, I would give you the land and bricks and mortar, and I would take the brands and trademarks, and I would fare better than you."[2]

What's new is the relatively recent proliferation of branding and a kind of bootstraps ingenuity in creating new territories to brand. Packaging, promotion, or technique can turn a commodity into a valuable brand almost overnight. In 2011, the U.S. Patent and Trademark Office issued 140,000 trademarks—100,000 more than in 1983.[3]

But it takes more than a catchy name for a brand to survive and thrive. Few people can create a brand that is relevant and evocative with minimal cost. Land grabbing and branding something that already exists, which has a product development cost of literally zero, will put anyone ahead of the game. But it's getting crowded out there in the brandscape. Now that stadiums, sidewalks, shopping carts, fruit, and even bathroom stalls are branded, what's left?

## GO SOUTH, YOUNG WOMAN

Beauty is in the eye of the beholder, women's mothers always told them. Do you think they had a clue that one day it would be in the hands of the Brazilians? Paris, move over. There's a new role model in fashion, and beauty branding and clothes have absolutely nothing to do with it.

From the blowout that promises to transform even the coarsest of manes into a frizz-free, pin-straight sheet of silk, down to the barely there, perfectly filed pedicure, the Brazilian brand is putting its stamp on women's bodies from Albuquerque to Zuma Beach. Scores of shampoos and conditioners containing natural products from Brazil—maracuja, Brazil nut, and acai, to name a few—line the shelves of the beauty aisles in stores, guaranteeing to deliver the Brazilian look. Brazilian blowouts have stormed into hair salons, and, for the rest of the body, a growing number of workouts promise to deliver that much-envied and coveted Brazilian derriere, some in as little time as a week. These days, the truly daring can even go for artificial implants that will result in something called a Brazilian butt lift.

What young woman outside of a nunnery wouldn't harbor some level of desire to strut her stuff with total confidence in a microbikini, like the tanned and gorgeous girls on Copacabana Beach? Brazilian women, like the supermodel Gisele Bündchen, have moved into the pole position for personal beauty brands. Gisele is a role model for business as well as beauty, a branding machine in her own right, steadily increasing her presence on the global fashion stage while managing her Ipanema sandal line, her Hope lingerie collection, and multiple endorsements for several designer powerhouses, including Versace and Dior.[4]

Brazil's obsession with physical perfection is no secret. This is a land where beauty is perceived as a basic human right, where wanting to look amazing and doing whatever it takes to achieve that is as valued as freedom of speech. In Brazil, cosmetic intervention is not just cultural, it's a social responsibility. While cosmetic surgery for any part of the body and face is de rigeur among the Brazilian elite, even the economically disadvantaged can perfect themselves through free treatments provided by institutions like the Brazilian Society of Aesthetic Medicine, which has treated free of cost more than 14,000 patients at its Rio de Janeiro branch since it was founded in 1997.[5]

When women beyond the borders of Brazil are aspiring to be branded beautiful in the Brazilian way—they may have their hair keratined and their toes pedicured—there's still plenty of real estate that can be converted to branded revenue potential.

Enter the J. Sisters.

The Seven Sisters once conjured a stately lineup of respected women's colleges: Barnard, Bryn Mawr, Mount Holyoke, Radcliffe, Smith, Vassar, and Wellesley, all founded between 1837 and 1889. But there's a new brand in town. The new Seven Sisters are the seven J. Sisters, midwives of the Brazilian bikini wax. Branded beauty à la Brazil really began in 1987, with these seven Brazilian siblings, whose first names—no surprise—all begin with the letter J. They came to New York City from the southeastern Brazilian province of Espírito Santo—a region renowned for its stunning beaches—to impart the beauty skills they'd learned at their family beauty salon in their native city of Vitória, Espírito Santo's capital.

"We spent our first years working in different salons, quietly researching to see what they had and what they didn't have," recalls Jonice Padilha, the siblings' official spokesperson and one of the sisters.[6]

The signature services the Sisters offered when they opened their own salon in midtown Manhattan were the hour-long Brazilian manicure and the Brazilian pedicure, a two-hour process in which a beautician thoroughly sloughs the skin off a client's feet and digs around her toenails to shove cuticles aside with instruments that look like something a dental hygienist would use.

The Brazilian nail treatments were runaway successes and quickly drew praise for the J. Sisters. The clients started to come by the droves, and the sisters' business and their name reached more epic proportions after 1994, when they introduced—and branded—that hallmark of Brazilian beauty, the infamous Brazilian bikini wax.

In Brazil, Jonice insists, the notion of a Brazilian bikini wax is redundant: It's just a "bikini wax," she says, "nothing more and nothing less." More is more, actually. The key is the size of Brazilian bikinis—akin to dental floss. As a result, waxing is a necessary part of a Brazilian woman's beauty regime. "The bikinis are tiny and it's summer all year long—we have to wax, we have no choice," says Jonice.

The J. Sisters didn't plan on branding the bikini wax—at least not at the outset. They certainly didn't think of qualifying it with the word "Brazilian," Jonice says. In fact, they were not even thinking of offering the wax as a service at all.

"But one day, I went to get my own bikini done, and the woman had so many questions for me about where to remove hair, how much hair should she remove, and she offered different prices for different parts," Jonice says indignantly. "I didn't get it."

That was the aha moment, when Jonice knew that what was "necessary" in her book was completely uncharted territory in American beauty.

"I was sure that other women would want to feel that feeling, even if they are not wearing tiny bikinis every day. We decided to offer the bikini wax, and we called it Brazilian Bikini Wax because—well, we are Brazilian."[7]

But selling that kind of bare beauty meant getting New York women to go for the bikini wax, which would require breaking through the boundaries of accepted beauty norms into what had previously been porn territory. Branding the procedure, selling it, and building awareness would mean changing existing mindsets and breaking through existing cultural taboos. Because as much as bikini waxes à la Brazilian may have been an accepted beauty ritual for regular Brazilian ladies from all walks of life, in the United States, porn stars were the only women who dared to bare to that extent.

There were other barriers to success as well. Brazilian waxes cost more than regular bikini waxes. And then, of course, there was the pain factor. Who would be willing to pay a premium for a feeling that approximates being dipped bottom-first into boiling oil?

Enter the counterweight that tipped the balance: the celebrity factor. In 2000, Sarah Jessica Parker's character Carrie Bradshaw got an on-camera Brazilian wax in an episode of *Sex and the City*, the girlfriends on the show joked about "going to Rio," and a new part of the anatomy was branded with its own geography. Today, an entire wall of the J. Sisters' 57th Street space is covered with signed photos of celebs, including Kirstie Alley, Cindy Crawford, Kim Catrall, Sarah Jessica Parker ("It was my first," she gushed sentimentally on her picture, reality apparently imitating TV fantasy), Gwyneth Paltrow, Uma Thurman, Lindsay Lohan, Avril Lavigne, and scores of other female stars. ("Not too many men," Jonice notes.) The J. Sisters have been featured on Oprah with supermodel Naomi Campbell and written about in publications across the world. Now, even business school students from Yale and Harvard have, according to Jonice, come to the J. Sisters to find out the story of their business success.

Perhaps if the procedure had had a name other than Brazilian bikini wax, it wouldn't have been so successful. "I would have patented it if I could have," Jonice says. "I couldn't, unfortunately, because you can't patent a nationality."

Today, just about every American neighborhood sports a beauty salon that offers the Brazilian wax. In the past few years, sales of razors for women have dropped 15 percent, as a painful procedure passes into lifestyle maintenance routine.[8]

For better or worse, the Brazilian has staked out a claim to the female body that previously seemed impervious to branding. It has even become an aspirational procedure, and a—some would say dubious—rite of passage to womanhood. One salon reported 500 twelve-year-old girls as clients for the Brazilian wax. "For waxing, 12 years old is the 'new normal,'" a Philadelphia esthetician told the *Today* show's website. And the bikini opened the door to the rest of the body. The word "Brazilian" now connotes a premium beauty service.[9]

Such is the power of branding. Or believing it's worth it, as the L'Oréal commercials say. As Jonice says, with a shrug, it's not really about the brand. "It's about you."[10]

## HOOK, LINE, AND SINKER

In 1977, Lee Lantz, a young seafood importer from Los Angeles, was trolling the hand-painted wooden boats in the waterside fish markets of Valparaiso, Chile, in search of new possibilities for import, when he found himself staring into the bulging eyes of a monster fish—blackish-gray, close to five feet long, over a hundred pounds, with a protruding lower jaw sporting a lineup of razor-sharp, pointy teeth. His first thought was, "What the hell is it?"

It was a fatty, oily white fish that could grow to two hundred pounds and live as long as fifty years, found in the waters off Chile and continental shelves off the sub-Antarctic islands. The fish was not eaten in Chile. Chileans near its home waters did not know what to do with it. In fact, if local fishermen caught a specimen, it was by accident. Nobody specifically fished for or ate this deepwater monster, which required long lines set 2,000 to 5,000 feet deep. However, Lantz knew that cultural tastes vary and that the Chileans' distaste for this fish did not necessarily mean it would suffer the same unpopular fate in the United States—especially with a little marketing savvy. And its unpopularity made it cheaper, a definite appeal for import. For instance, swordfish, not a favored fish in Chile, had hit the jackpot on foreign shores. And the new fish's bland taste meant that there were no immediate barriers—it could provide a blank palette for chefs in the newly emerging culinary market.[11]

The name of the fish was *bacalao de profundidad*, and it was also referred to as the Patagonian toothfish, for obvious reasons. Also for obvious reasons, Lantz knew that not many people in America were going to be excited to eat something called the toothfish, wherever it was from. In a stroke of marketing genius, he rechristened the fish the Chilean sea bass. OK, it wasn't strictly a "sea bass." But the meat was white and seemed sea bassesque. Close enough—and Chile had an exotic, yet specific ring to it. Chilean sea bass it was. The brand makeover of the Patagonian toothfish had begun. Lantz made a deal with a local processor and ventured forth to shepherd the Chilean sea bass into the choppy waters of the wholesale seafood market.[12]

Initially, the going was painfully slow. Lantz got exactly zero orders when he first pitched the new fish to his clients. Then some orders started to roll in—for a product that was used in frozen fish sticks—near the bottom of the culinary food chain—a place where an innocuous "mystery fish" could be sliced up, rolled into breadcrumb coatings, and passed off as McProtein. As for the higher rungs of the culinary ladder, the buyer who supplied seafood to the celebrity hangout Chasen's and other high-end venues summed it up: "Why would anybody want to eat this thing? It tastes like nothing. And I don't think it's a sea bass."

Eventually, shortages in other, more popular fish, combined with exhaustive sales efforts and the bargain price of Chilean sea bass, sparked some sales. Cantonese restaurants were an initial market, where the fish was usually described as "black cod." Meanwhile, the Chilean fisheries had hit on a mother lode of the deepwater fish thirty miles off an eight-hundred-mile stretch of Chilean coastline. In the open waters of the fishing industry, proprietary zones are designated and theoretically respected and maintained, according to maritime regulation and industry licensing. As Chilean sea bass began to pick up sales volume, a plethora of licenses was issued, and the scene was set for fierce commercial competition—as well as the inevitable poaching.[13]

The 1980s marked the beginning of the gourmet food movement in the United States, and the search for nature's perfect ingredients became a passion for a foodie nation. The stage was set for Chilean sea bass, once the ugly stepsister who needed her teeth fixed, to step into the limelight as the newest culinary star.

The wholesale price had jumped from $1.75 to $2.75 a pound.

Lights, camera, action: fast forward to 1991, the newly trendy Tribeca in New York, and the celebrity restaurant Tribeca Grill, fronted by Robert De Niro, who led an investor group that included Sean Penn, Mikhail Baryshnikov, and Bill Murray. Dressed up in a crust of crab and a port-wine glaze, Chilean sea bass hit the menu of Tribeca Grill's chef, Don Pintabona, to rave reviews. Pintabona had first been introduced to the fish while cooking on a charity trip to Santiago with another chef, Jean-Louis Paladin. Pintabona recalls,

> We tasted this fish and tried to figure out what the hell it was, but we could see it was the type of fish that is hardy, difficult to mess up, didn't overcook easily like some fish, and was nonoffensive to even nonfish lovers. And cheap. I put out feelers to fish purveyors and started buying it at $3.00 a pound. Also, about this time Nobu, the ultrahip Japanese celebrity restaurant, came along and started serving it as a Chinese sea bass

dish, substituting for cod—and saving half the price of the cod. That really started the buzz. Next thing you know, Chilean sea bass became a banquet hall fish—half the banquet halls in America were serving it.[14]

Other high-profile chefs and eateries debuted their own variations, and the fish's popularity soared. Consumer demand hit frenzy levels, and the Chilean sea bass craze was on. The fish quickly became a premium item, with wholesale prices and profits to match; the price per pound rocketed up to $8.99. The toothfish catch catapulted from 12,000 tons in 1992 to 34,000 tons by 1992. Black market sale was at par with or greater than the legal market, with the 1997 total illegal catch of Patagonian toothfish around 100,000 tons at a value of more than $500 million.[15] Fishing vessels, both legal and illegal, swarmed the native waters of the toothfish. The fish is slow to mature to reproductive age and as a result does not regenerate numbers quickly. In the late 1990s, Whole Foods actually stopped selling Chilean sea bass due to sustainability issues and rumors that the species was threatened with extinction due to overfishing, although it resurfaced in its seafood cases, sourced from approved and limited fisheries, by 2006. That same year, a manifesto signed by 1,000 chefs to "Take a Pass on Chilean Sea Bass" signaled that they were finally putting the brakes on the wholesale vacuuming of the deep ocean waters for this once-ignored fish.

"I started to use Chilean sea bass in 1992 or 1993, and it was a great fish, a beautiful fish," said Cesare Cassella, of the acclaimed Tuscan restaurant Beppe in New York City's Flatiron District. "In the last few years they have been getting smaller and smaller, while the quality is getting worse. Now, most of the Chilean sea bass on the market is illegal, and it has been frozen. I agree 100 percent with the campaign to improve the stocks of this fish for the future." He noted, "The chefs were responsible for creating a trend. But if we can stop the use of Chilean sea bass, the demand will drop for the illegal fish."[16]

In 2010, Greenpeace International added the Patagonian toothfish to its seafood red list, a list of fish that are commonly sold in supermarkets around the world and that have a high risk of being sourced from unsustainable fisheries. As of this writing, there are 374,000 listings on Google for "Save the Chilean Sea Bass."

Today, the harvesting of the Chilean sea bass is much more closely monitored, but you can still purchase it wholesale for between $28 and $35 a pound, depending on your location. As it turns out, the fish is high in mercury, inciting consumer education and warnings that have also helped diminish the demand. There is an interesting postscript that is indicative of the limits of consumer branding. In 1994, the U.S. government refused to rename the Patagonian toothfish the Chilean sea bass, although it agreed it could be used as an alternative name for marketing purposes. Still, the Chilean sea bass's is a cautionary tale that, with skill and determination, you can rebrand almost anything, serve it up in an orange-soy reduction, and market it nearly into extinction.[17]

## FROM DIRTY TO DELICIOUS: WHO DOESN'T LOVE CHOCOLATE?

They sound luscious, delectable, good enough to eat or sink a couple of thousand dollars into. But before people raved about their deep, rich color, before celebrities like Jennifer Aniston and Jennifer Lopez began sporting them at red carpet events, and before they were bestowed that mouthwatering moniker, the so-called "chocolate diamonds" that are so loved and desired today were little more than plain old brown diamonds—gemstones that, experts say, have always been as legitimate as any other diamond of any other color, but because of their brownish tints and yellowish undertones, they were deemed undesirable. These stones were the gem equivalent of Cinderella before the ball—on their knees, scrubbing the hearth, and definitely not invited to the ball.

Like other all-colored diamonds, brown diamonds owe their hue to a number of natural factors that occur during their formation period. But in the diamond hierarchy, brown diamonds somehow just couldn't make the cut with consumers. By virtue of their coloring, they were considered dirty and have always been overshadowed by the white diamond—the diamond of a million dreams. Let's face it: When Marilyn Monroe shimmied through "Diamonds Are a Girl's Best Friend," the bling that decked out her arms, neck, and ears was not brown. In the world of colored diamonds, it was the expensive and rare blue and pink diamonds that people coveted the most. Brown diamonds didn't stand a chance of getting noticed—except by heavy industry, which was where they were relegated.

And yet one of the largest diamonds ever mined to date was actually brown. The Golden Jubilee diamond, discovered in 1986 in South Africa's Premier Mine, was probably so disappointing a find because of its color that it was disparagingly christened Unnamed Brown. Weighing in at a hefty 755.50 carats, the stone was handed over by De Beers (its owners) to legendary, sixth-generation diamond cutter Gabi Tolkowsky—but not with the intent of having him fashion it into a piece of high-end jewelry. Quite the contrary. Tolkowsky was to use the hapless stone to test out new cutting tools and techniques that could not be tested on other, more high-profile, consumer-friendly stones.

Little did anyone know, though, that the cutting would yield unexpected results: Tolkowsky's talent transformed Unnamed Brown into a beautiful golden yellow color with a bright reddish center, which led De Beers to move the stone up the scale to the category of "fancy yellow brown."

Even so, it was not a stone that anyone outside of hard-core industry would want or that De Beers considered worthy of touting. And the poor stone was completely overshadowed at De Beers's centennial celebration in 1988 by the Centenary Diamond, which had also been found in South Africa's Premier Mine and been cut by Tolkowsky.[18]

In 1995, De Beers sold Unnamed Brown to Henry Ho, a Thai businessman, who then presented it as a gift from the Thai people to their king, Bhumibol Adulyadej, on the fiftieth anniversary of his coronation. Now known as Golden Jubilee, the diamond has found a home in the royal palace in Bangkok and is featured there as part of the crown jewels. Its value is estimated to be anywhere between $4 million and $12 million, and it has been on display at various museums around the world.[19]

Other than the Golden Jubilee, brown diamonds were supposedly quite rare until 1985, when millions of stones were discovered deep inside mining company Rio Tinto's Argyle Mine in Australia. This resulted in the creation of the Indo-Argyle Diamond Council in 1994, which put the brown stones in the hands of expert diamond cutters from India, with the goal of pushing the brown diamond out of the wings and into the limelight and to create a market in which to sell the now plentiful supply.[20]

But it would take a lot more than cunning craftsmanship, precision cutting, and diamond industry marketing to popularize the brown diamond. To elevate the gem's profile and turn it into something that people would not just want, but covet, it would take the branding genius of a jeweler named Eddie LeVian—a man who also had a flair for design and a long-standing family reputation in the jewelry world. Via an extremely clever marketing campaign, LeVian turned brown into white, as far as diamonds are concerned.

LeVian rebranded brown diamonds by trademarking the name Chocolate Diamond and, by so doing, elevated the plain-jane brown diamond into a totally different class. (Not unlike a jewelry version of the Chilean sea bass.) Suddenly, a brown diamond was no longer brown, but chocolate—something lush and rich, luscious, and desirable, a stone that would make women drool and celebrities flock.

LeVian capped off his coup by setting the stones in stunning cuts and styles, developed by the leading jewelry craftsmen of the world to enhance and bring out their warm, brown tones. LeVian's company puts only a few hundred designs into full production each year, but it has ensured their success by inextricably linking them to the world of fashion. Every year, LeVian stages a trends forecast show at the jewelry industry's premier event, the JCK show in Las Vegas, where Chocolate Diamonds are showcased to enhance the latest clothing styles, and vice versa. LeVian also brought Chocolate Diamonds to the masses when he joined forces with jewelry retailer Jared, for whom he does exclusive Chocolate Diamond collections.

Thanks to the metamorphosis of the brown diamond to the Chocolate Diamond, all those neglected brown/yellow diamonds were given a new lease on life. Like ugly ducklings suddenly turned into swans, they emerged on the world jewelry stage as "Champagne, Cognac, Clove, Honey, and Cinnamon" diamonds, even neutrals such as black or gray. Colors that had never been considered attractive were suddenly the talk of the town. From high-end bling to mass-market malls, everyone wanted them.

The perception of diamonds as being exclusively white or colorless gemstones was changed by introducing a fashion angle that was new to most consumers. And suddenly, consumers couldn't get enough.[21]

Another gemological rebranding success was the black diamond—long considered unattractive and even labeled industrial grade because it was so brittle and difficult to work with. It, too, became a fashion statement thanks to the likes of Fawaz Gruosi, an Italian-born jeweler in Geneva, Switzerland, who was the first to create an exclusive line of black diamond jewelry for his upscale Geneva boutique, De Grisogno. Gruosi has continued to actively promote and use the stones through the years in both jewelry and watches and has been much lauded for his work and his creativity.

Ask a gemologist what he thinks of all this bling transformation and he'll tell you most of it is hype, but hype that came about at the right time. Brown diamonds were abundant but had to be given appeal, says Alexandre de Miguel, a second-generation gemologist and numismatist based in Geneva, Switzerland. The hype worked, and the entire diamond industry—miners, merchants, and jewelers—loved it. Diamonds in every shade of brown were in, even though they had always been around and, in essence, are not much different from any other diamond. But so great has been the hype around brown diamonds (especially the deep brown ones—which have always been valuable, even though no one really cared, de Miguel says) that, today, there's an entire industry devoted to engineering and altering the color of brown diamonds to make them as rich and chocolaty looking as possible.

Although the lens of branding may make Chocolate Diamond buyers feel they're getting something totally unique, they're really not. "From the perspective of a gemologist, it's the quality and individual beauty of a particular gemstone that makes the difference, not what kind of stone or color it may be," de Miguel says. "Technically, a well-defined color in a diamond—that means the stone has intense hue, color and saturation—qualifies it as a fancy colored diamond. That distinction has always applied to dark brown diamonds, too, but there just wasn't a market to make them trendy and desirable."[22]

Those magic words clinched the deal: trendy and desirable. And what could be more desirable than a combination of bling and chocolate, presented as an irresistible fashion must-have, the new frontier in diamonds? Bingo, LeVian (which also has a trademark on the term "vanilla diamonds"). And people ate it up.

Diamonds that are good enough to eat—and affordable, too, because the price point at which Chocolate Diamonds sell is a big part of their appeal. On www.chocolatediamondrings.com, for example, consumers can get their fill through a repository of information for anything to do with brown diamond rings, including links to an exhaustive list of stores that sell the jewelry and show prices that range from $500 to $3,500.

In today's market, though, price is irrelevant. If people are buying a Chocolate Diamond because they believe it's a cheaper alternative to another kind, they're only seeing part of the picture, de Miguel says, because depending on where you shop and what you're prepared to pay, you can get any diamond for a wide range of prices.

"Diamonds are always worth less than the work that's necessary to manufacture jewelry," according to de Miguel. "A high-end jeweler would choose the perfect stone and have it cut and fashioned by high-end workers, but you can take the same stone and get it made cheaply in a factory somewhere, and then sell it at Walmart at that price point."[23]

The same applies to the brown diamond family: The source determines the price. At the higher end of the Chocolate Diamond scale, jewelers like LeVian put a great deal of effort and funds into not only choosing the best stones (the company is picky in its selection process), but also into the way in which they are cut and set, and the way the jewelry is designed. LeVian endeavors to increase the perceived value of his line of chocolate-branded stones by not only having them set in high-quality jewelry, but also by creating a desire among women to collect the jewelry and keep adding to what they have. As women aspire to more important pieces, he encourages them to upgrade by allowing full trade-in value at trunk shows. While the average piece of LeVian chocolate jewelry retails for a couple of thousand dollars, women who signed on have moved up the ranks, some buying pieces that cost as much as $20,000.[24]

And of course, celebrities (they're featured in great detail on Eddie LeVian's blog) add the greatest appeal of all.

"At the end of the day, you can buy a chocolate diamond at Walmart or you can buy it at LeVian or some other high-end place in just the same way as you would buy any other diamond," de Miguel says.

"Obviously, the Walmart diamond will cost less, the LeVian diamond will cost more, and that has to do again with workmanship, style, design and so on. But the 'chocolate' is what makes people feel they're buying something special. When you turn plain brown into chocolate, you've made a new market and you've turned something that no one wanted into something that appeals to all."[25]

A yummy prospect, indeed.

## LIQUID GOLD

In 1976, Americans drank an average of 1.6 gallons of bottled water every year. Roughly thirty years later, consumption increased to 30 gallons per person, according to the Earth Policy Institute—despite the fact that bottled water can cost anywhere from 240 to 10,000 times more than tap water, which is brought right to your home for pennies a gallon.[26]

But maybe you're, say, a celebrity who has turned away from the tap and bellied up to the bottle, paying $60 for 750 ml of Bling H2O, one of the world's most expensive bottled waters, created by a Hollywood producer and served at the Emmys (the most expensive will set you back $60,000, but I'm guessing even a celebrity would have to be crawling across the Gobi Desert in a sandstorm before that would pique his or her interest). Or maybe you're more discerning and want to do your research among the 3,000 varieties of bottled water available worldwide before laying out the serious coin. Water sommelier to the rescue! At least one representative of this burgeoning profession, Dr. Michael Mascha, a food anthropologist and author of the comprehensive book *Fine Waters: A Connoisseur's Guide to the World's Most Distinctive Bottled Waters,* has made it his mission "to educate people about premium bottled water" in hopes of "taking bottled water to the next level."[27]

Water, which is basically a free and natural resource, is now a $15 billion a year industry.[28]

Ask anyone if they prefer the taste and texture of a particular brand of bottled water over another and you'll probably both bemuse and amuse them. Water is just water, after all, to most people, no matter what the bottle or brand. Taste? Texture? Do they really exist with respect to water, and, if so, what are they worth?

There's a small but staunch coterie of global "water elite" who'd rather die than fill up their glass from the tap and who'd perhaps pay more for an obscure bottle of still or sparkling than they'd pay for a bottle of wine. These people firmly believe it's worth it to search for the perfect water, not just because premium waters can complement a gourmet meal, thereby enhancing a dining experience, but also because these waters are allegedly better for health than any run-of-the-mill bottled water.

Martin Riese is another water sommelier, albeit self-appointed (an unofficial designation that one can only earn, he says, by "drinking and drinking lots and lots of water"). Riese has recently moved to Los Angeles from his native Germany to spread the word on premium water. Riese, a wine sommelier by training and part of a small band of European wine sommeliers who have branched out into the world of rare and fine waters, can't bear drinking Poland Spring—the most ubiquitous brand in the United States. His water of choice is Iskilde, cork-sealed and drawn from an underground spring in the heart of Denmark, with, Reise claims, a distinctive taste that is far more pleasing to his palate than any other water. Although it's a costly proposition, Riese orders crates of Iskilde online and has them shipped over to L.A., although Iskilde is available in the United States at $60 for a 1,000 milliliter (about 33 fluid ounces) bottle. It's a worthwhile investment, he says, because for him, water isn't about quenching thirst, but about a deeper and more meaningful experience, a sensual pleasure that comes with added health benefits.[29]

Like other premium branded waters, Iskilde has a story to tell, designed to make consumers see its water differently. For a willing audience, stories always make for a strong selling point.

"[The spring] was found in 2002 centrally in the Mossø Reservation area, between Yding Skovhøj, which until recently was believed to be the highest point in Denmark, and Mossø Lake," the website fineh2o.com, the premier distributor of luxury bottled waters from around the globe, says about Iskilde. "The reservoir of the spring lies more than 50 meters below the ground, but the water is under so much pressure, that it would reach the surface as a fountain, if left on its own. The fact that the water-reservoir is under such pressure means that it is closed for penetration of new water. This is probably one of the reasons why the water is so pure. Ground water in Denmark has an average temperature of between 8 and 12 degrees all year round. With a temperature of below 8 degrees, Iskilde is an unusually cold spring."

Then there's the story of Cloud Juice, a premium brand of rainwater from King Island in Tasmania, bottled from one of the largest unspoiled expanses of water in the world. Cloud Juice founder Duncan McFie, a teacher on King Island, decided to get into the water business because his friends were always coming over to collect rainwater from a tank outside his house.

"I knew that we had the cleanest air in the world, and I knew that King Island had a superb reputation for fine quality food. It wasn't a big jump. I just had to find out if clean air equaled clean water—which of course it did—and then I had to figure out how to catch the water without affecting the taste," McFie said.[30]

What McFie ended up building was "was a very expensive, over-engineered, 10 square meter catchment. This should have caught sufficient water to service the King Island market but it didn't work out that way. Cloud Juice had to expand. And so the catchment grew. The new roof section was built on the southern tip of King Island, part of the Bowling Property, a 6,000 acre specialty beef farm adjacent to 11,100 kilometers of the Great Southern Ocean."[31]

As a water connoisseur—someone who has trained his tongue to distinguish the subtle and not-so-subtle differences between waters that most people couldn't detect—Riese can tell you with complete confidence that Tasmanian rainwater tastes completely different from any other water in the world.

"It is very, very smooth and pure because pure rainwater has no minerals in it and has very low carbonation," he says. "Tasmanian rainwater tastes like velvet."

Riese will also tell you that Tasmanian rainwater brings out the best in red wine. "It's unbelievable how the taste of wine can change in your mouth if you're drinking the wrong water. People think they're just drinking one red wine, but if they have two different waters with it, the wine will taste totally different," he says.[32]

Michael Mascha became a water sommelier somewhat by default. Mascha holds a PhD in food anthropology and was a wine collector until he found out in 2002 that he had an alcohol allergy that could stop his heart, at which point he transferred his interest to water.[33]

His website details the characteristics that distinguish different kinds of bottled waters: balance (the carbon content), virginality (the level of nitrate in a water, which determines how protected the water is from its surroundings), minerality (mineral content determines a water's taste and terroir), orientation (the pH level of a particular water determines whether it's sweeter or more sour in taste), hardness (the amount of calcium and magnesium in water determines how hard or soft it is—bottled water, which has lower levels of both, is naturally softer than tap water), and vintage (the younger a water, the lighter and cleaner it tastes).

However, most consumers don't have the opportunity to taste-test dozens of waters side by side. Instead, they choose by brand. Without branding, water is just a commodity that is almost impossible to differentiate.

Aquafina is a product of PepsiCo, which has the second-largest share of bottled water in the United States. "If there weren't any branding in the water category, the business would eventually go 100 percent to price and to private label," says Robert Lynn, executive vice president of sales and marketing for Global Beverage Systems. Aquafina's differentiation strategy includes its affiliation with PepsiCo, a trusted name, as well as its charcoal purification process, in which natural minerals are removed from the water.[34]

Distribution is a key strategic element in branding an elite water. If you want to taste Cloud Juice, you'll have to go to an überhigh-end establishment like one of the Mandarin Oriental Hotels, the Four Seasons, or the Ritz-Carlton.

Cloud Juice also sells at Dean and DeLuca, which is more accessible than a five-star hotel, but generally speaking, the company is picky about its retail partners, preferring to go with those who reflect the brand sensibility and are "serious" about quality water.

Over the years, several elite hotels around the world have made it a point to shine the light on water. As far back as 2001, the Ritz-Carlton in Battery Park, New York, became the first hotel to bring on board a water sommelier.[35]

And in 2007, the August Claridge's Hotel in London introduced a "Water Menu" that offered thirty different kinds of the finest in bottled water, priced, in some cases, as high as fifty pounds sterling a bottle.

Water on the Claridge's menu came from every corner of the world—Hawaii, Newfoundland, Japan, India—and the menu detailed the best ways to pair them up. "Just Born Spring Drops" from the Nilgiri Mountains in the south of India, for example, would apparently be best suited for "sensitive digestions," while France's Wattwiller water was said to be "ideal with fine foods and fine French cuisine." The menu suggested pairing Italian water Panna with seafood and white meat dishes, and it suggested that Llanllyr—a water from West Wales that apparently has a "very soft taste" despite being a mouthful to pronounce—was the perfect accompaniment to *amuses bouches* and salads.

According to Renaud Gregoire, Claridge's food and beverage director, "water is becoming like wine. Every guest has a particular opinion and asks for a brand."[36]

## WATER, WATER EVERYWHERE

The process of branding water has been going on almost since man could drink. There is evidence of waters with attributes dating back as far as the Etruscans. The ancient Romans became convinced that water had many health benefits and ranked or branded waters from different sources according to their effects on the skin and the hair or how they fortified different organs and body parts. Another of the earliest examples, says Jim Salzman, Samuel F. Mordecai Professor of Law and Nicholas Institute Professor of Environmental Policy at Duke University, who has written extensively on the history of bottled water, is the bottling of water from holy wells during the Middle Ages in order to capture the pilgrimage trade. Water from various holy wells was sealed in earthenware pots that were then marked with the name of the particular well it came from and sold to pilgrims.[37]

"Water of the sun," Chateldon 1650, a bottled mineral water that was served in the courts of French king Louis XIV, has been called the first bottled water ever.[38]

Some say that Louis XIV's personal physician suggested His Majesty drink Chateldon for health reasons. Others dispute that fact, asserting that Chateldon only had its claim to fame much later in history via French politician Pierre Laval, owner of the Chateldon castle, who served it regularly. But the unsavory Laval—a key figure in the Vichy government of Occupied France who signed papers authorizing the deportation of foreign Jews from French soil and was later found guilty of high treason and executed when France was liberated—was hardly in the same league as Louis XIV, which is probably why Chateldon's glass bottle comes emblazoned with the Sun King's emblem. The story has lifted the water to a special status, whereby it's only produced in limited quantities each year and is consumed by only a select few.[39]

In the twentieth century, strides in bottling technology gave a new burst of life to the bottled water business. But that bubble promptly deflated after the introduction of chlorination, which cleaned up municipal water supplies and made it more chic in an earthy/crunchy way to drink tap water than bottled.[40]

Then came the fitness boom of the 1970s, 1980s, and 1990s, when bottled water enjoyed the greatest success, particularly in the United States. Companies like Perrier invested heavily in their ad campaigns, bringing in celebrity endorsers—Orson Welles was the Perrier spokesperson. Once Coke and Pepsi entered the water picture, however, behemoths took over the market and have ruled it since.[41] Considering that the premium market represents only 6.3 percent of the bottled water market, it could be assumed that most people either don't want to pay the added price, buy into the hype, or follow trivia like the fact that Sophia Coppola and Penelope Cruz only drink Chateldon 1650.[42]

But elite designer waters can still stir up buzz, either because a celebrity is caught on camera drinking it, or a bottle catches on as being particularly cool, or both. Designer water Voss from Norway, for instance, was the talk of the town some years ago because of its beautiful bottle, created by former Calvin Klein designer Neil Kraft— and because it was Madonna's chosen water (until she switched to Kaballah water, which is claimed to have curative powers). For a while, Voss rode high among the hipsters on the combination of celebrity and design aesthetic.[43]

Whether the differences are real, if tasting is believing, bottled water has gained its converts. In his 2009 book, *Passion for Pinot*, wine expert and beverage writer Jordan Mackay talked about a dinner at Rome's famous La Pergola restaurant, where "I was presented with a wine list—a really long one—and then I realized that it was the water list. There were eight of us, all drinking the same wine, but different water. So everybody had their own bucket of ice behind them, and the dinner became all about tasting each other's waters."[44]

No one in Mackay's party knew anything about water, and he was shocked by how some of them tasted. "Some were sulfurous, some were salty," he said. After choosing a high-mineral-content wine, he recalled, "It coated my mouth, and the wine came off hard. Even the food didn't do a lot for me because the water was such an incredible presence."[45]

*Time*'s Joel Stein also overcame his skepticism during the course of a three-course lunch with Michael Mascha, the water sommelier, where each course was paired with a different kind of bottled water: "To my surprise, the waters did taste different. Or felt different."[46]

Mascha also writes about the differences between top-branded water and generic branded water—an important distinction he makes on his website and one that purists would certainly endorse.[47] For the rest of us, though, Evian or Poland Spring is probably as elite as it gets.

## YOU ARE WHAT YOU DRINK

Jim Salzman dismisses the elite level of water branding as something that appeals only to people in a self-contained universe of luxury. These avid luxurists wear expensive watches and couture and drive high-end cars. Only they, he feels, are likely to want to put their water where their wine is, if not higher.[48]

More to the point, Salzman believes that Americans are not really interested in drinking water for taste. Health and convenience more likely drive the purchase of bottled water, and, anyway, most Americans put ice in their water—something that makes the purists shudder as if someone had emptied the contents of an ice machine into a magnum of vintage Champagne. More important, it's hard to pinpoint or define brand loyalty when it comes to bottled water. "You do have a certain brand loyalty when it comes to higher waters like Fiji and others, but overall, that's a niche market and I don't see it expanding," Salzman says.[49]

Taste is just one of the factors relevant to brand differentiation among bottled waters. Flavoring, carbonation, or nutrients may be added, but overall, Americans are more likely to buy bottled water for portability, says John Sicher, editor of *Beverage Digest*, which means that the market for premium, pricey brands is constant, not likely to diminish but not likely to grow either, since most people don't really aspire to buy better water.[50]

Location is also a brand differentiator, be it an exotic town or island, an Alp, a spring, a glacier that presumably melted into the bottle, or an iconic venue. The city of Venice, Italy, launched a major rebranding and promotion campaign for its water supply. City officials renamed the municipal water Acqua Veritas and emphasized the fact that it was drawn from exactly the same source as San Benedetto, a bottled water from the same region.[51]

Increasingly, the taste factor of bottled water is being overshadowed by social issues. The bottle itself is a key brand differentiator that has moved beyond design into the area of ecosustainability. The major bottlers are responding to environmental claims by introducing eco-friendly bottles, such as Pepsi's first-ever PET bottle made from 100 percent plant materials, including switch grass, pine bark, and corn husks, and a fully recyclable bottle.[52]

Nobody can taste water online. But everyone can evaluate—or activate—a bottle. The Internet has provided a petri dish for the ongoing war between green advocates and bottle boosters.

In the predigital beverage market, the big consumer products companies fought for what they called the "share of liquid stomach." Whether working on the American Dairy Association's milk account, 7Up, or Tropicana, I saw innumerable pie charts that illustrated these statistics. They were always a one-way street—what the brand would tell consumers about the product. Consumers were relegated to "insights" from focus groups and research decks, not dialogue. But now the Internet provides opportunities for all sides of the conversation to line up and state their case—and add a new level of brand differentiation. Here, an individual has an advantage over a corporate brand. An individual is perceived as telling a story, representing a passion; a company is seen as pushing a product or an agenda—so companies will often hire individuals or experts to state their cases. A video called "The Story of Bottled Water," produced by a consumer activist, blasting the evils of bottled water, debuted on YouTube, only to be countered by a "mini-film" by the powerful International Bottled Water Association (IBWA), which highlighted the proactive sustainability practices of major brands such as Nestlé.

Within days, the activist's video had 120,000 hits on the Web; the IBWA's had 250.[53]

# Chapter 12

# RAISED BY WOLVES, PECKED TO DEATH BY GOSLINGS

A JetBlue pilot has a raving meltdown midflight and has to be carted off the plane by authorities. BATS Global Markets Inc. launches an initial public offering on its own stock exchange, which explodes after less than ten seconds due to a computer glitch. Netflix unexpectedly raises its prices and splits off its DVD rental service, inciting customer rebellion. Tiger Woods's love life implodes and, with it, his game. Of these brand disasters, as of this writing, only Tiger Woods's brand has suffered brand-killing damage, and even he has regained a number of sponsors. The fact is, although the potential to kill a brand has never been higher due to the Internet, where it only takes nine and a half seconds to upload a file that can snuff out a brand reputation, the damage can sometimes be mitigated by the same factor—the Internet. The forces that pull the brand train in cyberspace are a two-way street with increasingly powerful implications. Prescient marketers are learning to leverage both directions.

On March 28, 2012, just one day after a JetBlue pilot's rampage on a flight from New York to Las Vegas caused the copilot to lock his superior officer out of the cockpit and the flight to be diverted to Amarillo, Texas, the company's CEO, Dave Barger, spoke out on the *Today* show and also on a blog post. "It was a tough event, to say the least, as it was unfolding yesterday," Barger said. "But I think that…the training that took place with the copilot who became the pilot in command and the entire cabin crew and then working with the customers—that's the follow-up to this story." While moving to restore consumer confidence by reinforcing the professionalism of the crew, and even saying that the pilot, a twenty-year veteran and personally known to Barger, had until that point been a "consummate professional," Barger admitted that there was a spiraling situation. "What happened at altitude and the call into the FAA is that we had a medical situation and that's how we responded," he said. "Clearly, especially in today's [real-time] media, we know that it also became a security situation."[1]

Did this damage the brand? Not for long. The next day, JetBlue's stock was trading up 2 percent. On the company's official blog, *BlueTales*, the reaction of consumers was mixed, but many were enthusiastically supportive, focusing on the way the situation had been handled by the crew at 35,000 feet, as opposed to the meltdown of the pilot: "Seriously a huge applause to the guys who took over and landed the people safely!" was a typical comment. The diversion of potential brand damage was as successful as the diversion of the actual flight.[2]

JetBlue has masterfully managed its digital presence in such a way that when a potentially brand-breaking incident occurred, the brand had Teflon. This was a strategic marketing imperative, not a fan-fueled accident. For instance, in 2009, JetBlue sported 1.5 million followers on Twitter, but only 60,000 on Facebook. It didn't wait for a great social media migration to happen organically. Instead, the company swung into action and launched an "All-You-Can-Jet Fan Sweepstakes," where being a fan on Facebook made consumers eligible for free tickets and vacations.[3]

Not only that, but JetBlue has closed the loop to be certain that the customer experience matches the brand promise, as a recent in-flight blog post from a weary, delayed JetBlue flier illustrates. While trapped on the runway, the blogger heard the following announcement:

"Ladies and Gentlemen, we know we're late taking off, and even though it's the weather and not something we caused, we're going to comp everybody's movies for this flight. We know you've all had a long day and we want it to end with something nice and relaxing. And for those of you who were supposed to be on the Continental flight and ended up here, we don't ever want you to go back."

The mood on the flight—which could have been a rather dreary late evening affair—took an immediate upswing. People joked and smiled and made eye contact. They were noticeably brighter and calmer as the flight progressed. And I'm writing about the experience today and business travelers are reading about it.[4]

This blog post, describing an experience that occurred the previous month, was posted the day of the pilot meltdown. This consumer was riding to the virtual rescue of the brand, pounding on its virtual chest in the CPR effort that would counter the potential brand damage that had just occurred on a massive scale. One person? Yes, but one among many. Social media communications like this JetBlue blog post are insurance in the bank for a brand. And JetBlue was able to count on its store of stockpiled consumer goodwill to deflect the pilot meltdown and turn a serious fiasco into a brand enhancement, as opposed to the disaster it could well have become. The CEO's public comments were transparent and consistently on-message, aligned, in fact, with the themes of the in-flight announcement from the blog post quoted above: *There's been a problem. We acknowledge it. We're handling it professionally, and we have the assets to do so with your complete confidence. We want to keep you as a customer, so we are open and sharing this with you, personally.* Does it take guts to put your brand out there to consumers without makeup, with all its wrinkles and pimples? Yes. Guts and strategic smarts. But the glory in return is potentially great. And brand makeup today is widely perceived by today's supercynical consumers— particularly digitally savvy Gen Y—as lipstick on the pig.

BATS Global Markets was a hot new stock exchange that in 2012 became America's third-largest trading platform, behind the New York Stock Exchange and NASDAQ. The initial public offering on March 23, 2012, was supposed to cement the brand in the annals of Wall Street and the global marketplace; instead it imploded the high-frequency trading technology of a company ironically named Better

Alternative Trading System. Something went wrong in the computer systems, causing a "flash crash" in which all stocks with symbols between A and BFZZZ—including BATS's own—stopped trading, causing their prices to plummet. BATS's share price crashed from an opening level of $15.25 to $.02. A fail-safe was triggered that stopped all trading of the affected stocks, which included Apple. The computer glitch was quickly corrected, and BATS acted quickly to minimize investor confusion.

"We feel absolutely terrible about letting our customers down," said BATS chief executive Joe Ratterman. "The fact that our own stock was out there to be traded for the first time, and we showed system problems, eroded customer confidence." The founder of BATS demanded that all BATS executives forego their bonuses. Days after the flash crash, Ratterman was stripped of his chairman's role. Nonetheless, largely due to fears of brand damage to the share price, BATS's IPO was postponed indefinitely.[5]

In 2011, Netflix customers did not take it well when the company surprised them with a price hike of up to 60 percent and then, to put a cherry on it, announced it was splitting the DVD service into another brand called Quickster. *Quick! You now have two accounts!* This swift maneuver nearly sunk the brand by all estimations. In three months, from July to September, 800,000 U.S. customers fled. Netflix had badly betrayed the loyalty and trust that their red envelope had come to stand for.

The company actually underestimated the power of its brand and, by not being collaborative and open with its customers, turned this brand power against itself. In a week, the stock price tumbled 27 percent and outraged customers hit the blogosphere.[6]

The company did not respond strongly enough to the irate consumer base. Customers received a letter, but only after the fact. CEO Reed Hastings went the public flogging route and posted a blog apology that began: "I messed up. I owe everyone an explanation. It is clear from the feedback over the past two months that many members felt we lacked respect and humility in the way we announced the separation of DVD and streaming, and the price changes. That was certainly not our intent, and I offer my sincere apology." It appeared that the strategy behind this fiasco was basically an effort to put focus on the more profitable aspects of the business, with Netflix's marketing team brought in after the fact on damage-control patrol.[7]

"Netflix made a mistake and it was bad," says ThinkTank Digital founder and CEO Tynicka Battle. "But it's something they could have found out in advance, even with crowdsourcing. They could have determined that it wasn't going to be received very well. And it seemed like they just sprung this on everybody, although clearly it took them some time to come up with it, and no one liked it. Even myself—I put my account on hold, and I was like—*what??* Are you just telling me that my fee is doubling right now? That was just not smart."[8]

By early 2012, Netflix had spurred a recovery, adding almost 2 million new subscribers, and announced that, although the share price was down, optimism was up. The numbers backed them up. First-quarter revenue did better than expected, rising 21 percent from the previous year, losing eight cents a share in the face of predictions that the company would lose twenty-seven cents a share. "Our brand recovery is well under way," announced Hastings at the end of the first quarter of 2012. "We still have a ways to go, but we are working hard."[9] "Netflix slipped, but it is something that enjoys a really strong brand affinity with their consumers," says Battle. "It's just that in this economy, with the options, people will say, 'Not for now. I'll come back when you're making some kind of sense.'"

Battle points out that there are levels in the scale of consumer response and retribution. Customers can punish brands in a step that is not a complete absolution, but a hammer blow, stunning but not completely killing a brand. This was likely the Netflix scenario. "Netflix took a big hit," she says, "but they'll recover."

## SAVED BY THE BLOG

Why do some brands merit forgiveness, while others just crash and burn? It's not all about the dollars. "I think it really is about the tone and how you communicate with consumers," says Battle. "I find that some brands are inconsistent with this—for instance, they do some things really well, but their Facebook is lackluster."[10]

Tiger Woods? Battle comments,

I think the thing is, he just was not really likeable in the first place. That was the problem, whereby somebody else, like the singer Chris Brown, could make a mistake and people will sit and wait. The mainstream media just does not like Chris Brown, but he survived a scandal in 2009 in which he allegedly beat up his pop star girlfriend because his fans were waiting for the apology, that's what they wanted, and they waited to see if he was going to be humble, they waited to see if he was going to get back to work, and he really just talked to them. He was open with his fans, who call themselves Team Breezy. He told them he was really sorry, he even told them when he was tired of apologizing, he told them too much—and it actually worked. People wanted to be able to stand by him because he gave them everything, he was completely transparent. He was then able to put out and get support for his next album, which was a big success.

In 2009, Woods was embroiled in an explosive scandal involving his marriage, infidelity, and a portfolio of sex partners. His brand is still in recovery. Battle notes,

Tiger Woods didn't say anything for a while, until he figured out it was time to say something, and then he did. He said something his publicists clearly put together, and that was it. He didn't bother to make the connection before, and he certainly didn't bother to make the connection during. He definitely got banged up somehow, and I don't think we would actually even have known as much as we did if that hadn't happened. He doesn't owe us that. But in general, people want to know the story, as if you were the celebrity's brother or something. And unless you're a super sports enthusiast, you're hard pressed to find those comments on line where people will say, "Leave him alone, this is about golf." Most people will just never get over it.[11]

The consumer colosseum can make, break, or reinstate a brand. Dissing by bloggers has a cumulative impact that has been compared to death by a thousand cuts. A brand like Tiger Woods relied largely on the image consumers chose to attribute to the golfer because fans tend to ascribe personal attributes to athletes who professionally perform. Because the public had relatively little information from Tiger himself, they filled in the blanks themselves. Even George Washington would be on the digital block had he chopped down that cherry tree today.

Being honest, Battle notes, doesn't automatically get everybody an out-of-jail-free card. "Investors and people who are giving you money don't want to know that you have made a terrible mistake. So that can be a double-edged sword." It's possible that by being guarded, Woods may have lost ground with fans but salvaged some of his brand value. Even as he dropped out of the world's top fifty golfers ranking for the first time in fifteen years in 2011, he retained his position as *Forbes*'s top individual sports brand. Woods lost major sponsors like Gatorade and AT&T, but it was nonetheless estimated by *Forbes* that, although he lost $17 million in brand value (calculated by Eurosport Asia at $1 million per mistress), in 2011 he was still ranked $29 million higher than the next guy on the list, squeaky-clean tennis star Roger Federer.[12]

The public now expects the full-monty mea culpa if a brand goes off the rails—and even when it doesn't. To not do so is to put your brand at risk of, if not banishment, punishment, or a forced march through the virtual walk of shame. One ugly e-mail exposé or blog post is not going to bring a brand down—but it can bring it to its knees. See: "Why I Am Leaving Goldman Sachs," an op-ed piece published in the *Wall Street Journal* and on all relevant websites. On March 14, 2012, a departing twelve-year veteran employee blasted once-impenetrable Goldman for a variety of offenses, including calling its clients "Muppets." Within a month, Goldman announced that it was firing off a new PR initiative around its CEO, Lloyd Blankfein.[13]

This was hardly a secret, closed-door strategy, and it was, in fact, featured on AOL's home page for all to see. Taken in infinite multiples, bites out of any brand, no matter how august or seemingly invincible, can result in being pecked to death by goslings.

But the good news about being transparent from the get-go is that the blogosphere that made you can also save you. Although the CEO may not feel comfortable stripping naked and laying it all out for the consumers, it's now the expectation. But there's bad news, too: A brand born of consumers can be killed by consumers. And to assume less is the most predictable form of brand suicide.

## FACEBOOK TO THE TEST

Perhaps the ultimate test, to date, will be the net result of Facebook's IPO face plant—the stumble of the largest Internet IPO in the United States and the third largest in history. After Facebook CEO Mark Zuckerberg rang NASDAQ's opening bell on May 18, 2012, the stock emerged to a tumult of technical problems, process issues, and trading uncertainty that was just the start of a series of allegations, recriminations, revelations, apologies, and damage-control tactics. Facebook shares dropped 15 percent within the first week, in the midst of a simultaneous overall market decline. NASDAQ delivered a mea culpa, which did not stem the tide of lawsuits against it, with claims estimated to exceed $100 million.[14] Investors filed a class-action lawsuit against Facebook and its underwriters, including Morgan Stanley and Goldman Sachs, and there were calls for an investigation by the Securities and Exchange Commission regarding discrepancies in Facebook's financial disclosures in an amended prospectus prior to the IPO; in the prospectus, the company noted that revenue growth could slow as a result of increased use of mobile devices to access the site, due to reduced advertising revenues in mobile and tablet devices.[15] NASDAQ delivered a mea culpa, which did not stem the tide of lawsuits against it, with claims estimated to exceed $100 million. Trading losses climbed in the tens of millions of dollars.[16] This is hardly the ideal scenario for a golden-boy brand.

The question remains: How much of this potential damage will stick to the Facebook brand? At first blush, it would appear to be brand Armageddon. But maybe not. Unlike most corporate-driven brands, Facebook was already not just a Brandzilla, but a cultural-icon brand that was grandfathered in by the social culture, as opposed to industry or the corporate community. Everyone knows the modern myth of Facebook founder Mark Zuckerberg, the geeky boy wonder from Dobbs Ferry, New York. Zuckerberg epitomizes the power of modern mythmaking—few, especially few of those who use Facebook, would not aspire to have been the everyday, outsider kid who became the unlikely billionaire in a hoodie and jeans. He's a techie James Dean for the millennium, riding a mouse instead of a motorcycle—and a classic keystone element of icon branding, one that no industrial corporation could probably ever achieve. Consumers have basically been there since the birth of Facebook. They baptized the brand, dipping it in Teflon. And they live on it now—more than 900 million of them. As such, the consumer colosseum rules. They who made the brand hold in their hands the right to turn thumbs down—or up. It's likely that, no matter how apocalyptic the legal or financial turbulence, Facebook, one of their own, will get the thumbs up, survive—and, in the end, be pulled to shore.

# Chapter 13

# RAISING LAZARUS: THE DEAD LIVE AGAIN

When a brand has lost its luster, and no one is quite sure how that happened, but it feels like the forces it's up against—new and agile competitors, changing social mores, to name just a couple—are just too strong to contend with, what can be done?

Should the brand simply fade away into oblivion? Does it continue to putt-putt along in some lesser fashion, watching its revenues drain away and upstarts race ahead to where it may never reach? Or is there something that can be done to restore the brand's worth and take it in a new direction?

Brand reinvention is never an easy task. History, longevity, recognition, and reputation—all these elements matter in the resurrection of a brand, but it takes more than that to teach an old dog new tricks and make its tail wag in a different way. A successful brand comeback takes hard work, creativity, ingenuity, and a keen insight into where markets have headed and will continue to head. It takes a certain skill to tell new stories that cannot only revitalize and reinvigorate an old brand, but that also can leverage off its past success to build its future.

For Yardley, the centuries-old British fragrance and cosmetics brand, entering a new market with a new owner breathed new life into a moribund brand. Old Spice—the brand everyone's dad used—muscled up its dated image and powered into Generation Y through TV commercials and an online marketing campaign that totally inverted the way a whole new generation of consumers viewed the brand.

If all else fails, there's always the white knight: for example, struggling book retailer Barnes & Noble—a brand that had been more or less decimated by the relentless expansion of the digital book business led by Amazon. In April 2012, Barnes & Noble announced an unexpected partnership with tech giant Microsoft that instantaneously infused new life into the brand. The crash cart has arrived, and—*clear!*—Barnes & Noble has arisen, ready to walk, if not run, into profitability, if not immortality.

## GRANNY GOES BOLLYWOOD

Yardley. The name itself evokes a beautiful English garden in the summer. It titillates the senses with the scents of lavender and lily of the valley, of peony and rose, and it conjures up images of women in flowery dresses and long, pearl necklaces, their faces shielded from the sun by wide-brimmed hats as they delicately sip Darjeeling tea from bone china cups and elegantly nibble on perfectly cut crustless watercress sandwiches.

But fast-forward through the centuries, and you'll see that the venerable British fragrance and cosmetics brand—which dates back to 1770, making it one of the oldest brands in history—has moved far, far away from the English garden. Today, Yardley is growing by leaps and bounds in an avatar that would probably make its founder, William Yardley, turn in his grave, and the talcum-powdered, lavender-scented memsahibs of yore shudder in disbelief.

Because in 2012, Yardley of London is reinventing itself as Yardley of Mumbai.

Great leaping Lazarus! That's one way to save a brand that has been simply unable to keep up with the times in its core market. Now Yardley, which has languished in the doldrums for years due to poor marketing and lack of vision and foresight, is seeing a tremendous rebound in a booming market on the other side of the world. Under the stewardship of Indian consumer goods company Wipro, which in 2010 acquired the Yardley brand rights for Asia, Australia, and parts of Africa for $45 million, Yardley has grown by an impressive 60 percent in India alone and is slated to grow by another 25 percent per year wherever Wipro has the rights.

Call it reverse colonialism and have a chuckle that a brand reportedly born around the time Britain began to really expand its rule
across India—a brand that has not one but two royal warrants, one
that is as British as the Queen herself—should have found a new
lease on life in the crown jewel of the British Raj. Sizzling Bollywood
bombshell Katrina Kaif, one of the highest-paid actresses in the
Indian movie industry and the face of Yardley India, is about as far
removed from the Queen Mother (for whom Yardley made soaps) as
one could possibly imagine. But this reversal of fortune was probably
as inevitable, and welcome, as India's independence from the British
Empire because Yardley, though an old and established brand, had
progressively been losing touch with the twentieth century as times
changed.

Yardley was well aware of that, of course, and through the decades,
a string of owners tried to throw out lifelines in the form of different
product lines and various advertising campaigns that strove to connect
with the social buzz of the times. In the 1960s, Yardley was a fixture
in Swinging London, having forged a connection with the übermodels
Jean Shrimpton and Twiggy, both of whom took turns as faces of the
brand. It was Carnaby Street, miniskirts—and Yardley.

In the late 1990s, under the management of SmithKlineBeecham,
Yardley tried to lose the granny glasses by launching a costly marketing campaign around supermodel Linda Evangelista, the hallmark of
which was an ad featuring Evangelista shackled in chains and hand-
cuffs. The effort failed, while also alienating Yardley's core clientele of
British matrons.[1]

The company later sought to get more in line with the mass market
by increasing the distribution of products, particularly cosmetics, in
drugstores and discount stores. The results were disastrous. Yardley's
flagship London store closed down, and the brand vanished from
upper-end retailers.

The biggest problem that has plagued Yardley has been the inability
of marketers to parlay the brand's two-hundred-plus years of history
into something relevant for the present. In India, though, Yardley's
past is what has determined its future.

"We used Yardley's history as our launch pad," says Kumar
Chander, managing director of Wipro Unza (a Wipro subsidiary based

in Kuala Lumpur, Malaysia) and a key figure in the Yardley acquisition and marketing campaign.

While the quintessence of Old World Britain may no longer carry the same cachet in England, in India and in all the former colonies of the British Empire, there can be no better point from which to start reinventing a brand, Chander says.

"The fact that Yardley has gone from being one of the oldest living brands to the position it's in now in the West is to me a serious case of marketing gone wrong and marketers just not being able to connect the dots," he says.

> Yardley has gone from one corporate to another, but no one has been able to chase the right geographies. No one has realized that what you need to do is grow the brand in geographies where its history, equity, and heritage actually mean something. In India and in other former British colonies like Singapore and Malaysia, Yardley has always represented the best of the British Raj. It connoted luxury, pomp and circumstance. Royal warrants mean a great deal in these countries. For years, Indians had been buying Yardley products—soaps, fragrances, etc.—in the U.K. or the Middle East whenever they traveled to those places, and gifting them to relatives in India. Yardley is a name that people have always wanted and being able to buy Yardley in their home market means a great deal.[2]

But even in a market where British legacy and heritage mean much more than they do in England, Wipro nevertheless had to make the Yardley brand relevant to a new generation of Indian consumers. India, after all, has been an independent nation since 1947, and the generation whose lives were, for better or for worse, directly shaped by the Raj has all but disappeared now.

"We had the British connection firmly built into the brand, but we needed to make Yardley appeal to a generation of New Indians through both product as well as marketing," Chander says.

The product front was easy: "Today, talc is definitely out with young Indians who associate it with their grandmothers, so we decided we'd launch a line of aerosol deodorants at an affordable price point for the mass market, and those have been extremely successful," Chander says.

But the marketing front was perhaps even easier, owing to the magic of Bollywood—the most powerful tool in an Indian marketer's toolbox—and, of course, digital media.

"In India, Bollywood stars provide cut-through no matter where they are used," Chander says.

> On TV, particularly, there's a lot of clutter, but ads with celebrities get right through it all and capture everyone's attention. In India, too, the penetration of the Internet and the use of social media is most pronounced among young consumers. Those are the people we are targeting with a brand like Yardley, so the Internet is definitely part of our marketing mix, and it has played a key role in rebuilding the Yardley brand in India. It is difficult for us to quantify the impact of the different thrusts we have done in standard media versus the Internet, but a digital presence does modernize the brand, and allow it to be seen more as a contemporary brand—which was anyway one of the objectives in making Yardley "my brand versus my mother's brand."[3]

Overall, the success of the Yardley campaign in India can be credited to a seamless integration of advertising on various channels. From Facebook to Twitter to TV and back, Bollywood glamazon Katrina Kaif is the common link. But Kaif alone doesn't do the trick: "She actually works to bolster Yardley's English connection," Chander says.

Indeed, Kaif was carefully chosen to be Yardley's brand ambassador in India because it's a little-known secret in India that she is a British citizen. Born in Hong Kong, the gorgeous Kaif—whose luscious body, flawless skin, and lustrous locks have not gone unnoticed in the West either—is of mixed parentage (her mother is English), and she was a model in England before she came to Bollywood.

"The tag line we use for her is 'from London to Bombay, everything has changed but my Yardley,' so we're hitting all the points we want to hit," Chander says. "We have an iconic figure who's relevant to the youth in India and someone whose every move they're going to follow, but we're also keeping that link to London and England going strong."[4]

Yardley is looking to learn from the experience and is strategizing ways to retain its quintessentially British character while building on that to its advantage in overseas markets, even looking to enter countries like Chile, Mexico, Peru, Argentina, and Brazil, where it hasn't been visible in decades, with the right selection of products.

"The brand equity and heritage still exists, they just haven't seen us for a while," says Quentin Higham, Yardley's managing director. "The fact that in Yardley's case we have two royal warrants is a fantastic kudos for somebody who's living in Santiago—they love that. It might not always be so apparent at times but there's still a significant percentage of the population who are proud to be British."[5]

Yardley may even have a chance to capture some market share in the United States, thanks to the wildly popular Anglo-American TV series *Downton Abbey*, which seems to have spawned a whole new generation of Anglophiles. All of a sudden, the Web is afire with posts from women going gaga over the Downton look, who are wondering about Yardley's Lily of the Valley Eau de Toilette (*Downton*'s lead actresses must reportedly spritz it on the set). Some young women are even wondering what's what with talc. So even as a generation of young Indians eschews the fragrant powder their grandmothers wore for more trendy deodorants, Yardley talc may well be the Next Best Personal Care secret for a whole new generation of young Americans.

## OLD SPICE GETS A SIX PACK

Every morning, an immaculately groomed gentleman sits down in his favorite armchair, a cup of coffee or lemon tea by his side and the newspaper in his hand. He is impeccably dressed, his trousers are pressed, and his shoes are freshly polished. He even wears a tie.

This man isn't going anywhere special. Since he's retired, pretty much all he's going to be doing for most of the morning is sitting in his armchair and working his way through the crossword puzzle, displacing himself only to take down *Roget's Thesaurus* (an actual hard copy—he won't use the online version) from the bookshelf that's across the room to look up a five-letter synonym for "cold" (the word is "gelid"). All the same, he's freshly shaved because that's what he does, and he would never be able to imagine going through the day any other way.

You know this man. He's your father. He's your grandfather. You also know that little white bottle of aftershave that sat on the small shelf above the bathroom sink for as long as you can remember. That bottle, emblazoned with the logo of a blue ship, is etched like the Proustian madeleine into your brain, one of the scents you'll forever associate with your father and his father.

For some, Old Spice nostalgia is what has kept their faith in a product that has been on the aftershave market since the late 1930s. For example, look at this posting on Badger & Blade, an online discussion forum dedicated to shaving, by a presumably young man, about why he decided to buy Old Spice rather than any other aftershave:

> There on the shaving section were bottles of Brut and Old Spice aftershaves. My mind immediately wandered back to watching my Dad shave, and remembering the bottle of Brut I bought when I was younger, plumped to buy the Old Spice for nostalgia reasons. It has to be said, I normally invest in expensive designer aftershaves, and buying the Old Spice was something of a break from the norm for me, so when I got home, proceeded to have a perfect shave. I went through my post shave routine before opening that bottle of classic cologne and liberally splashing it over my face. Memories of Dad shaving came flooding back, and, thankfully, unlike my father, my lack of cuts made for a pleasant post shave splash on experience. Using aftershave isn't normally part of my post shave routine, but it was nice to follow in my father's footsteps.[6]

But no brand can forever rely on the past to sustain its future, and plenty of men out there did not want to smell like their fathers. Like most of Generation Y.

This is a classic by-product of success in the case of many brands. In the late 1990s, the ad agency that handled the Cadillac account noticed that sales were doing fine, but smoke was on the horizon—in actuality, a car crash. Research showed that Cadillac was indeed perceived as a gold standard brand by high-net-worth customers—a desirable audience. However, the bulk of this audience was men over fifty years old. Many were even older, in their sixties. This did not bode well for the future, with its giant generation of Baby Boomers and empowered women. The brand had a problem. Cut away from the long shots of the car cruising elegantly along and the close-ups of the leather upholstery. Cut instead to Cindy Crawford, in a leather-miniskirted-and-booted getup at the wheel of a Cadillac Catera in a commercial that premiered on the Super Bowl XXXI in 1997—and the beginning of a brand turnaround. Postscript: There was one brand hiccup, a classic case of know-your-client, which actually forced Cadillac to pull the Crawford commercial from the air. "The dominatrix outfit," as the general manager of Cadillac referred to it, and the wolf whistle in the music track did not endear the spot to the desired target market of women. I recall discussions of digital lengthening of the hem, but in the end, the spot was taken down. At least it was a beginning.[7]

Cadillac could probably have chugged along and gotten by with a modicum of support from an aging client base even as it watched other, hipper brands race ahead and reap the revenues. But it chose instead to take on the challenge of reinvention.

As did Old Spice, which, unlike Cadillac, had the advantage of nailing its new tone right out of the box when it suddenly and coun-terintuitively leapfrogged from grandpa's Barcalounger to the young male grooming market.

Old Spice's owner, Procter & Gamble (P&G) (which bought Old Spice from its original parent, the Shulton Company, in 1990) decided to make a radical change, completely revamping the brand. In 2006, P&G sent Madison Avenue into a tizzy when it took Old Spice out of the hands of the Starcom MediaVest Group and Saatchi and Saatchi and entrusted it to Weiden & Kennedy, the firm best known for a series of Nike ads taking off from the "Just Do It" campaign that aired on ESPN's *SportsCenter* show.[8]

But even as it sought to completely revamp Old Spice's image, Weiden & Kennedy wasn't about to erase Old Spice's brand legacy; research has shown that heritage is more of a benefit than a burden, as younger consumers tend to seek out venerable products they perceive as cool or hip because they are authentic.[9]

The aim of the campaign, then, was to harness the Old Spice pedigree in order to make the brand hip, current, and forward looking, without playing up the emotional and nostalgic elements of its history. The result: an extremely successful effort, almost a total reinvention, in fact, that added such a "swagger" to Old Spice that everyone wanted to hear the brand strut its stuff. Weiden & Kennedy completely revamped Old Spice in various product categories through the launch of an aggressive ad campaign across various media outlets.

The tipping point was Old Spice's "Smell Like a Man, Man" commercial.

First launched on TV and featuring a hunky actor sporting washboard six-pack abs, the campaign crescendoed on the Internet to a digital level few would have imagined. Barely a month after it was launched online in February 2010, the original thirty-second spot had logged 4.3 million hits to become the sixth-most-watched YouTube video over a thirty-day period, and it caused a ninefold increase in monthly traffic to OldSpice.com.[10]

And if things could get any wilder, the campaign then went viral, crazy and totally interactive, with its star, Isaiah Mustafa, showing up in personalized YouTube clips aimed at members of the public—celebrities like Ellen DeGeneres and George Stephanopoulos, as well as regular Joes—fielding questions from Reddit, Facebook, and Twitter. Hank Stewart, vice president of Green Team, a New York–based ad agency specializing in sustainable brands, noted, "People started tweeting about this commercial almost immediately. Within one day, the company sent out about 87 video responses to tweets that had been sent. What mattered was the quality of the tweet, and how to play off it, and did the person who sent that tweet have a large following. In that way, the company provided a social platform—but did not completely relinquish control."[11]

The cannonball-style campaign was a resounding success, but as quickly as it had begun, it ended. In a farewell video aimed at "everyone," the star took himself offline. But after dominating social media for about forty-eight hours, uploading nearly 200 viral response videos to YouTube, and receiving blog coverage and a barrage of comments

and tweets, the Smell Like a Man campaign was not about to be forgotten anytime soon.[12]

Rather, it forever locked Old Spice into the social media channels
by clearly proving its interactivity as a brand and proving that a brief
but intense online marketing campaign wields a great deal of power,
even in an age of information overload. Particularly one that's burst-
ing with muscle, attitude, and heat. But I don't need any of this proof.
I recall my college-age son, the blasé Cynic of All Time, grabbing me
and laughing hysterically as he showed me an Old Spice spot on his
Apple. The next thing I knew, a bottle of Old Spice found its way into
residence in his medicine cabinet. Mission accomplished.

## READ IT AND DON'T WEEP

Once upon a not-so-very long time ago, a New York City–based Barnes
& Noble set out to conquer the United States. Its modest goal: to bring
the book superstore to every corner of America.

Barnes & Noble was no upstart in the book business. The company had a long history and reputation behind it. More important,
its superstore strategy was enabled by a string of prior acquisitions
that gave the bookseller a strong platform from which to launch its
expansion.

But in cities and towns across the United States, many people
resented the idea of a book superstore. They mourned the loss of their
favorite regional and neighborhood bookstores that the giant had put
out of business. Some of them even cried out against it for debasing the
sanctity of the bookstore by converting it into a supermarket.

But Barnes & Noble didn't care. And after a while, neither did
consumers. In fact, the book superstore became the go-to place for
more than just discounted paperbacks. It was the place you'd quickly
nip into over your lunch break to check out wedding dresses in *Brides*
magazine. Its in-store cafes were a welcome sanctuary on a rainy or
frigid afternoon, the ideal venue to meet a guy or a girl you'd been set
up with on a blind date, the smart people's alternative to singles' bars.
It was where you'd take your Mac computer to work on your term
paper or the second draft of your novel, a Caramel Macchiato and a
scone by your side, or just to look cool.

Those were the good days, and anyone who said they didn't like the book superstore concept had to be kidding. Also, they simply had no idea of what was to come.

Barnes & Noble, like another brand that didn't make it, Kodak, was actually technologically ahead of its time, pioneering in the digital market, but nobody knew it. Who knew that the Rocket eBook, the very first e-reader, dating back to 1998, was launched by NuvoMedia, a company founded in 1997 in Palo Alto, California—and that, ironically, one of the main investors in NuvoMedia was Barnes & Noble?[13]

Rocket-compatible books were sold through the Barnes & Noble website, but at that time, the supply of digital titles was minimal. While publishers had an inkling of how the book world was going to change, they were still somewhat reluctantly testing the waters. But then in came Amazon with the first Kindle, in 2007, and everything came together—the device, the content, and a growing audience for both, all powered, of course, by Amazon's thrust—to forever change the world of books.

As book publishing went increasingly digital, the book superstore model teetered on the edge, doomed, it seemed, to failure. Borders, the other big superstore chain, acquiesced, admitted defeat, and exited stage left. But Barnes & Noble stayed in the game, launching the Nook, which competed favorably against the Kindle and other e-readers. With Amazon more or less the uncontested kingpin, today holding about two-thirds of the digital book business, Barnes & Noble had little choice but to downsize significantly in order to salvage whatever it could of its shrinking market share and shuttered an increasing number of stores across the country. As Barnes & Noble's stock price plummeted in early 2012, the company was more or less left for dead.

And then the miracle happened, in the form of a partnership that promised to change the course of Barnes & Noble's fate overnight. In April 2012, Microsoft came galloping in on a white horse with a boatload of cash. The $605 million deal sent Barnes & Noble stock soaring and speculation flying about what the new deal could mean for both companies, as well as the e-book industry as a whole.

The creation of a new subsidiary (in April 2012, it was referred to simply as "Newco") "will build upon the history of strong innovation in digital reading technologies from both companies," Microsoft said in a statement. "One of the first benefits for customers will be a NOOK application for Windows 8, which will extend the reach of Barnes & Noble's digital bookstore by providing one of the world's largest digital catalogues of e-Books, magazines and newspapers to hundreds of millions of Windows customers in the U.S. and internationally."[14]

The scope of the partnership is boundless, and beyond the creation of a Microsoft-powered Nook, it could parlay itself into ventures like the creation of new e-book publishing tools and increased overseas expansion possibilities for Barnes & Noble (the $25 million that Microsoft has agreed to commit annually would provide a leg up to catch up with Amazon). Some are even speculating about a Microsoft store inside Barnes & Noble.[15]

The partnership with Microsoft has reinvigorated the Barnes & Noble brand. Ironically, the misfortunes of the company that everyone loved to hate for gobbling up the independent bookstore have actually served to its benefit, as consumers and the book publishing industry became the retailer's greatest champions. With Microsoft in the picture, there's still a chance for the retail storefront, the increasing loss of which was a source of sadness for many consumers. The stores had also been subsidizing the Nook and providing a bricks-and-mortar location where people still on the fence about e-readers could visit, touch, and try, which made it much harder, from a cash perspective, to compete on the e-book front. Microsoft will ease that burden. The storefront has been saved, as has Barnes & Noble—at least for now.

Brand reinvention takes innovation and courage, but it is generally cheaper and easier than launching a brand from scratch. If a name is at least embedded somewhere deep in the consumer mindset, if it can be made relevant, and, unless it shoots itself in the foot, it can usually be sent on a path toward success, even surviving a stumble like the Cadillac "dominatrix" commercial. When brand relevance is lost, the emotional connection is cut. People no longer care. Strategic planning and creativity that speak to the audience can grab attention. Social media can be used to make people care again, but once you have their focus, handle with care. Because it's another thing to gain their trust and keep their hearts.

# Chapter 14

# REGULATORY MUSICAL CHAIRS: WHEN THE MUSIC STOPS

It's your birthday and—assuming she's a relatively hip mother—your mom posts a cute little video of herself and her Maltese puppy singing "Happy Birthday to You" on a social networking site. *BAM! Lawsuit!* Next thing you know, Mom is slapped with papers and sued for copyright infringement by a subsidiary of Time Warner, which owns the rights to the birthday song.

Yep, it could happen.

And, many say, it would have happened if the advocates of the Stop Online Piracy Act (SOPA) had their way. Sound far-fetched? When was the last time you heard "Happy Birthday" sung on TV? There's a reason for that—and it's called music rights. It's a highly valid concern. Protecting ownership rights to intellectual property is necessary. Entities that have copyrighted and trademarked their property did so to protect it. Just because those properties are now accessible through virtual distribution and access channels does not make this any less valid. The Web has been the Wild, Wild West of copyright law since its inception, but now regulators are moving in on Dodge City.

Imagine a virtual world—the one that has become so essential to business and marketing—where you couldn't advertise or conduct business with any website that infringes on the guidelines of SOPA.

Imagine a world where a law like SOPA, in its attempt to clamp down on what its proponents believe is rampant online piracy, could make it possible to ban Internet service providers from hosting websites that do not comply. The regulations have implications for both B2C and B2B relationships, and particularly for the point at which they both intersect on social media platforms.

"In this day and age, where just about every brand is using social media in one form or the other, where things like user ratings and reviews are not just good for brands but for other consumers too, this kind of regulation would really inhibit the conversation around brands," says Glenn Laudenslager, president of Charge Ahead Marketing.

In a SOPA kind of a world, a particular site would be responsible for any content posted to it that would be flagged as copyrighted. "If a user posted to the Facebook page of a particular brand and they had a link on their profile to an illegally downloaded song, would Facebook be liable for that posting?" Laudenslager asks. "According to the law, they would be. Take that example and extend it to wherever there's user-generated content. If someone tweets something that flags as copyrighted, would Twitter be responsible?"[1]

According to the law, yes. If SOPA regulations, as proposed, went through, then we would probably have to say good-bye to social media in its current form. Imagine a world where sites like Facebook, Twitter, and so on would be forced to sanitize their sites for anything to do with copyright. The essence of social media is content sharing. How would it even be possible for mainstream social media platforms like Facebook or Twitter to have gatekeepers for the millions of links and posts that are up on their sites faster than the eye can blink? Well, as of this writing, at least, Pinterest is trying. Pinterest's terms of use prohibit its members from posting copyrighted material without the copyright holder's permission. This is almost impossible to police, among other issues. Unlike most other social media sites, Pinterest's technology platform involves not just linking to images but copying, embedding, storing, and making them available for sale. One blogger who researched the issue found a hundred usages of her photos posted on Pinterest, with only five credited. This has implications for search, usage, and much else beyond creating a pinboard.

In a world governed by SOPA-type regulation, social media would require searches, approvals, releases, and watchdogs.

How mind boggling and onerous would that be?

Hence, on January 18, 2012, more than 75,000 websites (bolstered by 25,000 blogs) blocked their content in protest of the two laws—SOPA and its Senate counterpart, the Protect IP Act (PIPA)—that, if they had been passed in the United States, would have curbed the usage of the open Internet and changed forever the way people—whether they're individuals or businesses—have known and used it.

Google posted a black rectangle over its logo and collected 7 million signatures on a petition opposing the bills. Wikipedia blocked access to its content. Craigslist counted 30,000 phone calls to lawmakers, and there were 3.9 million tweets on Twitter about the bills, according to NetCoalition, which represents leading Internet and high-tech companies.[2]

Some sympathetic sites showcased information about the proposed laws and what they would do to inhibit the Internet, meaning to educate their users and rally support from them. Many websites, both large and small, encouraged users to contact their government representatives and protest the measures.

As those websites turned black, protesters took to the streets in major cities like New York, San Francisco, and Seattle, tweeting and texting back to their friends who couldn't make it out to keep them posted on how the "fight" against Internet regulation was proceeding. The real and virtual worlds were united, ready to bring down SOPA and PIPA. In both worlds, plenty of people didn't understand what the laws were even about and didn't care to read them, but were there to add their voice to the fight against what they believed to be Internet repression.

## LAYING DOWN THE LAW

The two proposed laws, SOPA and PIPA, had come to the fore with the purpose of curbing the online trafficking of copyrighted intellectual property and counterfeit goods, both of which have recently spun out of control. Proponents of the legislation alleged that it was necessary to protect the intellectual property market and its corresponding industry in order to safeguard both jobs and revenue in these areas and to add much-needed firepower to the enforcement of copyright laws, especially laws against foreign websites.

The visceral reaction that SOPA and PIPA elicited was completely unprecedented, far more vocal than opposition to any previous kind of regulation.

In Europe, the opposition was just as strong: In January 2012, thousands took to the streets, from Warsaw to Dublin, braving freezing temperatures to fight against the Anti-Counterfeiting Trade Agreement (ACTA), a multinational treaty conceived to strengthen the legal framework for intellectual property and crackdown on counterfeiting and online piracy. The ACTA has yet to be ratified by individual national parliaments, but as of October 2011, it had already been approved by eight countries, including the United States and Japan. More countries are sure to follow.

SOPA and PIPA, though, were not the first efforts by the U.S. government to regulate the Internet, or at any rate what it alleges to be those parts of the Internet that need to be regulated. Indeed, other measures had preceded them, such as the Communications Decency Act (CDA) of 1996, which by most accounts was the first real attempt by Congress to harness material on the Web. Tacked onto the Telecommunications Act of 1996, the CDA as law was, generally speaking, designed to control and regulate the transmission of pornography, obscenity, and generally indecent material on the Internet, particularly to children.

Naturally, advocates of free speech were quick to attack the measure as unconstitutional and were even successful in overturning parts of the CDA that related to "indecent" but not "obscene" speech. And in a 1997 Supreme Court decision (*Reno v. American Civil Liberties Union*), all nine justices voted to strike down the anti-indecency provisions of the CDA on the grounds that they violated the freedom of speech provisions of the First Amendment.

CDA had a clear and targeted focus, says Maura Corbett, spokesperson for Net Coalition, an organization that represents the interests of Internet and technology companies. Even the Internet purists recognize that its mandate was a single slice of the vast and complex Internet universe and that it was crafted to regulate a clearly defined piece of the pie.

SOPA and PIPA, by contrast, were, in Corbett's opinion, much wider in scope than the CDA. And more important, the world—real as well as virtual—is also different from what it was in 1996. Back then, the Internet was in its infancy; today, it is light years ahead and on a seemingly unstoppable course to become even bigger and more powerful. "Today, the Internet can almost be considered a third party, and it functions that way," Corbett says.[3]

Indeed, on January 18, the Internet proved to be just that—"an economic and social medium that can mobilize itself to protect itself," Corbett says. "And it's able to be that because of its technological strength—a strength that allows for self-correction, self-protection, and self-governance. Regulation, by nature, always looks backwards, but the Internet looks forward, and that's where the inherent disconnect lies and why there can't be these sorts of overarching laws with respect to the Internet."[4]

Marvin Amorri is a leading First Amendment lawyer and Internet policy expert who played a key role in the adoption of network neutrality rules in the United States—rules that advocate no restrictions by Internet service providers or governments on consumer access to networks that participate in the Internet. He was also instrumental to the defeat of SOPA and PIPA, and he believes that the Internet industry and all those who stand up for a free Internet have no choice but to play the D.C. game. Just as the content and cable companies will continue to invest more and more in D.C., so too must those defending the free Internet build up their lobbying strength, he says.

"The content industries—the studios and the cable companies—view the Internet as just a means to distribute content through different channels, and then the distribution is monetized. But then, on the other side, you have people for whom the Internet is basic infrastructure for all our speech, who view it as a way of connecting one person to another person to many people. Those people are saying: 'No one is an expert who deserves to speak more than me because they have money.' They are the people who rose up against SOPA and PIPA and asserted the vision of the Internet as an open platform," Amorri says.[5]

The fight for the Internet really gained momentum and force on January 18, as it spread from computer to computer, from iPhone to iPad and from iPad to iPhone, and back again—in a matter of seconds

it went viral. The backlash came with such powerful and unprecedented force that the proponents of the laws had no choice but to back
off in haste, take the measures off the table, and quickly tuck them at
the back of the cupboard.

Round One was over. Companies like Reddit—widely credited
with leading the protest movement—Google, Twitter, and Craigslist
had won the battle. But Rounds Two and Three loom.

## A CHANGED BRANDSCAPE, A DIFFERENT CONVERSATION

For brands, the consequences of broad-based regulation promise to be
life changing. If a copyright owner flags a site as guilty of copyright
infringement, for example, a judge could shut down the site—and the
conversation—immediately. "Brands would have to be sure that they're
not sharing anything online that is copyrighted material; they'd have
to be super careful in their interactions with both consumers and other
businesses to make sure they're not crossing any lines they shouldn't
be crossing," Laudenslager says.

SOPA-esque laws would also burden brands with extra governance costs that would impact their bottom line. "There would have
to be a much closer interplay between legal and marketing personnel,
because the legal requirements would dictate how marketing would
have to work in all online domains, whether that be company websites, social media, or any kind of information sharing or information
storing platform," Laudenslager says. "The financial impacts would be
huge because the level of resources required to monitor compliance
would be huge."[6]

The conversation that's happening around branding would completely change. Today, branding and brand building occur through a
multiple-party dialogue. User-generated content plays an important
part in the development of new products and services. Brands increasingly rely on the leverage provided by the Web.

A regulated world threatens to dramatically reduce that interactivity. In a world where "copyright" is a blinking yellow light, brands
and businesses may be reluctant to dig in online. The openness and
transparency that the Internet, in its present form, allows would be

lost in the drive to be more compliant and perhaps seek safer channels than social media.

"With millions of brands and billions of users generating content, how do we draw the line between copyright infringement and consumer content creators?" asks OgilvyEntertainment's Abigail Marks. "Furthermore, if we are deputizing sites like YouTube and Facebook to enforce these laws, how do we ensure that there is a consistent interpretation of the rules?"[7]

## HANDSLAPS, THE SLAMMER, AND SOCIAL MEDIA

- A Red Cross employee tweets something personal from the @RedCross Twitter account. Quickly, the Red Cross deletes the tweet and follows it up with something humorous that counters the offending tweet. The employee also tweets about her blunder and apologizes. Ha ha, mea culpa.
- The British High Street retailer Primark launches a publicized, brand-damaging staff investigation after employees posted vicious comments about customers on Facebook.[8]
- Starbucks employees appear in a minidocumentary on YouTube testifying to the company's unfair labor practices.[9]

Employees' participation in social media is impossible to monitor, but a single post or tweet could potentially bring down a brand. Employees have always been the single most influential ambassador of any brand—but undeniably that works both ways. A seemingly harmless e-gaffe can be the spark that ignites a million clicks.

Information governance is probably an even greater priority for brands these days than the impact of potential Virtual Big Brother-type Internet regulation that seeks to address copyright and privacy issues. Today, there's a pressing need exists for businesses to self-police on social media, not only for purposes of transparency but to avoid any potential legal repercussions. The haziness of the digital future makes that all the more critical. The information cloud around and behind online brands is so vast that it's almost impossible to know where it begins and where it ends. Even if things get deleted—have they really been deleted? Don't count on it. There are still imprints or threads in cyberspace that a brand may be unaware of, but that can surface at any point in time.

"Simply put, businesses cannot afford not to be social," writes *Forbes* magazine's Barry Murphy. "However, companies that dive into social media without the right policies and solutions to govern usage will encounter information governance and eDiscovery nightmares down the road."[10]

And the impact on brands could be devastating. Regulatory infringements and transgressions that lead to shutting down or heavily penalizing digital brands could lead to a cyberspace version of the financial crisis, where not only do some brands disappear literally overnight, in the midst of ongoing transactions—like Bear Stearns or Lehman Brothers—but consumer confidence and trust would similarly evaporate, never to be fully regained. Even if a limited number of brands served as canaries in the mine shaft, the contagion effect would poison the entire category, eradicating consumer confidence. Any comeback would doubtless be even more heavily regulated, with prohibitive costs for start-ups. Only large corporate budgets would be able to sustain this kind of scrutiny. The small, agile innovators with no to low budgets would be shut out—or co-opted by the corporate behemoths. In a world where authority is already suspect, the authorities would be providing oxygen to the smaller constituents. Remember how in the Old West, Shane or Matt Dillon or some sheriff would ride through that dusty main street and you'd notice that the buildings seemed to have these big false fronts that made the little buildings loom larger and give the little town an image of substance? This new street in cyberspace would be the reverse, with the larger, impersonal entities fronted by the smaller, more relatable ones.

One of the truths about brands is that the more awareness a brand has, the more difficult it is to change the perceptions about it. An unknown brand has little or no awareness, but it is much easier to create a perception. If larger brands dominated the Internet due to governance issues, they would, in one scenario, gain trust by proxy by sponsoring and standing behind smaller brands that sought their patronage to survive. You might not love Big Box, which is building a megastore where your park used to be, but it's hard not to like the sweet, industrious grandma it claims to support. In fact, we already see this trend emerging, as major brands feature bloggers as spokespeople in their commercials and on their websites. When the wolves are wearing sheepskin coats, Little Red Riding Hood better keep her eyes peeled.

## INTERNET FREEDOM VERSUS THE LAW

The fact that there was no immediate move by legislators to put SOPA and PIPA back on the table is in itself a victory because "it's a sign that the politicians really recognize that something has changed here and that the public really cares about using the Internet in the way that they have been used to using it," says attorney and author Mike Godwin, a former general counsel for the Wikimedia Foundation. But the story won't end here. The conflict between lawmakers on one side and Internet advocates, together with and spurred on by Internet companies like Reddit, is far from over.[11]

For Erik Martin, general manager at Reddit, the January events that led up to the blackout on the 18th of that month were "decentralized and organic. I didn't send e-mails out to people or call them asking to black out on the same day as us," he says, "but it ended up with us being the first ones to call for a blackout on that day because we decided to do what works for us. We're only twelve people, so logistically it worked for us."

Reddit felt it had a duty to get involved in the anti-SOPA movement because the company feels a legitimate responsibility toward the next generation of start-ups. Like so many other digital companies, Reddit at its inception in 2005 was just "two guys in a room at the University of Virginia," Martin says.[12]

A strict regulatory environment would seriously curtail the ability of companies to emerge and grow as quickly as Reddit has done, to create and put forth these kinds of online platforms that encourage innovation of any kind. New brands would be stillborn without the great enabler that is the Internet. Without digital venues like www.etsy.com, could single moms in Minnesota sell hip, handmade scarves; without www.kickstarter.com, where would fledgling artists raise funds globally to get a new single or film off the ground? It's because of the Internet that a woman in India can launch a brand named www. ipaidabribe.com, which collects anonymous reports of attempted bribery, a revelatory tool in a country where this information might otherwise never see the light of day.[13]

And a free and unfettered Internet enables its own. A "Boycott SOPA" Android phone app came out shortly before the January 18 blackouts. The free application—no doubt created in a matter of minutes, if not seconds—would allow users to scan bar codes to help them identify whether the products they buy are created by or intimately related to SOPA-supporting companies. "There are currently over 800 brands/companies on our list," the app's creators wrote on their website. Who are these creators? According to nomoresopa.com, "We are two college kids who are unimpressed with the current SOPA bill and want to discourage it from getting passed in any way possible."

# Chapter 15

# ON THE WAY TO—WHAT?

Step right up, ladies and gentlemen! Foursquare, Evernote, Dropbox, Spotify, Pinterest, Audioboo, Rara, Flickr, Tumblr, MySpace, YouTube, Friends Reunited. Following Facebook's $1 billion acquisition of Instagram, a gambling site placed odds on which of these twelve websites would be the next-up acquisition for Facebook—and invited users to place their bets. The post was accompanied by a picture of a roulette wheel. The visual was highly appropriate and, although unintended in this context, an apt metaphor for the role of the Internet in branding today—and probably for the indeterminate future—or at least as long as they keep inventing new technologies. Because where she stops, nobody knows. Almost daily, it seems, new Web brands are emerging. The Web has become a petri dish, as platforms breed, emerge, merge, and purge.

Take Pinterest, the game-changing online pinboard site. The Pinterest community grew tenfold in the seven months between September 2011 and April 2012, catapulting it into position as the third-most-popular social network. Growth slowed slightly at that point, but interest didn't. Here was a way to harness imagery to tell a story, and anyone could do it. It was like paint by numbers, without the paint or the numbers. Brands quickly jumped on board.

A search of the word "brand" on Pinterest turns up a plethora of images that span the gamut from the Nike swoosh to a photo of a condom in a pink packet sporting the Chanel logo. Pinterest became a darling of corporations as well as brides planning weddings and dudes

drooling over cars. Whole Foods was an early embracer, pinning
everything from recycling to holidays to cool kitchens, and, of course,
its own content.[1]

Here was virtual virtuosity at its best, with a brand playing platforms like an orchestra conductor and consumers as rapt participants
in the multimedia symphony. Marketing professionals and bloggers
alike laud Whole Foods for its excellent overall use of social media and
its ability to keep an active and spontaneous yet strategically calibrated
conversation on each of the key social media platforms. The company
has an extensive array of Twitter accounts, for instance, where its tweet-
ers tweet about different topics (cheese, wine, etc.), and the program
goes down to the local level in cities across the United States where
Whole Foods has a presence, so that customers from Austin to Boulder
to Chicago can relate. For instance, the company announced that it
had "successfully cracked open more than 305 wheels of Parmigiano-
Reggiano. That's one wheel for each of our stores…and then some!",
thus unofficially beating the Guinness world record for the number
of wheels of Parmigiano-Reggiano cracked open at the same time—
which record the store already held, in case you were wondering. To
celebrate, its website asked shoppers and Facebook and Twitter followers to share favorite Parm-Reg recipes, posted them online, and
selected the top recipes based on flavor, culinary appeal, and innovation—thus hopefully driving shoppers straight to their local stores to
try the recipes for themselves.[2]

The company implements Twitter and Facebook accounts for each
store in order to deliver more targeted information to customers. "One
of the best things about social media is that it allows us to connect
with people that enjoy eating food and sharing it with others as much
as we do," said Michael Bepko, Whole Foods's social media specialist.
The company doesn't just post coupons to download; it invites you to
"share the love." Overall, Whole Foods's logo resides among a social
community of more than 5 million friends, fans, and followers. The
company has more than 300 Twitter accounts and 250 local Facebook
pages. Its national Twitter account has more than 1.8 million followers, and the national Facebook account has more than 48,000 fans.
It holds photo contests on Flickr and offers deals for customers who
check in on the location-based Foursquare app.

Just reading the company's blog, with its numerous threads—I counted seventy, ranging far beyond food, to natural remedies for dog fleas and microlending—would exhaust Martha Stewart. But Bebko revels in the coverage. Noting that shoppers might be physically in the store only an hour or two a week, he notes, "Engaging with them on social media means that conversation can continue outside the four walls of the store. That's amazing."[3]

Now Whole Foods has dived into Pinterest, with its taste-tempting foods and recipes and cooking/entertaining ideas pinned to the boards of more than 13,000 followers. Disclaimer: By the time you read this—by tomorrow—these and all previously stated numbers will be woefully obsolete. These numbers might as well be written in sand, with an infinite tide washing them away with every new wave.

## LIBRETTO FOR A NEW KIND OF OPERA

The journey that starts online doesn't stay there, but continues offline and then circles back online, in a continuous ellipse. Whereas marketing previously relied on the cut-through power of staccato and interruptive messages, like a series of exclamation points designed to grab attention, today's connection is interwoven, embedded, and experiential. In the new paradigm, the consumer is seamlessly involved and is often the originator instead of the target. The marketplace has evolved to a kind of virtual opera, where the purveyor and the consumer trade arias and, occasionally, merge voices in harmony, joined by a chorus of participants.

"Classic advertising goes on a propaganda-type philosophy, where a simple message is repeated continuously in areas where you live your life, where in the social media world and the Internet world, it's a pull market philosophy where you should be doing things that are interesting so people come to you, and start following you and start wanting to learn more about you. So it's opened the doors for a whole new way to communicate, and brands can use that now. But now they have to be responsible for doing very interesting things and finding ways to connect them," says Chad Jackson, cofounder of The 88, a bespoke digital agency. This might take the form of working with influencers to create content videos, editorial shoots, or promoting brands. The

result of leveraging social media in this way is, Jackson says, "the purest form of endorsement. People might come to a blogger because this
person expresses a point of view and people appreciate that point of
view—then you're getting a really direct connection with that audience. It has to feel natural, authentic, and not reek of endorsement or
seem misleading. You have to give back more to the audience."

And this information flow is not limited to the Web, Harry
Bernstein, cofounder of The 88 with Jackson, adds. "I've worked with
very credible people who don't even have computers, but the live social
network around them is very connected and influential. You have to
go out and give them printed copies, and that can also be effective."[4]

Adrian Ho, founding partner of Minneapolis-based Zeus Jones, is
a new kind of navigator. His is one of a growing number of companies
whose expertise lies in guiding brands, new and established, around
the Internet and social media. In his opinion, what matters is not the
delivery system, but the approach—and he believes that many brands
are still clinging to an obsolete idea, of branding as a communication practice or construct, based on getting a one-way message across,
as opposed to forming a two-way relationship. Today's brands should
be built on purpose and experience, Ho believes, rather than words
and messages, and Zeus Jones has infused this model into the entire
branding process, from product development to design to strategy.

"Communication has become much less relevant to the way brands
are perceived and it's much more about the experiences people have
had with a particular product—their own direct relationships and the
relationships that others have had and that they have shared," Ho says.
"If a brand wants to optimize all the different touchpoints that are
important for succeeding today and in the future, it's impossible to do
so from a communication framework. To even think of digital interaction as starting with communication is ridiculous. This is a framework
that allows for greater flexibility in bringing a brand to life."

Ho cites Google as an example. "Google's purpose is to organize
information and make it more accessible to people, so it needs to be
in all the different areas where organization can help provide value to
customers," he says. "If Google had tried to define itself in the classic
way, by positioning itself around a message that says, 'This is what we
do,' it would have been very difficult for it to move into all the different

areas it's now in. So clearly, having a purpose and not a position has been key in making Google so successful."

Ho's theory is that the purpose versus positioning approach allows for greater flexibility in brand building, but it's also important because of the way people are choosing their products and services. Increasingly, consumers (particularly Generations X and Y) are making their choices based on an alignment of values. So while a positioning statement may explain very well what a company does, it doesn't explain *why* it does that. Without the "why," there's no differentiator, and that can doom a brand to failure.

"There are millions of companies that sell shoes, for example, but I as a consumer want to know why a particular company is selling shoes, and that reason would be the differentiator for me," Ho says. "So not only does having a purpose as opposed to a position mean that things have changed for the brand manager, it shows that there's been a big change on the consumer side as well, and so building a brand around a purpose is a far more effective strategy."

"Modern branding, of course, is still evolving, and we are still trying to figure out its context as social media and technology continue to change," Ho notes. "We do a lot of experiments with clients where we work on their different brands and say, 'Here's a model that we think makes sense, let's put it into practice, let's measure it and learn from it.'"[5]

This approach applies even to venerable companies like General Mills, a client of Zeus Jones. Think that Cheerios, the cereal generations of Americans grew up on, is just lying there basking in a bowl of milk, immune to the changed world of branding, smug in the dream that its reputation, history, and status in American society have given it some kind of immunity? Hardly. In today's brandosphere, where the conversations take place both online and in the real world, nobody's impervious.

"Every brand has to invent purpose and faces different reasons to invent it," Ho notes. "For a brand like Cheerios, there's a huge amount of change coming from the rise of private labels, so General Mills has realized that the only way their brands can survive is by building direct relationships with customers, because if they don't have that, they're at the mercy of their retail partners. This has been a huge impetus for General

Mills and Cheerios, but also for brands in other categories. There's now an opportunity to have a direct relationship with customers, and the brands that have seized that opportunity are the ones that are thriving."[6]

The Cheerios website reflects this. Cheerios clearly has a purpose—to start and keep a dialogue going through a forum for shared experiences and stories. Burning consumer issues such as environmentalism and health are open for discussion. A key feature of the site is called "The Story of Cheerios As Told by You" and connects to consumers' stories about Cheerios on Facebook. Granted, these stories are curated, but the overall impact embodies the trend—that the brand stewardship gauntlet has passed from the company to the consumer.

## REARRANGING THE DECK CHAIRS ON THE *TITANIC*

Along the way, some brands developed a kind of *Titanic* complex—brands that thought their stars would never fade, that they were too dominant in their space to fail (remember Blockbuster?), or that rested on their laurels sailed forth without sufficient sensitivity or prescience to a potential doomsday scenario (icebergs ahead, Netflix!). Brands so comfortable in their own skin somehow convinced themselves they were immune to the danger lurking just below the surface if they did not make a course correction.

Real-time data has allowed both companies and consumers alike to see trends and movements and be proactive in reacting to them, point out The 88's Bernstein and Jackson. Having realized that the same consumers who had adored a particular brand, stayed loyal to it, and bolstered its image and reputation, who had boosted its sales and stoked the egos of the brand managers, could just as quickly turn on them, and that their negativity could spread and sink the ship, brands quickly fled to the social media lifeboats—often forced to choose between the devil and the deep blue sea because avoiding the social media universe entirely would result in equal, if not worse, results.

A survey conducted by the U.K. firms Content & Motion and Toluna, based on the responses of 3,000 international consumers, has shown that this is indeed just the tip of the iceberg. This survey illuminated the fact that many brands have rushed blindly into the social media arena, failing to seek either a relevant strategy or authentic consumer connectivity simply because they didn't want to miss the boat. Nor did they understand why and how they were being followed by social media users, says Roger Warner, Content & Motion's CEO.[7]

How could such superficial initiatives succeed?

Facebook believes most brand managers and marketers are not getting it. Facebook's brand manager, Paul Adams, claims that the old paradigms of branding are still being applied via Facebook, which completely defeats the purpose. Facebook isn't about instantly grabbing someone's attention and immediately converting it into a sale, Adams says; it's softer and more subtle that than that, more about how we build relationships with one another in the physical world, through "many lightweight interactions over time." Avoiding social media overkill means using it to build a relationship first, over time, and only then leveraging it for marketing purposes. The "hot spot" in the relationship is more toward the middle of the continuum and beyond, not at the beginning, Adams says.[8]

Connect first. Earn trust. Successful branding in cyberspace places sales as the last, not the first, port of call.

## IT'S A LAYER CAKE

"The important things brands need to figure out are where their customers are and how they can add value to the communications they have with their customers and be relevant to them on a social media platform," Content & Motion's Warner says. "Some brands make more sense than others, but if you are talking about butter or sausages on Facebook, you'd have to think pretty hard to get the right social media strategy. There's been a crazy rush to be where the customers are, which at a very high level does make sense, but the questions brands need to ask themselves is whether there is customer relevance for them to be on a particular platform. Just being on Facebook doesn't mean that you add value to your brand, and lots of brands rush in, build a presence and then start building all these wonderful apps that are never used because they are just not relevant.

"It's not about getting as many people as possible to look at you on Facebook—it's about strengthening the bonds of the social network and adding value to the persona of the consumer," Warner says.[9]

It's also not just about social media, but about integrated strategies. As the Content & Motion and Toluna study confirms, TV is still universally critical. Fifty percent of respondents still cherish TV as their prime media source, and traditional ads/product reviews still influence 60 percent of their purchasing decisions.

Marketers and brand managers may believe that social media users are constantly connecting with each other, sharing information, opinions, and news, but actually they're only going to let a brand in if its interactions can deliver added value. Most people use social media to connect first with their friends, and only 20 percent said they interacted with a brand at least once a day online. If they're going to follow a brand and stay engaged with it, people need to really feel its value. How a brand chooses to showcase its value addition and then convey that message is the differentiator.[10]

For Craig Dubitsky, chairman of the board of advisers of Lexicon Branding, a global leader in product and brand naming, "relevance" is the buzzword for branding today. And that applies to both a brand's online presence and its footing in the real world. "There is a lot of room for improvement in helping consumers go from doing online research to in-store purchases," according to research firm Forrester's five-year e-commerce forecast, released in 2010. "Only 61% of consumers who cross over from one to the other are satisfied with their buying experience, compared to 82% for those who end up buying online." Satisfaction is key to customer loyalty and brand affinity, so the numbers would indicate that the Internet can be a powerful tool in achieving brand loyalty.

In 2010, Forrester said that retail stores needed to do a better job in appealing to customers. Today, Dubitsky says that's still the case, and the essence of getting it right is featuring products that shine off the shelves in the store as well as generate a buzz online. Doing that right is all about relevance.

"No brand can hope to succeed today unless it's economically and socially relevant to everyone," Dubitsky says. "There has to be some perceived value beyond what a consumer pays for something, otherwise a brand's authenticity is irrelevant. If something isn't relevant, then it won't catch my attention because everything is vying for my attention.

"Today's world offers brands the chance to elevate what's normal and everyday and make it into something special," Dubitsky observes. "That to me is the future, where brands realize that relevance lies in making what's every day into something magic."

This is largely due to the great demystifying power of the Internet. No longer does the image of an exotic island in some far-flung corner of the world carry the same cachet as it did when you saw it in a magazine. Geographies level; borders disappear. Superior technology allows us to peer into the exotic hideaways of rock stars and billionaires and see their bathing suits hanging out to dry. Maybe you can't get there physically, but technology has made it such that virtually, the far-flung places of the world are more tangible, accessible, and attainable. This, Dubitsky feels, has taken away the magic associated with what only a select few elites could reach.[11]

Today, branding magic is all about the banal. It's about making the ordinary seem extraordinary, through a layered and interwoven process of design and execution, innovation, and creativity of expression, that ultimately will result in relevance—both offline and online. Let's take something scraping the bottom of the excitement scale like home cleaning products, a category of products that are the epitome of drudgery. Method, a hot household brand that Dubitsky helped launch, offers a line of nontoxic, environmentally friendly detergents and cleaning products. Method's brainparents, two young guns named Adam Lowry and Eric Ryan, did not turn toxic products green or grant them "the ability to talk to fish." This was truly putting lipstick on the pig: These guys decided to focus on cleaning up the cleaning products space, so to speak, and giving it the extreme makeover that it so desperately needed.

"Eric knew people wanted cleaning products they didn't have to hide under their sinks. And Adam knew how to make them without any dirty ingredients. Their powers combined, they set out to save the world and create an entire line of home-care products that were more powerful than a bottle of sodium hypochlorite. Gentler than a thousand puppy licks. Able to detox tall homes in a single afternoon," according to their website, www.methodhome.com.

The duo also made it a point to zone in on design and aesthetics— with beautifully shaped bottles and liquids in Alice in Wonderland–type mouthwatering shades of purple and red that seem to call out "drink me and I will change your world."

Method released cleaning products from the shackles of drudgery and infused cleaning your house or washing your dishes with a modern, cool, nonchemical feel. Their Facebook page is as fresh and clean as the products it sells. And the brand goes beyond soap and laundry products, with a consumer conversation that aims to be not only reflective of the brand's relevance to everyday life, but to elevate that life by infusing it with something special. Nontoxic—check. But not just cleaning—"happy cleaning," including sleek, simple packaging and a website featuring videos of crazy, dumb dancing. "Give your nose a hug and clean happy," chuckles the site. If you gotta clean your house, you might as well do it dancing.

"Today, anything can be made better, no matter what it is," Dubitsky says.[12]

The challenge for modern-day branding is just that: creating seamless, end-to-end magic that can bridge two worlds, the real and the virtual.

# Chapter 16

# THE YELLOW BRICK ROAD

Futurist Watts Wacker puts it out there: "What are the new aspirations, and where do our perceptions exist that are and are not able to change? A perception is a belief, based on your instincts, not your intellect. And the hardest thing to change is a perception, period. The world as it presents itself and the world as it is are not in synch.... This is not about the rate of change or the cause of change, it's beyond that. It's a conspiring of the economic, technological, and social agendas, all adjusting at one time."

Wacker believes that those people and institutions in power try to prohibit change and maintain the status quo, creating stagnation. "We have this terrible conflict of the world moving toward new social norms, and our institutions trying to delay or stop them," he says. Wacker calls this the Epoch of Uncertainty, and that's where we find ourselves now. He opines, "It's time for a new story."

"All institutions have to change and prepare for the future," says Wacker.[1] In a change environment, people don't desire further instability; they seek the security of others like themselves—a scenario that is throwing fuel on the blogging and reality trends. Authority becomes suspect—and who is an authority, anyway? There is a tear in the fabric, and a blogger less than a year out of college, working out of her bedroom, can attract more blog followers than the editor in chief of *Vogue*. In this light, the power of popular culture makes eminent sense: Authenticity trumps celebrity. If it's time for a new story, the dominant force, those with the most impact and influence, will be the storytellers. In an environment of socioeconomic drift, connecting becomes a "sacred religion," to use Wacker's term. Initiatives like the Occupy movements gain massive traction, as people interweave agendas and demand accountability and transparency. Look for new leaders and content functions to emerge to support a range of marketing disciplines and community programs. They will also impart new ways to help teams understand how content plays holistically within plans to reflect the way people now consume and share it.

Additionally, new roles will evolve to develop, curate, and activate the intersection of marketing and storytelling. In an effort to better understand consumer behavior, the role of research director has evolved to nomenclature including chief insight officer, head of planning, or even, in the case of one Fortune 500 company, chief scientist.

As storytelling gains in perceived value to the business community, chief content officer (CCO) will become a revered and aspirational role. The CCO will hold the keystone position in the Venn diagram of marketing, strategy, research, and media, and, most important, a seat at the top management table.

"Content is at the center of it all," notes Chris Perry, who leads the digital practice for Weber Shandwick and contributes to Forbes.com. "Few organizations have an overarching strategy that channels all this branded content into a consolidated planning model. In parallel, we see lack of defined leadership for overall orchestration and accountability for content-driven programs. This will become a business priority as companies seek more discipline in how stories are conveyed—not to mention cost savings that come with more disciplined sourcing, curating and production."[2]

## BRAND WALDEN

The question is open—will the focus on the new and the innovative continue in the face of consolidation headwinds? There are a number of potential outcomes. Some say that digital innovation as we know it will be endangered if the Internet succumbs to brand consolidation— with Brandzillas gobbling up or partnering with smaller brands.

Others say the support of larger, better-funded brands will enable even greater development.

Robert C. Blattberg, Timothy W. McGuire Distinguished Service Professor of Marketing at the Carnegie Mellon University's Tepper School of Business, sees branding as increasingly critical as the Internet evolves. "Brands will be more important than ever as the Web evolves," he believes, "because if you don't know what the product is physically, the brand will help impart that information. The aspects' and values of the brand equity will transfer to the product."

"What kind of marketing strategies will emerging products need to have in order to succeed virtually?" Blattberg asks. One is a hot-house approach: "Create a small brand, like Under Armour, and figure out how to get, for example, pro athletes or the high school athletic community to accept the brand. There are all kinds of sampling plans that can evolve, and from these come word of mouth." The Internet can also be leveraged to create a go-to brand for education on a product or topic, particularly if the audience is laser-targeted. Blattberg cites Blue Nile as a company that has done a good job of that in the diamond category. "It figured out that a lot of men who know next to nothing about jewelry but who also are comfortable with the Internet buy diamonds, so it created an online informational strategy." Blattberg also identifies a kind of wingman strategy, which eases the path to consumer acceptance by partnering with brands, products, or personalities or authorities that already have a high degree of recognition and trust.[3]

The Luxury Institute's Milton Pedraza sees partnering, and even being tucked under larger and robustly funded corporate umbrellas, as viable avenues, especially for the luxury category. "Many luxury brands need nurturing, and one of the advantages of being part of a conglomerate is nurturing and spreading of the brand. There's no question that there is a huge advantage to being part of a conglomerate."[4]

"You have the big companies on the high end," says Harry Bernstein of The 88, "but they can't possibly cater to everyone, and then at the very low end, you have all of these individuals, mom-and-pop companies that have been able to give it a go. Kickstarter is a fantastic example of a technology—it's called crowdfunding—that enabled people with an idea to get an audience and eventually fund their product."[5]

Sometimes, it's not a matter of either/or, but *and*—a new kind of brand hybridization may evolve. For example, "A guy in Portland wasn't happy with iPhone docks," says Chad Jackson of The 88. "And he came up with a way to make [his own]. He did a prototype, he put it on the Internet, and within a month he'd gotten $1 million worth of funding, and people saying he did a better job of creating Apple products than Apple. Even two years ago, that was unheard of—you didn't have the channels to go direct to consumers and scale for it on a large level."[6]

Following the brand implosion, we could see a feeding frenzy; similar to the consolidation in the financial world, where a Pac-Man effect is rolling along like an avalanche, with larger brands devouring smaller ones like hard candies—Wells Fargo devours Wachovia, Merrill Lynch swallows Smith Barney, Citi envelops everybody. Much of history is the result of reactions rather than actions. The immediate end result of brand consolidation can only be fewer brands. And a kind of relief from the breeding frenzy that comes before natural selection comes into play. As brands evolve and consolidate, we can anticipate a forced return to fewer brands—but they'll be überbrands—and a backlash from exhausted, overstimulated consumers seeking simplicity. This stage of seeking authenticity is surfacing in the reality phenomenon, paradoxically in spite of a current addiction to brands. One also breeds the other. Super successful authenticity often results, by popular or self-declaration, in a brand.

The future would then become bifurcated: on one side, a megabrand monster mash, and on the other side, a kind of brand Walden, its shores lined with microbrands as consumers seek an oasis of calm and authenticity from the noise put out by the Brandzillas. "Yes, I buy the kids' sweaters from Big Box City, and their issues concern me, but I feel good because I also buy hand-knit sweaters from this fisherman's family in Ireland—look, they post pictures on their blog of the grandma shearing the wool. I'm supporting this kind of sustainability." The next step in this continuum is that Big Box City contracts the Irish grandma to "design" and endorses her boutique line of hand-knit sweaters. What if Grandma goes viral? A brand going viral is both a dream and nightmare—depending on who's looking at it. Who owns the brand here? Big Box or Grandma? And who owns the brand equity? Grandma gives Big Box, with its cavernous stores, a certain connection to intimacy and craft, while Big Box gives Grandma awareness and business credibility—but how authentic is that trade-off? The melding of two brands can make or break both the individual brands and their biological brandchild. So, you might think it's always Grandma who has the most to gain in a partnership with Big Box. But not necessarily.

When the Kardashians, partnering with the bank University National, launched a prepaid debit Kardashian Kard in November 2010, the financial terms were deemed usurious, consumer outcry occurred over the obvious targeting of teens and the cash challenged, and it was quickly pulled. It was called possibly "the worst card ever," "predatory," and, as the Connecticut attorney general put it, "outrageous"—among a barrage of many other negative comments.[7]

But was the real issue the terms, the audience, or the brand associations? When Chase announced plans to launch the JPMorgan Chase Liquid debit card in summer 2012, with celebrity financial adviser Suze Orman, among others, attached as a spokesperson, nobody was calling for cancellation. In fact, the card was positioned as a boon to the cash poor. The terms varied, and, overall, the monthly fees and other criteria were indeed higher for the Kardashian Kard, but the transaction fees were actually less (depending on variables). And similar products without any fees attached exist from competitors, including American Express and Western Union. Yet none of these was dunked in boiling oil by the court of public opinion or any attorneys general. (Note: the prepaid market is not regulated in any way.) The JPMorgan Chase card also states it is targeting consumers over age eighteen, while the Kardashian Kard, by way of it being branded Kardashian, had a fairly obvious youth target. However—did replacing Kim with Suze make one card more clearly valid to consumers by way of brand sense as opposed to dollars and cents?[8]

Clearly, partnering, like membership, has its benefits. But in the nine-and-a-half-second world, marketers must be increasingly aware of all the nuances of their partnerships. Brand has never been more impactful because of the unprecedented levels of transparency.

The conversation, as well as the product, is available for all to see and evaluate. If a celebrity partner or spokesperson lends his or her brand, or two brands converge, marketers can monitor consumer and investor reaction in real time on the Web, through blogs, videos, and all manner of postings. You can focus-group all you want, but today the consumer colosseum awaits beyond the focus room door. One can imagine the prelaunch focus groups for the concept of the Kardashian Kard—rooms full of teenage girls, responding like the sorority cast in the movie *Legally Blonde*, squealing with joy at the prospect of having their role model on a credit card, maybe even willing to pay a premium for the privilege of having Kim tucked into their Prada (or knockoff) purse. But then the consumer colosseum spoke: thumbs down.

No matter how brilliant the brand, a core issue in the digital space is monetization. In a seminal case in 1999, a teenager broke through and redefined how we think about music, only to see his business end up in a blizzard of lawsuits over who owned what—and we all saw Sean Fanning's peer-to-peer file-sharing site, Napster, get shut down, only to reopen as a pay-per-download revenue model. That was in the 1990s—and nobody has yet figured out a sustainable model. After years of unprofitability, YouTube ramped up a platform for advertisers on Web-hosted videos, but it is not connected to YouTube's TV app and still does not provide a real answer to the revenue-model issue. And just because we *can* get the content we want without paying for it—*should* we?[9]

Massive questions swirl around ownership and revenues regarding intellectual property, copyright, ownership, distribution, and revenue models. In the United States, the FTC Endorsement Guidelines clarify boundaries for best practices and require clear disclosures about partnerships, product commentary, claims or reviews, and fees paid for Web postings. Bloggers who do not disclose that they have been compensated have been fined $250,000. However, although it will investigate complaints, the FTC does not consistently monitor blogs. Still, the ring-fencing of cyberspace has only just begun.[10]

Marketers can develop integrated plans; but, with the digital revenue platform still uncertain, few can afford to stake the bottom line on unproven revenue models. Marketers are under more pressure than ever to meet targets and maximize return on investment. As a result, while digital brand investment is growing, as we move into the second decade of a new century, the Internet is still by no means the dominant element of most marketing strategies. The downside is often a piecemeal adaptation of digital strategies and channels. For this reason, for now at least, integrated strategies prevail. It's still all about the layer cake. But that's not to say that everybody likes chocolate.

## CUSTOMIZATION VERSUS CARPET BOMBING

For brands to succeed, they must, above all, be relevant. Some brands, like Apple, do it by coming out with new products and innovations every quarter; others, like Coca-Cola, whose formula has remained the same for 126 years, remain relevant by remaining constant. In either of these cases, to do the opposite would surely be detrimental to the brand—as New Coke so vividly proved. Relevance builds the emotional connection with the consumer and triggers motivation—to consider, to buy, to prefer, to recommend. The closer a brand can get to the individual needs of the consumer or client, the more relevant it is to his or her life or business.

If you are, say, a suburban soccer mom in your late thirties shopping for a purse and you walked into a store where the music is set at eardrum-puncturing decibel levels, fogged over with some kind of smoky incense, and the salespeople, who all ignored you, all looked like they just rolled up in an Airstream trailer from a long, spiritual weekend at Joshua Tree, you would probably turn around and walk straight out of the store. The customer experience just would not align with who you are. That store would never get five cents worth of business from you. In the real world, customers are increasingly empowered, and their experience, both in and out of the store, is critical to cementing their relationship with the brand and their propensity to do business with it.

The digital tail of the experiential comet is websites, blogs, tweets, e-mail messages, newsletters, promotions, and even what is happening

in the parking lot. Some Whole Foods locations host weekly farmers'
markets featuring local food and goods in their parking lots. Rather
than competing with in-store sales, they feel it enhances the brand
and provides a gateway that bonds the brand and the retail experience, drawing even more customers into the store. Personalizing the
Whole Foods mission and customizing it to the needs and personalities of individual communities is part of the Whole Foods strategy.
In Northern California, for instance, the Roseville store prides itself
on "paying tribute to Roseville's heritage…the store evokes the look
and feel of a rustic 1940s farmers' market. Historic photos of Roseville
orchards and ranchers are featured throughout the store…and décor
elements were all custom built using barn wood and reclaimed cedar
lumber from old fences."[11]

The next great frontier for marketers is transferring this kind of
customer experience to the Web. As Milton Pedraza of the Luxury
Institute says, "The needs of humanity don't change, just the way they
are achieved. It's not just the product, it's the experience."[12]

Personalization is one of the great advantages of digital media. A
Whole Foods farmers' market in the parking lot can create a push program and drive people into the parking lot, but if they're not already
in the customer database, the company still has to hope that a percentage of those people will take the next step, grab a shopping cart,
and walk in the door. If not this time, next time. Marketers can set up
the affinities and add-on brand impressions, but, especially with new
customers, they are still fishing with a wide net. That's where digital
media steps up to close the gap. That e-mail is going straight to *your*
mailbox. *Your* electronic footprint has told the brand where *you* have
been in cyberspace, what *you* have bought, who is like *you*, and who
*you* like.

In the B2B world, personalization hones in on the company and
involves the ability to target firmographically—title, function, company size, industry sector—the more information that is known, the
more relevant everything from the greeting to the message to the
follow-up. Customer or client experience opportunities have infinite
variations, but as both consumers and digital profiling grow ever
more sophisticated, the targeting needs to be equally precise. This
requires the medium and the message working in concert to tap into

the consumer/client mindset and behavior. Once the relevance vein is tapped, the floodgates open much more easily. M&C Saatchi CEO Moray MacLennan cites RS Components as an example.

> Three years ago, RS Components, the world's largest distributor of electronics and maintenance products, was facing a challenge in engaging with its customer base of design engineers. They valued the RS-Components.com website as a quick and efficient catalogue for picking up the parts they needed, but not as a place to commune with others. In fact, they reported they were largely "antisocial" with little interest in Facebook, Twitter, or YouTube. Yet RS Components understood that it was vital to connect with these engineers early in the design process, as it is often too late to change a component once a design is well advanced. Further investigation showed that these "antisocial" individuals could indeed be social, but this was most likely in forums where they could swap ideas with peers and trusted experts.[13]

And now that it has made the connection, the company can roll out a broader program. In 2010, RS Components launched a humorous viral video campaign championing both its new digital catalog and geek power, which it ran on YouTube, in English and Chinese. The video is a mock instructional clip featuring directions on how to rip up your old doorstop-sized TS catalog. The intrinsic brand idea is that sometimes ingenuity trumps brute strength. A geeky engineering type is shown facing off against a company muscleman to rip up the company's previous monster catalog—and, smart guy that he is, the engineer can do it in single rip because it's the downloadable version. Viewers are invited to send in their own ideas for creative uses of the old catalog, with chances to win prizes. The video "not only enables us to build stronger bonds with our customers but also provides lighthearted entertainment along with the new catalogue launch," said Richard Huxley, regional general manager, Asia Pacific, at RS Components.[14]

This triple brand play was terrific. By leveraging humor, the company effectively closed both the digital and human gaps, gave the brand a smart, contemporary personality, and began a dialogue with customers.

The more personal and customized, however, the more constant the curation must be. Louis XIV was relevant to an entire country. The Sun King brand is still as relevant to a child as to a businessman. Walking through Versailles, even today, occupied only by tourists and ghosts, the experience is curated, consistent—and relevant. However, one targeted e-mail with a misspelled name or title can make any message irrelevant before it is even opened. Relevant website content, which leads to higher conversion rates and increased return on marketing investment, is increasingly precision tuned for maximum efficiency and effectiveness. More than half of all companies are working to improve their Web content, with 70 percent of top performers making the commitment.[15]

If today's poster-child marketing strategy is to leverage the layer cake, then the bomb, literally, of tomorrow's will be carpet bombing, or total immersion. As former Undersecretary of State Charlotte Beers notes, "The ultimate goal is something that's experiential. To have your own experience with a brand, as opposed to being a spectator. So you have to move a product along the line until it ceases to be a spectator and becomes a participant in your life. That would be the standard."[16]

If you've ever had a dog or cat with fleas, you can imagine the extent of the immersion program, infiltrating every possible inch of a lifestyle, habitat, and physical being. This is not unlike what flea remedies need to do to be effective. The instructions tell you to set off an invasive vapor fog bomb on the premises that will seep into every nook and crevasse, including under the couch and the cushions. Humans are supposedly somewhat resistant or unappealing to fleas, and hundreds may be rebuffed, but as any animal owner can attest, you're going to end up with twenty-two bites on your legs anyhow.

This is a strategy to not just reach, but to envelop, consumers. It's not so much reaching out and grabbing as infusing, yet somehow it is infinitely more intrusive. From a marketing perspective, this approach offers infinitely more opportunities to connect than the good old antique roadblock media strategy. Then, you could turn off the TV. But how can you turn off your life?

# BO'S BLOG

Orwell's *1984* had Big Brother watching us all. The truth is, he never imagined that Big Brother would have it so easy. Big Brother can put his feet up in the hammock these days because we're doing most of the work for him ourselves. The digital footprint and data trail that consumers are leaving in cyberspace provide a virtual map to our entire lives. Consumer behavior is now mapped from the womb to the coffin, and a digital footprint lives forever in cyberspace. Every move you make, every breath you take. Big Brother doesn't have to watch you, all he has to do is gather your digital data. Privacy laws are still more suggestive than real, and superior technology allows the possessor to access almost anything. Every day, more and more data on every individual is being gathered, bundled, sorted, shared, and hacked. The emerging patterns give marketers advantages that are only limited by technology and budget.

For example, right now, retailers can predetermine buying behavior based on weather reporting, and police can predict crime patterns using statistical analysis. This "bodes well for behavior profiling based on social media," says one report on behavioral profiling. "Our digital footprints are as predictive in cyberspace as our product purchasing or crime patterns are in the physical realm. The ability to leverage big data sets containing both structured and unstructured information, such as credit card records, Facebook/LinkedIn profiles, websites, friends of friends, etc., creates the linkages to combine with advanced software and human experience to profile and predict behavior."[17]

Whether they are Democrats, Republicans, or simply residents of the planet, most professional observers would agree that Barack Obama's first presidential election campaign was one of the most brilliant examples of branding in recent history. His masterful use of the "Change" theme and his gathering and deployment of digital data and its matrixed analyses enabled strategic landmark communication initiatives with multiple constituencies. Obama's digital strategy team tested every possible combination of data and strategic iterations to fine-tune and optimize messaging and execution. They introduced the idea of "A/B" testing to Obama's staff, using live Web trials to find

out how different website colors, messages, and pictures affected dona-
tions and volunteer sign-ups.[18]

Next up could be even greater degrees of laser-targeting. By tapping
into even more extensive data—for example, Facebook's Timeline—
strategists will get to know their audiences as individuals and communicate in that way. Imagine, for instance, the Bo Strategy.

I have a dog, Waffles, whose picture appears on Facebook, and
I order dog food online. Suddenly, Waffles gets an e-mail from Bo
Obama, the Obama family's Portuguese water dog. Turns out that Bo
has a blog. How cute is that? Even the kids want to see this. "Bo" and
"Waffles" begin a line of communication. They exchange photos. Bo
talks about his adventures as First Dog, and the strategists behind the
campaign get to know a little more about Waffles's family. Next, because
I order organic vegetables from a website, my digital profile includes
that information, and I get an e-mail from, say, Michelle Obama—aka
the First Gardener. There are luscious pictures of the picture-perfect
White House organic vegetable garden and mouthwatering recipes.
And that's just the beginning. There could be links to other websites
with social responsibility implications—animal rescue or feeding the
hungry. A bumper sticker might arrive in the mail—or in downloadable format. T-shirts with pictures of Bo? Why not? Suddenly, I'm both
microtargeted and carpet bombed—and Brand Obama, heretofore
only seen by me on TV, is integrated into my family's everyday life.
That's not to say that the Obama administration would activate the Bo
Strategy—but, the point is, it could. Any marketer today with access to
the data and the capability to activate it could. You could.

## NEW RULES OF THE ROAD

Numerous initiatives are afoot to securitize and police consumer rights
on the Web. But not brand power. Brand power is much more indirect.
Yet brand power is a straight line to profits or losses. So it's inevitable
that some entity at some point will seek to control how brands behave
in cyberspace. Perhaps because the Internet has been slow to figure
out the revenue models, the brand police have not felt the urgent need
to pull together a posse. But where there's money, there are sure to be
rules. And the more money, usually, the more rules.

A classic way to solve a problem is to put a badge on the solution. When I was the ad agency creative director for the American Dairy Association (ADA) account, technologies had evolved that resulted in a proliferation of imitation dairy products, which were at the time somewhat new to the market. Research showed that consumers were basically unaware of or, due to lack of knowledge, blasé about this encroachment. But, when informed that they might be inadvertently purchasing imitations, they responded strongly. Who wanted to inadvertently feed their family plastic cheese? Consumers wanted the facts. But, short of scanning the fine print on every label, there was no easy process for identifying real from fake, and, frankly, consumers felt no compulsion to do so. The result was an assault on dairy product sales by the imitator industry. You'd better believe the dairy industry was not going to sit around and let its market share erode. But getting enough critical mass among individual companies was like herding cows, if not cats, and there was the question of how to handle the fact that the ADA represented the industry in general, not any specific product messaging that it could control.

The answer was the creation of an innovative program to "umbrella brand" real dairy products of every imaginable variety and product brand with a "Real Seal" insignia. This would be made available by the ADA to all member organizations, along with a detailed package of ad templates and information, backed up by a multimillion-dollar ad campaign run by the association. As in most association programs, members who wished to participate in the program would be assessed a share of the costs as part of their membership obligations.

Whether you were Kraft, McDonald's, or a local milk producer, you made room for that insignia on your packaging where consumers could see it. Response was not instantaneous—nobody is ever anxious to spend money—but very quickly, the benefits of being part of the program, and the detriments of not being part of it, became clear, and the program rolled out. Consumers had to understand it, so we at the ad agency created the theme line "When you see the Seal, you know it's Real." We shot a campaign of print and TV commercials introducing the Seal. To build awareness quickly, the commercials featured actor Vincent Price, who, in addition to his heritage as a dramatic and horror actor, had a successful side career as a gourmet and cookbook author—sort of like the Barefoot Contessa meets Count Dracula. (Out of character, Price was actually an erudite and cultured man, and his cookbook remains a classic.) Price's ads and commercials educated the public on how to identify a real dairy product by simply looking for the Seal. Alluding to his horror film roots, he intoned in his cut-glass accent, "Frightfully simple, isn't it?" Price also appeared on *The Tonight Show*, pointing out the Real Seal on packaging to Johnny Carson and millions of viewers. Soon, consumers were scrutinizing everything from cheese to ice cream to restaurant menus to see whether the dairy products they were purchasing, or the ingredients of products, sported the Seal. If not, hopefully a silent alarm went off in their minds: *FAKE! FAKE!* And they would drop the product as if the ingredients included plutonium.

It went way beyond the milk carton and even the dairy case. Fast foods and even movie popcorn butter got Sealed. Restaurants featured tent-cards with the Real Seal insignia on their tables. Ultimately, the member organizations of the ADA flocked to the program, and virtually every consumer and trade product that included a dairy product sported the Seal, leaving those that lacked it, well, suspect. Look on any dairy product you happen to have in your home or purchase today—I promise you'll see the Real Seal insignia. The Real Seal became what is still considered one of the most successful trade marketing campaigns in the United States and a Harvard Business School case history. The point of this story is that when critical mass, confusion, and potential profitability create a delta around the need for an organization or order around a proliferation, those with revenues on the line will create it. This kind of advocacy on the Internet cannot be far off.

For brands now swept into or born of cyberspace proliferation, what form might this take? Perhaps we will see a Brand Commission or a governing body of branding. A seal of approval structure may emerge, with disclosures and information, such as that currently found on nutrition labels and cigarette packaging, that will become a standard aspect of all products and services. There may also be a need to evolve a Consumer's Brand Bill of Rights. For instance, you may have the right to know whether a product is a commercially sponsored entity, and an insignia, like the Woolmark logo or the Real Seal, will be developed to give instant and transparent identification. There are already FTC regulations dealing with this; however, they are neither mandatory nor easy for consumers to navigate. Conversely, small brands may band together proactively to form an association in hopes of gaining greater powers than they would have standing alone.

Of course, these entities will all need to brand themselves, adding yet more notches to the brand proliferation headcount.

## WRESTLING WITH THE OCTOPUS

For marketers who have to show up and deliver results for brands, whether their own or their clients', there is a dazzling—to the point of blinding—array of options. Moray MacLennan of M&C Saatchi notes, "Every electronic interaction is a collectible datapoint, from online purchases to liking a brand, contributing to a forum or just searching for your name. Efficiency, opportunity, customer journey, location targeting, behaviour are just some of the brand benefits. If anything, there is too much data exhaust."[19]

Just as the Internet has opened up direct and transparent communication with consumers, it has also opened up transparency for brands. If you are steering a brand ship, be it battleship or dinghy, you no longer have to hire the Navy Seals diving team to plunge into the murky deep and probe what is unseen at the bottom of the sea—and then take their word for it. The water is crystal clear, and your boat has a glass bottom. You can see for yourself. You begin to think that you don't have to rely on the brilliance of your marketing or communications teams to address these things because you can see and do everything in real time, without filtering. The question is, do these brand captains have the capacity and capability to forge through hundreds or thousands of blog posts to see what the real sentiment is? Is there some kind of sympathy or touchpoint for the brand? If so, then they have an opportunity to take advantage of that opportunity, in that very moment. But then—do they have the scope and the stamina?

The Internet is a monster engine that requires constant care and feeding. But this is often overlooked in the rush to be digitally present. ThinkTank Digital's Tynicka Battle says, "I think it's excellent to see these things in real time, but it also means that a marketer's job is essentially 24/7. As if it wasn't already stressful enough—now, they

have to have eyeballs everywhere, every hour. It's too much for any
one digital shop to handle. It's one thing to monitor, another thing
to analyze, and another thing to address what you've just found out.
And everything's happening so quickly that it's difficult, even for the
brands that are very good at it, to address everything. It's definitely
hard to measure the success of all this engagement and interaction
because if you've got this network of 41 million people, and you can't
sell 200,000 downloads, it becomes frustrating."[20]

Building and defending a brand on the digital front lines is still,
in the end, a human effort, and the intensity takes a human toll. So,
of course, does any business, and hard work is always a prerequisite
to success. But the infinite aspects of cyberspace are both the greatest opportunity and the greatest challenge to marketers. There was
a story in the *New York Times Magazine* on May 6, 2012, about two
extreme couponers who were motivated by extreme financial anxieties to start a couponing blog called *Fabulously Frugal* in 2008. By
spring 2012, the blog was getting 900,000 page views a month, and its
little two-woman business had grown to include thirteen other part-
time workers and annual revenues in the low six-figures. The world
of couponing is a lot more than just clipping coupons; it involves
exhaustive, laborious 24/7 searching of cross-referenced deals and
free or discounted product opportunities, as well as combining of
various promotions and coupons in numerous publications, websites,
brands, and geographies. The women also teach couponing classes
and live the coupon life themselves, strategically attacking sales at
midnight, armed with thick clipping books stuffed with coupons to
score a year's worth of free tuna fish. Then they blog about it. It's
seamless—work and life. And endless. Yes, they created a business
success that helped haul them back from the financial brink. But to
do this required complete, 360-degree immersion in couponing to
the point where one of the partners had to call a time-out and take
a break.[21]

Today, content creation is inextricably fused with the marketing process, and the content-creation machine is not just voracious,
it's insatiable. Even brand-name professional authors, traditionally
involved in a one-person operation—the writer and the page, be it
paper or a screen—are expected to alter their creative dynamic and

pace in order to meet the demands of the raging digital-content inferno. In the past, readers waited expectantly but patiently for their favorite authors to release a new book. People still wait—for a nanosecond. "Today the culture is a big hungry maw," said best-selling thriller author Lisa Scottoline, "and you have to feed it." Authors who once considered a book a year to be a breakneck pace are now churning out supplementary content as if they were on a speeded-up assembly line, producing short stories, essays, novellas, and content that is trolled like literary chum that will build and hold an audience before and after the big strike of a book. If they wish to compete in the world of disposable content and the e-book, authors may be forced to churn out 2,000 words a day, seven days a week. These additional products, which can be downloaded for 99 cents, don't even make much in the way of revenue for most authors, but they are increasingly necessary just to keep pace in a medium where for an author to be absent is to be nonexistent.[22]

Then there's Joe Weisenthal, the lead financial blogger for *Business Insider*, a website that covers technology and finance. Weisenthal sends out fifty Twitter posts a day to his 19,000 followers, as well as fifteen lengthier posts; works sixteen hours a day; starts posting before he's out of his pajamas at 4 A.M.; and is afraid of what he will miss when he is in the bathroom.[23]

It could be said that these are examples of driven professionals trying to create competitive brand advantage. But isn't that true of all marketing? What kind of expectations does this set? And if this is point A, what is point C? Delegation can help, but only to a point, when the point is to get personal—with a point of view, an attitude, a relationship. How sustainable is all this ubiquity for marketers?

It's not.

In 2004, the *New York Times* blew the whistle on Amazon.com, the largest single source of Internet consumer reviews, reporting that a number of Amazon's so-called layman book reviews were not written by avid readers, but professional writers who were paid, if not in cash, in trade. Other exposés subsequently revealed that PR firms had been hired to post reviews, and that, of those surveyed, 85 percent of Amazon's "Top 1,000 Reviewers" had received some kind of compensation.[24]

In researching this book, I spoke to at least one "layman" blogger who claimed to create all his or her own blog posts. Then, when interviewing creative resources, I spoke to an agency that, as it happened, created videos for this blogger. Marketing and creative professionals should not be put in the position of being Cyrano de Bergerac, hidden behind consumers. Although some marketers obviously see this as an avenue to revenue, it's short-term thinking. In the end, it can only lead to one thing: the devaluation of the role of those professionals in brand stewardship. With the Web still largely unregulated and the guidelines issues raging, there are no easy answers. Building awareness around these issues is the first step. And marketers need to make clients acutely aware of the cost/value equation, not just the cost. They need to know that brands are built not just from best practices, but from strategic programs that include ongoing testing, accountability, and data reporting. Without this, the octopus wins.

The good thing about total connectivity is total connectivity. That's also the bad thing. Much about building brands in the digital world is double edged. The tools and technologies are massively empowering, but, until we figure out how to harness them and put the systems in place to manage them, they also have us at their mercy. As with all change manifestations, there is a transition point, and we seem to be there now—somewhere between the beginning and the breakthrough. With the exception of innovators and early adopters such as Apple, most businesses have not been led by a Steve Jobs or a media visionary and have simply not yet caught up with the structures and nuance required to optimize and even leverage these opportunities. Or maybe, as Watts Wacker noted, we are at that change-resistant point that marks the end of one era and the start of another.

Often, there is a paradox—the company is large and well monetized, but the digital aspects are without speed or finesse, thus losing advantage; or the company is small and well versed in digital aspects, but it lacks the resources to fully deploy its skills. In between is the opportunity for partnerships, where one brand piggybacks on another to fill in the gaps. Marketers increasingly see these benefits, as well as the chance to enhance brand equity with supportive partnerships that bring new aspects to the equity—for instance, (Product)RED, which brought a social responsibility imprimatur to a spectrum of brand partners and raised more than $150 million to fight HIV/AIDs in Africa, while lending the cachet of Bono and other supportive stars, as well as the cool factor, along with its program logo.

Then there is the philosophy that if the Internet is accessible to anyone, anyone can do it. "A curated point of view is important because the democracy of the Web has made things so accessible that everyone thinks they can do it," comments Richard Kirshenbaum. "This in turn impacts—and implodes—the value equation." Everyone can do everything today so easily. Everyone can create their own logo. My 11-year-old can create software programs and videos on his computer. A $25,000 website is considered expensive. But if you're providing real service in the e-commerce space, companies can and should be able to charge a premium. Few people have the gravitas to charge for expertise, although if they have it, they will do well. A small number of well-known bloggers, for instance, will be able to charge accordingly. But this is like the story you always hear about the one guy in Hollywood who sold a script, and then everyone thinks they can sell a script."[25]

"It's very important who brands pick as partners," says Tynicka Battle. "For instance, someone who is very technical may say the sentiment is positive for this new 30-second TV spot you put out there for the brand, but a technically driven person who might, say, be responding just to the number of site visits, may not pick up on the nuance of the response in the way someone who is familiar with brand dynamics and communications might be—they might say, 'Wait a minute. People are excited, but they're also expecting more. Oh-oh, how will we address that?' So it's really key that you're not just getting these spreadsheets with data points, but you are actually working with people who are reading the comments and picking out the highlights that you can review and figure out how to address."

Like Wacker, Battle feels that brand marketing may be at the end of one cycle and the beginning of another. "I've been doing this since 1999, and I have noticed that some of this is cyclical," she says.

As brand marketers, we go in and out of these stages where we want to be the first to do something, and then we go back to the stage where we want to hone in on best practices. I feel like a lot of brands are back to honing in on best practices, and making sure they know exactly what they are doing to leverage each and every network, and then as we're starting to move more into cloud computing, we'll see people doing some interesting things again. Cloud computing is going to change everything as to how people communicate. Now, it's on Facebook, as opposed to using your desktop for applications and software for communications, we're definitely going to see most of our communications, whether it be for work or personal, move to cloud computing. It's different in the fact that people will collaborate, for instance, on documents, rather than e-mail or Twitter back and forth. Even though we're still in the early stages, people aren't e-mailing each other as much, or IMing each other as often as they would on Facebook and Twitter. It's going to be really hard to control what is happening, Battle adds, because, unlike Facebook, the cloud is not highly transparent—if someone is doing some kind of collaborative document, you won't know how your brand is going to be discussed.[26]

Communications are moving onto separate online platforms. People are no longer limited to technology that shackles them to their desktops. Mobile? Bring it on. And every day a new app emerges that may or may not change your life. "Productivity is increasing, the entertainment industry is more mobile, people are communicating with certain things in their house or at work from their phones—so people will be relying more and more on their phones." says Battle, "The ease of tablet computing is, I can access all my stuff from several devices. There are so many different purposes, and if we can predict anything, it's that we know a lot of our communications will live in this whole cloud world in the very near future."

For all its promise, there are, and probably always will be, audiences that are not easily reachable by digital marketing. This is why social log-ins are emerging and growing—allowing people to access a digital program via, say, their Facebook account or some other account that is already part of their lifestyle. Still, as much as people are online, a lot of people—aren't. "Some people just cannot be reached through those means," says Battle. "Be honest with who your audience is and how you're going to reach them. You'd be surprised how many people think Facebook is going to be the answer. But a lot of people don't connect with their favorite brands on Facebook. For a lot of people, that's not the majority of their life, by a vast margin. You still have the work of converting those people. We're not there yet."[27]

Even for those vast numbers who do connect via the Web, it can't be viewed as a brand panacea. Marketers who jumped in headfirst have at times been forced to dog paddle back to the surface. Laurie Ashcraft of Ashcraft Research, who reports that 80 percent of the research she conducts is on the Web, recounts her experience with a Fortune 500 company that jumped into crowdsourcing by conducting a consumer brand study reached by a link on the company website. Expectations were high—this was new (to them), exciting, and, best of all, inexpensive compared with traditional quantitative surveys, which were conducted using costly consumer panels composed to achieve quantitatively projectable results. "They got a thousand responses," says Ashcraft, but the coding supervisor, the person who looked at the e-mails to tabulate them, reported a lot of junk in the responses and came up with a lot of comments unrelated to the questions. It seemed like there were also a large number of silly or nasty responses. Ashcraft notes a few of these: "'I like ca ca'; 'I like big poop'; 'You could be killed if you do not read this entire response.' A few just said generically, 'I love the product.' What the client then realized was that this was not a great way to survey their customers, that in order to find out anything, they needed to go to a panel of households that are nationally projectable. If you just viewed this as qualitative, like focus groups, crowdsourcing would be fine. Or if you just wanted to get a whole lot of ideas, that's fine."

"Another route is to curate the blogosphere," Ashcraft says. "Companies that specialize in a process called 'scraping' will monitor all relevant blogs to see if a brand is mentioned and 'scrape off' what is said about it. Then they can code it by positive versus negative, that sort of thing. That's good to monitor positives versus negatives about a brand, or new ideas that are popping up out there, and, if there are comments about your brand, you can respond. And there's a rapidity of information. So, instantly, if someone's upset about something, it gets viral, and people get up in arms. So if you are making a major change, such as what Netflix attempted to do, you could float the idea in a smaller area, or to a smaller audience in focus groups, including online focus groups to see how strong the reaction is." But, Ashcraft admits, there is still a wild card element. "It is hard to test with a regular projectable poll if something is going to go viral."[28]

"The critical issue," says marketing professor Robert Blattberg, "is how companies manage and respond to random consumer observations—not only regulated, crafted surveys. They have to control the risk, and this involves a lot of monitoring." Marketers need to be sure there are reliable, honest brand reviews that are not Pollyannaish, but, it is impossible—not to mention risky and potentially unethical—to try to literally control the messaging. "This has forced marketers to be highly proactive," Blattberg says. "But how do you control the outlier observation?"[29]

The audience is more fragmented than ever, and reaching it is not as simple as a strategy built around keystrokes. In many ways, the phase we are in now with digital media is mimicking the marketing era of vertical print proliferation—the good old days just before the advent of the Web, before the print business went to hell in a handbasket.

Charlotte Beers sees the parallels. "You have now got as fragmented, or more fragmented, a world in social media than you ever had in even the wide array of cable and television and the days when print went into a thousand slices of fragmentation. So part of the challenge for the clients and their media-placers is where you're going to go where you have a quality of dialogue and how you can really understand the audience. If you have a product that has a very narrow user base, I think that social media's a dream solution because you can actually talk to them yourself and solicit them and narrow it down."

Today's brands encounter a pyramid-shaped access model. At the broader base of the pyramid is the mass market, which is generally most accessible to social media. The higher up the pyramid goes, the more narrow, and the less accessible, the constituency becomes—the world of the high and higher net worth. There, the platform increasingly shifts to personal relationship marketing, and the Web reenters the picture, but on a one-to-one, rather than a mass, basis.

Beers illustrates this point: "When I was on the board of Gulfstream, and we were selling a $35 million airplane, that was a very, very narrow market and it was so exclusive, I was not going to be able to reach them in any traditional social media and so in that case, the members of the board became the sales team because they were very connected people who themselves had airplanes—except me. But if you ratchet down, you have the parameter of the price point. Then when you get into price leveling, you can't cut the assets any further. I'm not so sure that there is a readily available social media outlet for very high-income products, for instance."

Beers also sees social media as providing the kind of connectivity that may be best leveraged to build on brand equity and imagery that have been built via other or integrated platforms. "Somewhere there is always going to be this huge need to first create the atmosphere and aura, the intangible aspects of the brand, before you can take advantage of some of the shorthand that is in social media."[30]

The Web is a tool, an innovative and evolving delivery system, but technology has not evolved to the point where it is so experiential that brands can rely on it to replace other media—particularly not the in-person customer experience. As technology advances, however, that may not change. It's also probable, not just possible, that new, unimagined forms of social experience will instead replace those we currently know. It's interesting to think back to the days when the telephone in every home with teenagers constantly rang. Now, the phone rings less, even as teenagers may be on it more—because they're texting, e-mailing, or doing some other form of connecting.

In Victorian times, letter writing was a major form of communication. From the middle of the last century, it was the telephone. People refer to letter writing as a "lost art." In fact, there may be a case for the fact that, because the Web relies on written communications, we are now in the technological equivalent of the Victorian epistolary society. The Victorians wrote handwritten letters; we write e-mails, text messages, and blogs. AT&T has already spent more than a million hours developing its pioneering speech-recognition technology. It plans to release a kit that will allow users to capture their own voice and send it back into the network for transcription capabilities for use in their own apps.[31] But video is also on a rocket, with more than 8 billion videos viewed on YouTube every day.[32]

If Watts Wacker and those of his school of thought are correct—that we are at the end of one era and the beginning of another—technology may actually be taking human communication back to a more primeval time, when spoken and visual communication were the primary platforms. The written communications, texts, and e-mails that now inundate our lives and permeate our brands may soon become as quaint as Victorian love letters. For Generation V, those raised in the virtual world, online relationships are as common as offline. Danah Boyd, a senior researcher at Microsoft Research, notes that for young people in relationships today, who have limited real time to see each other alone and without adult supervision, digital communication is the path to intimacy rather than a distraction from it.[33]

This rising generation, already comfortable with brands as part of their lifestyle and raised with them online since they could first touch a screen and make something happen, has an open two-way highway of virtual communication, with few, if any, red or even yellow lights. But to build and maintain relationships necessary for building and maintaining brands, we may revert to some form of the commercial, embedded or blatant. Already, blog posts could often be called testimonials, especially if they are housed on sponsored sites. Right now, they're mostly unpaid. But that is already changing.

## AT THE BRANDZILLAS' BALL

"These things are definitely going to change life and work, and they already have, but it won't change the fact that brands talk with people," says Tynicka Battle.[34]

Just as technology has accelerated the speed and changed the face of everything else, it has swept marketing into the brandstorm, a tornado that has picked us up and swirled us into cyberspace. We are on a yellow brick road to we know not where. Any road map would be obsolete by the time it is written. Yesterday, there was no Internet. Today, there is. Yesterday, there was no social media. Today, we live on it. Yesterday, there was no Pinterest, and only art directors or crafters made "mood boards" or visual montages. Overnight, pinboards are rampant. And then there's Twitter. It has never been more important to know what's next, but the fact is, nobody does (well, maybe Steve Jobs did). Even the CEO of Microsoft, in 2008, said about the future of apps: "Let's look at the facts. Nobody uses those things." And then the Android app store reached 10 billion app downloads in February 2012, and the Apple App Store reported more than 100 million downloads in 2011.[35]

The two most important words for anyone involved in branding and marketing today are probably simply: "Be ready."

Today's barriers and challenges are tomorrow's gateways and opportunities. Who's to say that someday soon technology won't take us to an avatar world that is fully capable of experientially building brands, relationships, and dialogues? A world where Brandzillas prowl alongside Irish grandmas, where Louis XIV lives forever, presiding over a perpetual fashion show at Versailles, where intergalactic travel is taught in virtual space? A world where we can taste the food, try on the jewelry, sing with Elvis, travel through time? A never-ending candy box for brands.

We have great expectations.

# NOTES

## INTRODUCTION

1. "Kantar Media Reports U.S. Advertising Expenditures Increased 6.5 Percent in 2010," March 17, 2011, http://www.kantarmediana.com.
2. Doug Hall, interview with Liz Nickles, January 15, 2012.
3. Douglas B. Holt, "What Is an Iconic Brand?", excerpted from *How Brands Become Icons: The Principles of Cultural Branding* (Boston: Harvard Business Press, 2008), p. 10.
4. Adam Wood, "Biggest Brands: Top 100 Online Advertisers 2011," *Marketing*, March 22, 2011, http://www.marketingmagazine.co.uk/news/login/1061098/.
5. Watts Wacker, interview with Liz Nickles, May 2, 2012.

## CHAPTER 1: THE BRANDZILLA EFFECT

1. Lisa Robinson, "Lady Gaga's Cultural Revolution," *Vanity Fair*, September 2010, http://www.vanityfair.com/hollywood/features/2010/09/lady-gaga-201009.
2. Christopher Robbins, "'Science' Says SpongeBob SquarePants Makes Kids Dumber," *Gothamist*, September 12, 2011, http://gothamist.com/2011/09/12/science_says_spongebob_squarepants.php.
3. Meghan Casserly, "The New Celebrity Money Makers," *Forbes*, June 2011; "The World's Most Powerful Celebrities," *Forbes*, May 16, 2012, http://www.forbes.com/celebrities/list/.
4. Jim Hopkins, "Billion-Dollar Twins Take Business Seriously," *USA Today*, May 6, 2005, http://www.usatoday.com/money/media/2005-05-06-olsens-twins-business_x.htm.
5. Tamara Scheitzer Raben, "Mary-Kate and Ashley Olsen Build a $1 Billion Fashion Empire," *AOL Small Business*, March 23, 2011, http://smallbusiness.aol.com/2011/03/23/mary-kate-and-ashley-olsen-build-1-billion-fashion-empire/.
6. Jeremy Olshan, "A Rabbi's Mints a Mitzah for Your Mouth," *New York Post*, April 4, 2011, http://failedmessiah.typepad.com/failed_messiahcom/2011/04/rabbis-mints-a-mitzvah-for-your-mouth-23.
7. Richard Kirshenbaum, interview with Liz Nickles, January 31, 2012.

## CHAPTER 2: BRAVE NEW BRAND WORLD

1. Richard Kirshenbaum, interview with Liz Nickles, January 31, 2012.

2. Tara Palmieri, "Summer Babies Born Losers, Posh Moms Fear," *New York Post*, March 26, 2012, http://www.nypost.com/p/news/local/manhattan/summer_babies_born_losers_posh_moms_Gl6YuLf7h5RP2x1mB5Jn5M.
3. Terri Reid, "Branding Your Funeral Home," *Director*, August 2005, http://www.nfda.org/articles-arrangingafuneral/article/1595-.htm.
4. "Back with a Brand: Troubled Tiger Woods Is Still on Top," CNN.com, October 4, 2011, http://articles.cnn.com/2011–10-04/golf/sport_golf_golf-tiger-woods-forbes_1_elin-nordegren-brand-value-golfers?_s=PM:GOLF.
5. Kirshenbaum, interview with Liz Nickles, January 31, 2012.

CHAPTER 3: ONCE UPON A TIME

1. James Theall, "CSI: PowerPoint Reuse Design Crimes," *SlideManager*, n.d., http://www.slidemanager.biz/slidemanager%20powerpoint%20reuse%20crimes.html.
2. Renie McClay, ed., *Sales Training Solutions* (New York: Kaplan Publishing, 2006).
3. *Think Geek*, http://www.thinkgeek.com/geektoys/cubegoodies/c208/.
4. Dan Lyons, "Facebook Busted in Clumsy Smear on Google," *Daily Beast*, May 11, 2011, http://www.thedailybeast.com/articles/2011/05/12/facebook-busted-in-clumsy-smear-attempt-on-google.html.
5. Jonathan Gottschall, *The Storytelling Animal: How Stories Make Us Human* (Boston/New York: Houghton Mifflin Harcourt, 2012) pp. 148, 149.
6. Douglas B. Holt, "What Is an Iconic Brand?", excerpted from *How Brands Become Icons: The Principles of Cultural Branding* (Boston: Harvard Business Press, 2008).
7. Ray Gaulke, interview with Liz Nickles, December 20, 2011.
8. Julia Boorstin, "Pinterest's Growth Comes Back to Earth," *Media Money with Julia Boorstin*, CNBC, March 29, 2012, http://www.cnbc.com/id/46892680/Pinterest_s_Growth_Comes_Back_to_Earth.
9. Jason Damata, interview with Liz Nickles, January 20, 2012.
10. Charlotte Beers, interview with Liz Nickles, February 10, 2012, www.charlottebeers.com.
11. Rolf Jensen, *The Dream Society: How the Coming Shift from Information to Imagination Will Transform Your Business* (New York: McGraw-Hill, 1999), pp. 17–18.
12. Meghan Casserly, "Bethenny Frankel's (Skinnygirl) Family Expands to Include Wine…and Vodka!", *Forbes*, February 24, 2012, http://www.forbes.com/sites/meghancasserly/2012/02/24/bethenny-frankels-skinnygirl-family-expands-to-include-wine-and-vodka/; "Fastest Growing Liquor Brands: Bethenny Frankel's Skinnygirl Takes the Lead," *Huffington Post*, April 9, 2012, http://www.huffingtonpost.com/2012/04/09/fastest-growing-liquor-brands_n_1412417.html.
13. Rolf Jensen, interview with Liz Nickles January 10, 2012.
14. The World Factbook, Central Intelligence Agency, https://www.cia.gov/library/publications/the-world-factbook/fields/2177.html.
15. Beers, interview with Liz Nickles, February 10, 2012.
16. Rolf Jensen, interview with Liz Nickles, January 10, 2012.
17. Damata, interview with Liz Nickles, January 20, 2012.

18. Jensen, interview with Liz Nickles, January 10, 2012.
19. Watts Wacker, interview with Liz Nickles, May 2, 2012.
20. Ibid.
21. Todd Semrau, "Dust in the Wind," April 6, 2012, http://www.urbaneats.net/dust-in-the-wind/.

## CHAPTER 4: IF BIEBER WAS A BURGER

1. Evan Jacobs, "Eight Brand Success Pointers From Coca-Cola: Insight from ad:tech, New York, Brafton News, November 11, 2011, http://www.brafton.com/blog/eight-brand-success-pointers-from-coca-cola-insight-from-adtech-new-york.
2. Robert Dougherty, "Justin Bieber New Haircut Loses Twitter Fans," February 24, 2011, Yahoo! Contributor Network, http://voices.yahoo.com/shared/orint.shtml?content_type=article&content.
3. Dan Schawbel, "Inside the World of Justin Bieber: An Interview with Manager Scooter Braun," *Forbes*, February 11, 2012, http://www.forbes.com/sites/danschawbel/2011/02/11/inside-the-brand-of-justin-bieber-an-interview-with-manager-scooter-braun/.
4. Ibid.
5. Simon Owens, "The Secrets of Lady Gaga's Social Media Success," The Next Web, March 15, 2011, http://thenextweb.com/media/2011/03/15/the-secrets-of-lady-gagas-social-media-success/.
6. https://twitter.com/ladygaga/status/45770377338695680.
7. Tynicka Battle, interview with Liz Nickles, May 8, 2012.
8. Schawbel, "Inside the World of Justin Bieber; An Interview with Manager Scooter Braun."
9. Dan Schawbel, interview with Liz Nickles January 20, 2012.
10. Doug Hall, interview with Liz Nickles January 15, 2012.
11. Jason Damata, interview with Liz Nickles, January 20, 2012.
12. Battle, interview with Liz Nickles, May 8, 2012.
13. Marissa Bronfman, "The Undeniably Quirky Charm of the Man Repeller," *Huffington Post*, May 3, 2011, http://www.huffingtonpost.com/marissa-bronfman/the-undeniably-quirky-cha_b_856427.html.
14. Milton Pedraza, interview with Liz Nickles, April 18, 2012.
15. Antonia Fraser, *Marie Antoinette: The Journey* (New York: N. A. Talese/Doubleday, 2001).
16. Stephen Hess, interview with Liz Nickles, February 2, 2012.
17. Laurie Ashcraft, interview with Liz Nickles, May 12, 2012.
18. "Coke Lore: The Real Story of New Coke," Coca-Cola Company, n.d., http://www.thecoca-colacompany.com/heritage/cokelore_newcoke.html.
19. Damata, interview with Liz Nickles, January 20, 2012.
20. Robin Jay Miller, "Coke's Fantastic Social 'Un-Commercial' Rewards Honesty," December 7, 2011, http://www.socialmediatoday.com.
21. Jeffrey Graham, "Coke Is a Winner on Facebook, Twitter," *USA Today*, November 8, 2011, http://www.usatoday.com/tech/columnist/talkingtech/story/2011–11-08/coca-cola-social-media/51127040/1.

22. Wendy Clark, "Clark on Coca-Cola's Use of Social Media," Coca-Cola Company, December 9, 2011, http://www.thecoca-colacompany.com/dynamic/leadershipviewpoints/2011/12/clark-on-coca-colas-use-of-social-media.html.
23. Richard Kirshenbaum, interview with Liz Nickles, January 31, 2012.


CHAPTER 5: "OH THIS IS GOING TO BE ADDICTIVE"

1. Dom Sagolla, "How Twitter Was Born," *140characters*, January 30, 2009, http://www.140characters.com.
2. David Sano, "Twitter Creator Jack Dorsey Illuminates the Site's Founding Document," *Los Angeles Times*, February 18, 2009, http://latimesblogs.latimes.com/technology/2009/02/twitter-creator.html.
3. "Women's World Cup Final Breaks Twitter Record," *ESPN*, July 18, 2011, http://espn.go.com/sports/soccer/news/_/id/6779582/women-world-cup-final-breaks-Twitter-record.
4. "Average Time Spent Online per U.S. Visitor in 2010," *comScore Data Mine*, January 13, 2011, http://www.comscoredatamine.com.
5. "Generation M2: Media in the Lives of 8- to 18-Year-Olds," Kaiser Family Foundation, http://www.kff.org/entmedia/mh012010pkg.cfm.
6. April Dembosky, "With Friends Like These…," *FT Weekend Magazine*, May 19–20, 2012, p. 22.
7. "Addiction to Social Networking Causes Serious Mental Health Issues According to a New Study," Center for Internet Addiction Recovery blog post, October 27, 2011, http://netaddictionrecovery.blogspot.com/2011_10_01_archive.html.
8. "Internet Addiction Among College Students: 10 Startling Trends," August 30, 2011, Center for Internet Addiction recovery blog post, http://netaddictionrecovery.blogspot.com/2011_08_01_archive.html.
9. "A Growing Epidemic," http://www.netaddiction.com.
10. Kimberly S. Young, *Caught in the Net: How to Recognize the Signs of Internet Addiction—And a Winning Strategy for Recovery* (New York: John Wiley, 1998).
11. Kimberly S. Young, interview with Liz Nickles, February 2, 2012.
12. "A New Breed: Opportunities for Wealth Managers to Connect with Gen X and Y," Deloitte, 2008, http://www.deloitte.com/view/en_us/us/f52afd0057101210-VgnVCM100000ba42f00aRCRD.htm.
13. "Daily Media Use Among Children and Teens Up Dramatically from Five Years Ago," Henry J. Kaiser Family Foundation, January 20, 2010, http://http://www.kff.org/entmedia/entmedia012010nr.cfm.
14. P&G corporate website, P&G Views, http://news.pg.com/pg_views.
15. Doug Hall, interview with Liz Nickles, January 20, 2010.
16. Christopher Rick, "56 Million Americans Beyond TV Advertising's Reach Says SAY Media," *REELSEO*, http://www.reelseo.com/beyond-tv-ad-reach/.
17. Jason Damata, interview with Liz Nickles, January 20, 2012.
18. Stuart Feil, "The Time for Tablets," *Adweek*, February 13–19, 2012, pp. M1–M5.
19. Ibid., p. M5.

## CHAPTER 6: BURY ME BRANDED

1. Dan Schawbel, interview with Liz Nickles, January 20, 2012.
2. Catherine L. Mann, "Start-up Firms in the Financial Crisis," *Communities and Banking*, Federal Reserve Bank of Boston, Fall 2011.
3. "Red Sox Fans Can Get Logo on Coffins," *UPI.com*, December 1, 2008, http://www.upi.com/Odd_News/2008/12/01/Red-Sox-fans-can-get-logo-on-coffins/UPI-97801228152833/.
4. Christine Pepper, interview with Liz Nickles.
5. Edwards, Elizabeth, *Resilience: Reflections on the Burdens and Gifts of Facing Life's Adversities* (New York: Broadway Books, 2009) Chapter 7, pp 92, 93.
6. Richard Kirshenbaum, interview with Liz Nickles, January 31, 2012.
7. Chad Jackson and Harry Bernstein, interview with Liz Nickles, February 9, 2012.

## CHAPTER 7: A TALE OF THREE KINGS

1. Tony Spawforth, *Versailles: A Biography of a Palace* (New York: St. Martin's Griffin, 2008).
2. Suzy Menkes, "When Branding Was Fit for a King," *New York Times,* December 14, 2009, http://www.nytimes.com/2009/12/15/fashion/15iht-flouis.html.
3. Caroline Roux, "Steve Jobs—The Sun King of Cupertino," *Phaidon*, October 6, 2011, http://www.phaidon.com/agenda/design/articles/2011/october/06/steve-jobs-the-sun-king-of-cupertino/.
4. Elaine Louie, "New Sunrise for Palace," *New York Times*, December 12, 1991, http://www.nytimes.com/1991/12/12/garden/currents-new-sunrise-for-palace.html.
5. Alan Hanson, "The Amazing Comeback of Colonel Tom Parker," *Elvis History Blog,* http://www.elvis-history-blog.com/colonel-tom-parker.html.
6. Sean Donnelly, "Elvis: The King of Rock 'n' Roll (and Branding)," *GS Design*, January 12, 2010, http://www.gsdesign.com/blog/Elvis-king-rockpn-roll-and-branding.
7. "The World Factbook," Central Intelligence Agency, https://www.cia.gov/library/publications/the-world-factbook/fields/2177.html.
8. John Egan, "Viva Elvis!" *Technorati*, February 7, 2011, http://technorati.com/business/article/viva-elvis-company-adds-licensing-deals/#ixzz1qBu60IvZ; "About the King," *Elvis Presley: Official Site of the King of Rock 'n' Roll*, http://www.elvis.com/about-the-king/.
9. "Jackson Earnings Grow by Millions after Death by Tim Arango," *New York Times*, August 12, 2009, http://www.nytimes.com/2009/08/13/business/media/13jackson.html.
10. Scott Williams, interview with Liz Nickles, April 10, 2012.
11. Ibid.
12. *Elvis Presley: Official Site of the King of Rock 'n' Roll*, http://www.elvis.com/about-the-king/.
13. Williams, interview with Liz Nickles, April 10, 2012.
14. James Sullivan, "Twisted Tales: Elvis Impersonators Come in All sizes, Colors and Genders," *Spinner*, January 8, 2010, http://www.spinner.com/2010/01/08/twisted-tales-elvis-impersonators-come-in-all-sizes-colors/.

15. "75,000 Elvis Fans Attend Vigil", *Elvis Presley: Official Site of the King of Rock 'n' Roll*, August 16, 2012, http://www.elvis.com/news/detail.aspx?id=6560.

16. Williams, interview with Liz Nickles, April 10, 2012.

17. Ibid.

18. Kim Hartman, "American Idol Introduces Fans to Facebook Voting," *Digital Journal*, March 1, 2011, http://wwwdigitaljournal.com/article/304158#ixzz1q BxW6fTO.

19. Aileen Jacobsen, "Kennedys Continue to Be a Popular Topic," *Baltimore Sun*, October 23, 2001, http://articles.baltimoresun.com/keyword/jacqueline-kennedy -onassis.

20. Tina Cassidy, *Jackie After O: One Remarkable Year When Jacqueline Kennedy Onassis Defied Expectations and Rediscovered Her Dreams*, (New York: HarperCollins It Books, 2012), p. 243.

21. Tim Raphael, "Opinion: JFK-Nixon Debates at 50: A Defining Moment," *Northjersey.com*, September 26, 2010, http://www.northjersey.com/news/opin-ions/debates_092610.html.

22. James Piereson, *Camelot and the Cultural Revolution: How the Assassination of John F. Kennedy Shattered American Liberalism* (New York: Encounter Books, 2007).

23. Ibid.

24. James Pierson, interview with Liz Nickles, March 23, 2012.

25. Sally Bedell Smith, *Grace and Power: The Private World of the Kennedy White House*, (New York: Random House, 2004).

26. John J. Miller and James Piereson, NPR interview, "The Day the Music Died," June 19, 2007.

27. Piereson, interview with Liz Nickles, March 23, 2012.

28. Ibid.

29. Ibid.

30. John J. Miller and James Piereson, "The Day the Music Died," NPR Interview, June 19, 2007.

31. Michael O'Brien, *John F. Kennedy: A Biography* (New York: St. Martin's Press, 2005).

32. Susan Boer, "Jacqueline Kennedy Helped Define the Terms History Uses about JFK—The Mystique of Camelot," *Baltimore Sun*, May 27, 1995.

33. O'Brien, *John F. Kennedy: A Biography*.

34. Alice Kaplan, *Dreaming in French: The Paris Years of Jacqueline Bouvier Kennedy, Susan Sontag and Angela Davis* (Chicago: University of Chicago Press, 2012).

35. J. Randy Taraborrelli, *After Camelot: A Personal History of the Kennedy Family 1958 to the Present* (New York: Grand Central Publishing, 2012), p. xviii.

36. Piereson, interview with Liz Nickles, March 23, 2012.

## CHAPTER 8: FROM BOATERS TO BLOGGERS

1. "Oh, He's a Lying, Cheating…What? Stella McCartney on the Job Offer from Tom Ford (That He Denies) and Her First Flop," *Daily Mail Online*, February 25,

2012, http://www.dailymail.co.uk/femail/article-2106021/Stella-McCartney-job-offer-Tom-Ford-denies-flop.html.

2. Edmonde Charles-Roux, *Chanel and Her World* (New York: Vendome Press, 2005), 94.
3. Ibid.
4. Tilar J. Mazzeo, *The Secret of Chanel No. 5: The Intimate History of the World's Most Famous Perfume* (New York: Harper Perennial, 2011), p. 215.
5. Leandra Medine, interview with Liz Nickles, March 30, 2012.
6. Meredith Galante, "The Man Repeller: How a 23-Year-Old Blogger Wound Up on the Runway at New York Fashion Week," *Business Insider*, September 26, 2011, http://www.businessinsider.com/man-repeller-leandra-medine-blogger-fashion-2011–9.
7. Stephanie Kelly, "Student Guest Post: The Man Repeller Kicks It Up a Notch," *Editor's Desk*, March 25, 2012, http://editdesk.wordpress.com/2012/03/24/man-repeller/.
8. Medine, interview with Liz Nickles March 30, 2012.
9. Ibid.
10. Ibid.
11. Ibid.
12. Ibid.
13. Ibid.
14. Ibid.
15. Marissa Bronfman, "The Undeniably Quirky Charm of the Man Repeller," *Huffington Post*, April 8, 2012, http://www.huffingtonpost.com/marissa-bronfman/the-undeniably-quirky-cha_b_856427.html.
16. Medine, interview with Liz Nickles, March 30. 2012.

## CHAPTER 9: DIAMOND DUST

1. Susan Gunelius, interview with Savita Iyer, April 2, 2012.
2. Giselle Abramovich, "Battle of the Digital Brands, Tiffany vs. Zales," *Digiday*, April 24, 2012, http://www.digiday.com/brands/battle-of-the-digital-brands-tiffany-vs-zales/.
3. Lauren Indvik, "Tiffany & Co. Releases a User-Generated Map of the World's Most Romantic Moments," *Mashable Business*, June 1, 2011, http://mashable.com/2011/06/01/tiffany-what-makes-love-true/.
4. Gunelius, interview with Savita Iyer, April 2, 2012.
5. Rimma Katz, "Tiffany & Co., Marries Mobile with Interactive to Sell Engagement Rings," *Mobile Marketer*, January 15, 2010, http://www.mobile-marketer.com/cms/news/content/6548.html.
6. "Supply Chain Management of Harry Winston," Elements of Logistics forums, *Management Paradise*, January 10, 2011, http://www.managementparadise.com/forums/elements-logistics/212492-supply-chain-management-harry-winston.html.
7. Robert Scott, interview with Liz Nickles, May 11, 2012.
8. Ibid.

9. Harry Winston, "Commitment to Philanthropy," n.d., http://www.harrywinston.com/charitablegiving.
10. Scott, interview with Liz Nickles, May 11, 2012.
11. "Tate and BMW announce major new international partnership: BMW Tate Live," Art Daily, http://www.artdaily.com/section/lastweek/index.asp?int_sec=11&int_new=51126&int_modo=2#.UC1qoaAmySo.
12. Anna Rudenko, "BMW Guggenheim Lab Opens in New York, Launching Six-Year Worldwide Tour," Popsop, August 3, 2011, http://popsop.com/48148; "What Is the Lab?", 2012, http://www.bmwguggenheimlab.org/what-is-the-lab; Josh Rubin, "BMW Launches Their Bold Six-Year-Long Program to Dissect Urban Culture," BMW Guggenheim Lab, August 4, 2011, http://www.coolhunting.com/culture/bmw-guggenheim-lab-nyc.php.
13. "About Hermès," http://www.hermesfan.com.
14. Robin Givhan, "Oprah and the View from Outside Hermes' Paris Door," Washington Post, June 24, 2005, http://www.washingtonpost.com/wp-dyn/content/article/2005/06/23/AR2005062302086.html.
15. Milton Pedraza, interview with Liz Nickles, April 18, 2012.
16. Josephine Lipp, "Burberry Wants to Keep Its Digital Lead in the Luxury Industry," Social Media and Luxury, June 27, 2010, http://luxurysocialmedia.wordpress.com/2010/06/27/burberry-wants-to-keep-its-digital-lead-in-the-luxury-industry/.
17. Aimee Groth, "LVMH/Louis Vuitton is Redefining Luxury Marketing with NOWNESS.com," Business Insider, August 2, 2011, http://articles.businessinsider.com/2011-08-02/strategy/30063180_1_bernard-arnault-lvmh-louis-vuitton.
18. Pedraza, interview with Liz Nickles, April 18, 2012.
19. Jason Chow, "Dolce & Gabbana Apologizes for Photo Spat," Wall Street Journal, January 18, 2012, http://blogs.wsj.com/scene/2012/01/18/dolce-gabbana-apologizes-for-photo-spat/.
20. Pedraza, interview with Liz Nickles, April 18, 2012.
21. Miguel Levia-Gomez, "A-Class Mercedes Uses QR Codes in 2013 Model," TCMnet, January 24, 2012, http://www.tmcnet.com/topics/articles/258846-a-class-mercedes-uses-qr-codes-2013-model.htm.

## CHAPTER 10: THE VIRTUAL GOLD RUSH

1. Steve Wiegand, "The California Gold Rush: An Era Remembered," originally published in the Sacramento Bee, January 18, 1998, http://www.calgoldrush.com/part1/01overview.html.
2. Ibid.
3. "A Lesson from a Gold Rush Millionaire," Prospector Site, http://www.theprospectorsite.com/blog/?p=1704.
4. "Straus, Levi, (1829–1902)," German American History & Heritage, n.d., http://www.germanheritage.com/biographies/mtoz/strauss.html.
5. "Worldwide 220 Million Domain Names Registered," Networking4All, December 23, 2011, http://www.networking4all.com/en/domain+names/news/worldwide+220+million+domain+names+registered/.

6. Nao Matsukata and Josh Bourne, "Are More Domain Names Better for the Internet?", *CNN*, January 9, 2012, http://globalpublicsquare.blogs.cnn.com/2012/01/09/are-more-domain-names-better-for-the-internet/.

7. Scott Pinzon, "Predicting the Future," *Scott Pinzon's Blog*, September 19, 2011, http://newgtlds.icann.org/en/blog/predicting-the-future-19sep11-en.

8. Vance Hedderel, interview with Savita Iyer, April 19, 2012.

9. "Envisioning Your Dot BRAND New World: A Field Guide for Brand Builders," Afilias, http://www.afilias.org/dotbrand.

10. Hedderel, interview with Savita Iyer, April 19, 2012.

11. Erick Schonfeld, "Forrester Forecast: Online Retail Sales Will Grow to $250 Billion by 2014," *TechCrunch*, March 8, 2010, http://techcrunch.com/2010/03/08/forrester-forecast-online-retail-sales-will-grow-to-250-billion-by-2014/.

12. Scott Pinzon, "Predicting the Future," Scott Pinzon's Blog, September 19, 2011, http://newgtlds.icann.org/en/blog/predicting-the-future-19sep11-en.

13. Mary Helen Bowers, interview with Savita Iyer, April 17, 2012.

14. Ibid.

15. Ibid.

## CHAPTER 11: BRAND ALCHEMY

1. Erica Swallow, "What's the Value in a Brand Name," *Mashable Business*, November 6, 2010, http://mashable.com/2010/11/06/value-of-brand-names/.

2. Interbrand, "Brand Valuation, the Financial Value of Brands," *Brandchannel*, http://www.brandchannel.com/papers_review.asp?sp_id=357.

3. James Surowiecki, "The Decline of Brands," Wired, November 2004, http://www.wired.com/wired/archive/12.11/brands.html.

4. Herald Wire Services, "Gisele Bündchen's Brand Could Be Worth Billions," *Boston Herald*, June 2, 2011, http://bostonherald.com/track/star_tracks/view/2011_0602headlinegoes.

5. "Is That Really What They Need? Brazilian Surgery Offers Free Plastic Surgery to the Poor," *Daily Mail*, March 23, 2012, http://www.dailymail.co.uk/news/article-2119099/Beauty-right-Brazils-poor-FREE-plastic-surgery-make-look-better.html.

6. Jonice Padilha, interview with Savita Iyer, April 11, 2012.

7. Padilha, interview with Savita Iyer, April 11, 2012.

8. Paton Jackson, "Brazilian Wax for a Brazilian Bikini Line," *Brazilian Wax— Answers!*, n.d., http://www.brazilian-wax.net/Brazilian-Wax-for-a-Brazilian-Bikini-Line.html.

9. Jennifer Armstrong, "12 Year Olds Getting Bikini Waxes: Why Do Women Do Such Terrible Things to Their Vaginas?", *Alternet* (originally published at sirensmag.com), December 15, 2010, http://www.alternet.org/sex/149191/12_year_olds_getting_bikini_waxes%3A_why_do_women_do_such_terrible_things_to_their_vaginas/?page=entire.

10. Padilha, interview with Savita Iyer, April 11, 2012.

11. G. Bruce Knecht, *Hooked: Pirates, Poaching and the Perfect Fish* (New York: Rodale Books, 2006), pp. 5–10.

12. National Oceanic and Atmospheric Administration Fisheries Service, "Chilean Sea Bass: Frequently Asked Questions," http://www.nmfs.noaa.gov/trade/chile.pdf.
13. Ibid.
14. Don Pintabona, interview with Liz Nickles, April 29, 2012.
15. "Patagonian Toothfish," Greenpeace, August 26, 2003, http://www.greenpeace.org/usa/Global/usa/report/2007/8/patagonian-toothfish.html.
16. Brian Handwerk, "U.S. Chefs Join Campaign To Save Chilean Sea Bass," *National Geographic News*, May 22, 2002, http://news.nationalgeographic.com/news/2002/05/0522_020522_seabass.html.
17. Knecht, *Hooked: Pirates, Poaching, and the Perfect Fish.*
18. "The Golden Jubilee," *Diamond-Jewelry-pedia.com*, 2010, http://www.diamond-jewelry-pedia.com/golden-jubilee.html.
19. Ibid.
20. Ettagale Blauer, "Colored Diamonds' Mass Appeal," Rapaport Diamind Trading Network,, March 1, 2012, http://www.diamonds.net/news/ExportItem.aspx?ArticleID=39199&Action=Print.
21. Ibid.
22. Alexandre de Miguel, interview with Savita Iyer, May 2, 2012.
23. Ibid.
24. Blauer, "Colored Diamonds' Mass Appeal."
25. de Miguel, interview with Savita Iyer, May 2, 2012.
26. Suzanna Didier, "Water Bottle Pollution Facts," *Green Living*, http://greenliving.nationalgeographic.com/water-bottle-pollution-2947.html.
27. Alexa Weibel, "Meet the World's Water Sommelier," *Slashfood*, November 13, 2009, http://www.slashfood.com/2009/11/13/water-sommelier-michael-mascha/.
28. "Bottled Waters: The Best Mineral Waters & Spring Waters," *The Nibble*, http://www.thenibble.com/reviews/main/beverages/waters/index.asp.
29. Martin Riese, interview with Savita Iyer, April 10, 2012.
30. "The Story Behind Cloud Juice," www.cloudjuice.com.au/The_Story.html.
31. Ibid.
32. Riese, interview with Savita Iyer, April 10, 2012.
33. Joel Stein, "The Making of a Water Snob," *Time*, June 7, 2007, http://www.time.com/time/magazine/article/0,9171,1630570,00.html.
34. Samantha Slabaugh, "How Is Aquafina Marketed?" eHow.com, n.d., http://www.ehow.com/facts_7228149_aquafina-marketed_.html#ixzz1tOFSb8oo.
35. Caroline Gammell, "Claridges Sells Luxury Water at £50 per Litre," *Telegraph*, October 10, 2007, http://www.telegraph.co.uk/news/uknews/1565964/Claridges-sells-luxury-water-at-50-per-litre.html.
36. Ibid.
37. Jim Salzman, interview with Savita Iyer, April 12, 2011.
38. Le Blog Du Storytelling, http://lestorytelling.com/blog/2008/07/28/chateldon-leau-de-louis-xiv-a-moins-que/.
39. Ibid.
40. Salzman, interview with Savita Iyer, April 12, 2011.
41. Ibid.

42. Le Blog Du Storytelling, http://lestorytelling.com/blog/2008/07/28/chateldon-leau-de-louis-xiv-a-moins-que/.
43. Kitty Bean Yancey, "Sleek Cylinders Have Us Gushing over Norwegian Water," *USA Today*, August 14, 2001.
44. Doug Frost, "Water Sommeliers: Do They (Should They) Exist?" *Sommelier Journal*, August 2009, pp.59-63, http://www.sommelierjournal.com/articles/article.aspx?year=2009&month=08&articlenum=59.
45. Ibid.
46. Stein, "The Making of a Water Snob."
47. Bottled Water of the World, www.finewaters.com.
48. Salzman, interview with Savita Iyer, April 12, 2011.
49. Ibid.
50. John Sicher, interview with Savita Iyer, April 11, 2011.
51. Elizabeth Rosenthal, "City Known for Its Water Turns to Tap to Cut Trash," *New York Times*, June 11, 2009, http://www.nytimes.com/2009/06/12/world/europe/12venice.html; www.acquaveritas.it.
52. "PepsiCo and Evian 'Go Green,'" *Filtered Files*, March 23,2011, http://www.filtersfast.com/blog/index.php/tag/green-bottled-water.
53. Sindya N. Bhanoo, "The Battle Over Bottled Water," *New York Times*, March 24, 2010, http://green.blogs.nytimes.com/2010/03/24/the-battle-over-bottled-water/.

## CHAPTER 12: RAISED BY WOLVES, PECKED TO DEATH BY GOSLINGS

1. Dylan Stableford, "JetBlue Pilot's Midair Meltdown: It Started Medical but Clearly More Than That," *Yahoo! News*, March 28, 2012, http://news.yahoo.com/blogs/lookout/jetblue-ceo-pilot-mid-air-meltdown-started-medical-125331181.html.
2. Ben Rooney, "JetBlue Brand Tarnished but Not Destroyed," *CNNMoney*, March 28, 2012, http://money.cnn.com/2012/03/28/markets/jetblue/index.htm.
3. Jennifer Van Grove, "Become JetBlue's Facebook Fan, Win Free Travel for a Year," *Mashable Business*, December 10, 2009, http://mashable.com/2009/12/10/jetblue-all-you-can-travel/.
4. "A Story of JetBlue's Customer Experience Strategy," *Digital Spark Marketing*, March 27, 2012, http://www.digitalsparkmarketing.com/2012/03/27/a-story-of-jetblues-customer-experience-strategy/.
5. "BATS Global Markets: The 'Spectacularly Botched' IPO," *The Week*, March 26, 2012, http://theweek.com/article/index/226041/bats-global-markets-the-spectacularly-botched-ipo; Brian Bremmer, "The Bats Affair: When Machines Humiliate Their Masters," *Business Week*, March 23, 2012, http://www.businessweek.com/articles/2012–03-23/the-bats-affair-when-machines-humiliate-their-masters; Rhodri Preece, "Three Lessons from the Failed BATS IPO," CFA Institute, April 2, 2012, http://blogs.cfainstitute.org/marketintegrity/2012/04/02/three-lessons-from-the-failed-bats-ipo/; J. McKrank and A. Nandakumar, "BATS Strips Ratterman of Chairman Role by Reuters," *Yahoo! Finance*, March 27, 2012, http://finance.yahoo.com/news/bats-strips-ratterman-chairman-role-000146848.html.

6. Dave Wieneke, "Netflix Fragments Its Brand in a Self-Made Disaster," *eConsultancy Digital Marketers United*, September 20, 2011, http://econsultancy.com/us/blog/8031-netflix-fragments-its-brand-in-a-self-made-disaster.

7. Kern Lewis, "Brand Disasters for 2011," *Growth Focus*, November 3, 2011, http://growthfocus.net/marketing-strategy-blog/uncategorized/brand-disasters-for-2011/; "Top 10 Brand Disasters of 2011," *Inc.*, November 23, 2011, http://www.inc.com/ss/geoffrey-james/top-10-brand-disasters-2011.

8. Tynicka Battle, interview with Liz Nickles, May 8, 2012.

9. Michael Liedke, "Netflix Q1 2012: Millions of New Subscribers Added," *Huffington Post*, April 23, 2012, http://www.huffingtonpost.com/2012/04/23/netflix-q1-2012_n_1447123.html.

10. Battle, interview with Liz Nickles, May 8, 2012.

11. "Back with a Brand: Tiger Woods Is Still on Top," *CNN.com*, October 4, 2011, http://articles.cnn.com/2011-10-04/golf/sport_golf_golf-tiger-woods-forbes_1_elin-nordegren-brand-value-golfers?.

12. "Tiger Woods Has a Deal with Rolex," *ESPN Golf*, October 5, 2011, http://espn.go.com/golf/story/_/id/7062562/tiger-woods-endorsement-deal-rolex; "Tiger Woods Cheating Cost $1 Million per Mistress," *Eurosport Asia*, April 4, 2011, http://asia.eurosport.com/golf/'1m-a-mistress'-for-tiger_sto2735176/story.shtml.

13. Charlie Gasparino, "Goldman Hopes Image Overhaul Will Save Blankfein," *Fox Business*, April 25, 2012, http://www.foxbusiness.com/2012/04/25/exclusive-goldman-board-hopes-pr-boost-will-save-blankfein/.

14. Jenny Strasburg and Jacob Bunge, "Nasdaq: Hindsight Says to Delay IPO," *Wall Street Journal*, May 27, 2012, http://online.wsj.com/article/SB10001424052702303610504577420683577782546.html; "Facebook IPO: The Fallout Continues," *Washington Post*, May 24, 2012, updated May 25, 2012, http://www.washingtonpost.com/business/economy/facebook-ipo-fallout-continues/2012/05/24/gJQAJcTxnU_story.html.

15. Maureen Farrell, "Facebook IPO: Wall Street Losses Mount," *CNNMoney*, May 25, 2012, updated June 6, 2012, reprinted from *Campaign*, http://money.cnn.com/2012/05/25/investing/nasdaq-facebook/.

16. Ibid.

CHAPTER 13: RAISING LAZARUS

1. Emma Hall, "Linda Evangelista Stars in Yardley Launch Ad," *BrandRepublic*, September 13, 1996, http://www.brandrepublic.com/news/22987/NEWS-Linda-Evangelista-stars-Yardley-launch-ad/?DCMP=ILC-SEARCH.

2. Kumar Chander, interview with Savita Iyer, May 2, 2012.

3. Ibid.

4. Ibid.

5. Julia Wray, "Yardley—Quintessentially British," *Cosmetics Business* January 6, 2011, http://www.cosmeticsbusiness.com/technical/article_page/Yardley__quintessentially_British/58536.

6. "Old Spice: A Trip down Memory Lane," Badger & Blade, http://badgerandblade.com/vb/showthread.php/152669-Old-Spice-A-Trip-Down-memory-lane.

7. "Catera Ad Pulled by Cadillac," *New York Times*, February 19, 1997, http://www.nytimes.com/1997/02/19/business/catera-ad-pulled-by-cadillac.html.

8. Stuart Elliott, "Old Spice Tries a Dash of Humor to Draw Young Men," *New York Times*, January 8, 2007, http://www.nytimes.com/2007/01/08/business/media/08adcol.html.

9. Ibid.

10. Adam Tschorn, "Old Spice Talks to the Ladies, Man," *Los Angeles Times*, March 6, 2010, http://articles.latimes.com/2010/mar/06/image/la-ig-oldspice-20100306.

11. Hank Stewart, interview with Liz Nickles, May 6, 2012.

12. Megan O'Neill, "Old Spice Guy Bids Farewell to Fans After Achieving Social Media Domination," *Social Times*, July 15, 2010, http://socialtimes.com/old-spice-guy-bids-farewell-to-fans-after-achieving-social-media-domination_b17527.

13. "eBooks: 1998—The First eBook Readers," *Project Gutenberg News*, July 16, 2011, http://www.gutenbergnews.org/20110716/ebooks-1998-the-first-ebook-readers/.

14. "Barnes & Noble, Microsoft Form Strategic Partnership to Advance World-Class Digital Reading Experiences for Consumers," press release, April 30, 2012, www.microsoft.com.

15. Jeremy Greenfield, "Possibilities Abound in Microsoft, Barnes & Noble Deal,"*DWB*, May 1, 2012, http://www.digitalbookworld.com/2012/possibilities-abound-in-microsoft-barnes-noble-deal/.

## CHAPTER 14: REGULATORY MUSICAL CHAIRS

1. Glenn Laudenslager, interview with Savita Iyer, April 27, 2012.

2. Associated Press, "Influence Game: Online Companies Win Piracy Fight," January 21, 2012, *FOXNEWS.com*, http://www.foxnews.com/us/2012/01/21/influence-game-online-companies-win-piracy-fight/.

3. Maura Corbett, interview with Savita Iyer, February 6, 2012.

4. Ibid.

5. Marvin Amorri, interview with Savita Iyer, February 27, 2012.

6. Laudenslager, interview with Savita Iyer, April 27, 2012.

7. Abigail Marks, "Why SOPA and PIPA Are Bad for Brands," *Tweed*, January 19, 2012, http://ogilvyentertainmentblog.com/2012/01/why-sopa-and-pipa-are-bad-for-brands/.

8. Chris Garrett, "When Social Media Campaigns Go Bad," *Blog Herald*, May 22, 2009. http://www.blogherald.com/2009/05/22/when-social-media-campaigns-go-bad/.

9. Chris Garrett, "Is Untamed Social Media Damaging Your Brand," *Blog Herald*, July 8, 2009, http://www.blogherald.com/2009/07/08/is-untamed-social-media-damaging-your-brand/.

10. Barry Murphy, "The Next Governance Frontier: Social Media," *Forbes*, February 28, 2012, http://www.forbes.com/sites/barrymurphy/2012/02/28/the-next-governance-frontier-social-media/.

11. Mike Godwin, interview with Savita Iyer, February 27, 2012.

12. Erik Martin, interview with Savita Iyer, March 8, 2012.

232                                    NOTES

13. Stephanie Strom, "Web Site Shines Light on Petty Bribery Worldwide," *New York Times*, March 7, 2012, http://www.nytimes.com/2012/03/07/business/web-sites-shine-light-on-petty-bribery-worldwide.html?pagewanted=all.

## CHAPTER 15: ON THE WAY TO—WHAT?

1. Susan Gunelius, "5 Brands Using Pinterest Brilliantly," *Sprout Social*, February 13, 2012, www.sproutsocial.com.
2. Whole Story: *The Official Whole Foods Market Blog*, http://www.wholefoods-market.com/blog/whole-story/25-ways-enjoy-king-cheese.
3. Brian Gaar, "Whole Foods Wins Overall Title in *Statesman*'s Social Media Awards," *Statesman.com*, March 11, 2011, http://www.statesman.com/business/whole-foods-wins-overall-title-in-statesmans-social-1312933.html?printArticle=y.
4. Chad Jackson and Harry Bernstein, interview with Liz Nickles, February 10, 2012.
5. Adrian Ho, interview with Savita Iyer, March 22, 2012.
6. Ibid.
7. Roger Warner, interview with Savita Iyer, April 17, 2012.
8. Andre Bourque, "Facebook to Marketers: 'You're Going About It the Wrong Way,'" *Technocrati*, March 27, 2012, http://technorati.com/social-media/article/facebook-to-marketers-youre-going-about/.
9. Warner, interview with Savita Iyer, April 17, 2012.
10. "The C&M/Toluna Best Practise Guide to Social Media Marketing and Planning," SlideShare, Feb 29, 2012, http://www.slideshare.net/contentandmotion/toluna-cm-social-media-marketing-best-practise-guide.
11. Craig Dubitsky, interview with Savita Iyer, April 10, 2012; Erick Schonfeld, "Forrester Forecast: Online Retail Sales Will Grow to $250 Billion by 2014," *TechCrunch*, March 8, 2010, http://techcrunch.com/2010/03/08/forrester-forecast-online-retail-sales-will-grow-to-250-billion-by-2014/.
12. Dubitsky, interview with Savita Iyer, April 10, 2012.

## CHAPTER 16: THE YELLOW BRICK ROAD

1. Watts Wacker, interview with Liz Nickles, May 2, 2012.
2. Chris Perry, "Do Organizations Need a Chief Content Officer?", *Forbes.com*, October 27, 2011, http://www.forbes.com/sites/chrisperry/2011/10/27/do-organizations-need-a-chief-content-officer/.
3. Robert Blattberg, interview with Liz Nickles, May 19, 2012.
4. Milton Pedraza, interview with Liz Nickles, April 18, 2012.
5. Chad Jackson and Harry Bernstein, interview with Liz Nickles, February 9, 2012.
6. Ibid.
7. "Kim Kardashian's Credit Card May Be the Worst Credit Card Ever," *Gawker*, November 18, 2010, http://gawker.com/5693964/kim-kardashians-credit-card-may-be-the-worst-credit-card-ever; "Kardashians Cancel Predatory Credit

Card," *NewsOne*, November 30, 2010, http://newsone.com/880805/kardashian-credit-card/.

8. Mark DeCambre, "Chase Card Game: JP Morgan's 'Liquid' Targets Cash Poor Users," *New York Post*, May 12, 2012, http://www.nypost.com/p/news/business/chase_card_game_tmG3NTUgziiOAwxmOxlqgI; Catherine New, "Chase Liquid: JPMorgan Chase's Play for Low Income Customers," *Huffington Post*, May 10, 2012, http://www.huffingtonpost.com/2012/05/08/chase-liquid-card-jp-morgan-chase_n_1501065.html.

9. Robert Andrews, "YouTube's Missing Monetization Makes Its Internet TV Prospects Patchy," *Paid Content*, February 15, 2012, http://paidcontent.org/2012/02/15/419-youtubes-missing-monetisation-makes-its-internet-tv-prospects-patchy/.

10. "The FTC's Revised Endorsement Guides: What People Are Asking," U.S. Federal Trade Commission, Bureau of Consumer Protection Business Center, June 2010, http://business.ftc.gov/documents/bus71-ftcs-revised-endorsement-guideswhat-people-are-asking.

11. "Whole Foods Market® Opens Its Doors to Roseville Community," press release, November 5, 2008, http://media.wholefoodsmarket.com/news/whole-foods-market-opens-its-doors-to-roseville-community/.

12. Pedraza, interview with Liz Nickles, April 18, 2012.

13. Moray MacLennan, interview with Liz Nickles, May 14, 2012.

14. "RS Components Launches New 2010 Catalog," rs-online, RS press release, March 29, 2010, http://hongkong01.rs-online.com/web/generalDisplay.html?id=footer1/release/100329_cat2010launch.

15. Gleanster, "Harnessing the Power of Website Personalization to Drive B2B Marketing Improvement," *ClickZ*, 2011, http://whitepapers.clickz.com/content18189.

16. Charlotte Beers, interview with Liz Nickles, February 10, 2012.

17. Dan Dunkel, "Integration Intelligence," SDM, November 2012, http://digital.bnpmedia.com/article/Integration+Intelligence/881684/0/article.html.

18. Laurie Segall, "Optimizely Aims to Give Obama 2012 a Data Edge," *CNNMoney*, May 2, 2012, http://money.cnn.com/2012/04/23/technology/startups/optimizely-election/index.htm. These techniques, carried over to politics from industry, are now prevalent on the political scene.

19. MacLennan, interview with Liz Nickles, May 14, 2012.

20. Tynicka Battle, interview with Liz Nickles, May 8, 2012.

21. Amanda Fortini, "Honey, I Got a Year's Worth of Tuna Fish," *New York Times Magazine*, May 6, 2012, p. 59.

22. Julie Bosman, "Writer's Cramp: In the E-Reader Era, a Book a Year Is Slacking," *New York Times*, May 13, 2012, p. 1.

23. Binyamin Applebaum, "It's 4:30 in the Morning. Do You Know What the Jobless Claims Are Going to Come in At?", *New York Times Magazine*, May 13, 2012, p. 28.

24. Amy Harmon, "Amazon Glitch Unmasks War of Reviewers," *New York Times*, February 14, 2012, http://www.nytimes.com/2004/02/14/us/amazon-glitch-unmasks-war-of-reviewers.html?scp=6&sq=amazon+book+reviews&st=nyt;

George Lowery, "Study Unmasks Secret World of Amazon's Reviewers," *Cornell University Chronicle Online*, June 14, 2011, http://www.news.cornell.edu/stories/June11/PinchAmazon.html.

25. Richard Kirschenbaum, interview with Liz Nickles, April 8, 2012.
26. Battle, interview with Liz Nickles, May 8, 2012.
27. Ibid.
28. Laurie Ashcraft, interview with Liz Nickles, May 12, 2012.
29. Blattberg, interview with Liz Nickles, May 19, 2012.
30. Beers, interview with Liz Nickles, February 10, 2012.
31. Alex Armstrong, "AT&T Voice Recognition API Is Available in June," *I Programmer*, April 24, 2012, http://www.i-programmer.info/news/105-artificial-intelligence/4112-atat-voice-recognition-api-available-in-june.html.
32. "Statistics," undated YouTube press release, http://www.youtube.com/t/press_statistics.
33. April Dembosky, "With Friends Like These…," *FT Weekend Magazine*, May 19–20, 2012, p. 21.
34. Battle, interview with Liz Nickles, May 8, 2012.
35. Cody Willard, "Top Dumbest Tech Predictions of All Times," *Wall Street Journal* Market Watch blog, January 4, 2011, http://blogs.marketwatch.com/cody/2011/01/04/top-10-worst-tech-predictions-of-all-time-updated/; "How Many Apps Are Available in the Android Market?", *Wall Street Journal* Market Watch blog, January 4, 2011, http://blogs.marketwatch.com/cody/2011/01/04/top-10-worst-tech-predictions-of-all-time-updated/; Robin Wauters, "Apple: 100 Million Downloads from Apple Apps in Less than One Year," *TechCrunch*, December 20, 2011, http://techcrunch.com/2011/12/12/apple-500000-apps-in-mac-app-store-100-million-downloads-to-date/.

# ADDITIONAL SOURCES

Beers, Charlotte. *I'd Rather Be in Charge*. New York: Vanguard Press, 2012.

Chaney, Lisa. *Coco Chanel: An Intimate Life*. New York: Viking, 2011.

Charles-Roux, Edmonde. *Chanel and Her World: Friends, Fashion and Fame*. New York: Vendome Press, 2004.

Clark, Kevin. *Brandescence: Three Essential Elements of Enduring Brands*. Chicago: Kaplan Trade Press, 2004.

Fraser, Antonia. *Love and Louis XIV*. New York: Anchor Books, 2006.

Fraser, Antonia. *Marie Antoinette: The Journey*. New York: Anchor Books, 2001.

Gleik, Peter H. *Bottled and Sold: The Story Behind Our Obsession with Bottled Water*. Washington, DC: Island Press, 2010.

Gottschall, Jonathan. *The Storytelling Animal: How Stories Make Us Human*. Boston: Houghton Mifflin Harcourt, 2012.

Holt, Douglas. *How Brands Became Icons*. Boston: Harvard Business School Press, 2004.

Jensen, Rolf. *The Dream Society: How the Coming Shift from Information to Imagination Will Transform Your Business*. New York: McGraw-Hill, 1999.

Madsen, Axel. *Coco Chanel: A Biography*. New York: Bloomsbury, 1990.

Mascha, Michael. *Fine Waters: A Connoisseur's Guide to the World's Most Distinctive Bottled Waters*. Philadelphia: Quirk Books, 2006.

Mazzeo, Tilar J. *The Secret of Chanel No. 5: The Intimate History of the World's Most Famous Perfume*. New York: HarperPerennial, 2010.

Micek, Deborah, and Warren Whitlock. *Twitter Revolution: How Social Media and Mobile Marketing Is Changing the Way We Do Business and Market Online*. Las Vegas: Xeno Press, 2008.

Morgan, Adam. *Eating the Big Fish: How Challenger Brands Can Compete Against Brand Leaders*. Hoboken, NJ: John Wiley, 2009.

Picardie, Justine. *Coco Chanel: The Legend and the Life*. London: HarperCollins It Books, 2010.

Piereson, James. *Camelot and the Cultural Revolution*. New York: Encounter Books, 2007; new material, 2009.

Pine, B. Joseph II, and James H. Gilmore. *The Experience Economy*. Boston: Harvard Business Review Press, 2011.

Spawforth, Tony. *Versailles: A Biography of a Palace*. New York: St. Martin's Press, 2008.

Thomas, Dana. *Deluxe: How Luxury Lost Its Luster*. New York: Penguin Group, 2007.

Torrenzano, Richard, and Davis, Mark. *Digital Assassination: Protecting Your Reputation, Brand, or Business Against Online Attacks.* New York: St. Martin's Press, 2011.

Tungate, Mark. *Luxury World: The Past, Present, and Future of Luxury Brands.* Philadelphia: Kogan Page, 2009.

Weber, Caroline. *Queen of Fashion: What Marie Antoinette Wore to the Revolution.* New York: Picador, 2006.

Young, Kimberly S. *Caught in the Net.* New York: John Wiley, 1998.

# INDEX